Sex Differences
in Britain

EDITED BY

Ivan Reid and *Eileen Wormald*

*socialist
extraventialist
radical*

GRANT
MCINTYRE

First published in 1982 by
Grant McIntyre Publishing Limited
90–91 Great Russell Street
London WC1B 3PY

British Library Cataloguing in Publication Data

Reid, Ivan
  Sex differences in Britain.
  1. Sex role
  I. Title   II. Wormald, Eileen
  305.3.   HQ1075

  ISBN 0-86216-064-2
  ISBN 0-86216-065-0 pbk

Photoset in Times by Oxford Publishing Services
Printed and bound in Great Britain
by Billing and Sons Limited
London   and   Worcester

Contents

Contents

Contents

Acknowledgements

Eileen Wormald is grateful for the constant support she has received in her diverse roles from her colleagues, some of whose names appear elsewhere in this book, as well as from June Clayton whose activities underpin the whole enterprise, and from her family—Harry, Sara and David.

Ivan Reid is grateful to all those who helped him, directly or indirectly, in the writing and compilation of this book: first to Pat, Diane and Helen, for the several times they must have felt they came last, as well as for their support; to Lesley Howson and Brenda Carrington for happily and accurately typing parts of the manuscript and to Jennifer Kenyon not only for that task but particularly for her invaluable secretarial services; to those colleagues and students who have provided insights into sex differences; and to Sheila Allen and Jalna Hanmer who made valuable bibliographical suggestion.

Ivan Reid and Eileen Wormald are most grateful to Linden Stafford for her invaluable and constructive persistence with the minutiae of manuscript and proofs.

The author and publisher would like to thank the following for permission to use data presented in this book: Athlone Press, London, for data from E. Vallance, *Women in the House* (1979); Bell and Sons Ltd, London, for data from H. Land *Large Families in London* 1969); the editor of the *British Journal of Sociology*, for data from R. Mawby, 'Sex and Crime: The Results of a Self-Report Study', *British Journal of Sociology*, 31 (1980); Cambridge University Press, Cambridge, for data from C. Greenhalgh, 'Male/Female Wage Differentials in Great Britain', *Economic Journal*, 90 (1980); the Commission for Racial Equality, for data from M. J. Le Lohe, 'Sex Discrimintion and Under-Representation of

Women in Politics', *New Community* (Summer 1976); Conservative Women's National Advisory Council, for data from *Women in Politics* (1980); the editor of the *County Councils Gazette*, for data from S. L. Bristow, 'Women Councillors', *County Councils Gazette* (May, November and December 1978); Croom Helm Ltd, London, for data from M. Currell, *Political Woman* (1974), and M. Elston, 'Medicine: Half our Future Doctors?, in R. Silverstone and A. Ward, *Careers of Professional Women* (1980); the Managing Director of Dod's, for data from *Dod's Parliamentary Companion* (anually); the Equal Opportunities Commission, for data from *Women in the Legal Services* (1978), *The Experience of Caring for Elderly and Handicapped Dependants* (1980), *EOC Annual Report 1979* (1980) and *EOC Annual Report 1980* (1981); the European Economic Commission, for data from *Women and Employment in the United Kingdom, Ireland and Denmark* (1974); Gower Publishing Co. Ltd, London, for data from C. Mellors, *The British MP* (1978); the Hansard Society and the author, for data from R. Stradling, *The Political Awareness of the School Leaver* (1978); the Controller of Publishing, Her Majesty's Stationery Office, London, for data from *Annual Abstract of Statistics* (1979, 1980, 1981), Civil Service, *The Employment of Women in the Civil Service* (1971), *Civil Service Statistics* (1980), *Criminal Statistics for England and Wales 1979* (1981), *Curricular Differences for Boys and Girls* (1975), *Employment Gazette* (January 1976, June 1980, August 1980, October 1980, November 1980, January 1981, February 1981, June 1981, August 1981), *Family Expenditure Survey* (1979), Fulton Committee, *The Civil Service* (1968), *General Household Survey 1976, 1977, 1978* (1978, 1979, 1980), C. Hakim, *Occupational Segregation* (1980), L. Hamill, *Wives as Sole and Joint Breadwinners* (1978) and *An Exploration of the Incrase in Female 1-Parent Families Receiving Supplementary Benefit* (1978), *Health and Personal Social Services Statistics for England 1978* (1980), A. Hunt, *A Survey of Women's Employment* (1968), *In-Patient Statistics from the Mental Health Enquiry for England 1977* (1980), *Labour Force Survey 1973, 1975, 1977* (1980), *Life Tables* (1979), *Marriage and Divorce Statistics 1978* (1980), Maud Committee, *Royal Commission on Local Government* (196–9), *Monthly Digest of Statistics, Morbidity Statistics from General Practice 1971–72* (1979), *Mortality Statistics 1979* (1981), *New Earnings Survey* (1980), *Occupational Mortality* (1978), *OPCS*

Monitor, PP1 78/2 and FM2 78/2 (1978), *Report of the Work of the Prison Department: Statistical Tables* (1979), Robinson Committee, *Committee of Inquiry into the System of Remuneration of Members of Local Authorities* (1977), Royal Commission on the Distribution of Income and Wealth (1978), *Social Trends No. 9* (1978) and *No. 10* (1979), *Statistics of Education 1977* (1979–80) and *1978* (1980–1), J. E. Todd and L. N. Jones, *Matrimonial Property* (1972), *Women and Work: A Review* (1975); the Institute for the Study and Treatment of Delinquency, for data from C. Smart, 'The New Female Criminal: Reality or Myth', *British Journal of Criminology*, 19 (1979), and M. Maguire, 'The Impact of Burglary Upon Victims', *British Journal of Criminology*, 20 (1980); Dr Edward Keer, for permission to quote from private correspondence; the editor of *Local Government Studies* and the author, for data from S. L. Bristow, 'Women Councillors: An Explanation of the Under-Representation of Women in Local Government', *Local Government Studies* (May–June 1980); the author, for data from N. E. McIntosh, 'Women in Distance Education: The Open University Experience', *Educational Broadcasting International*, 12 (1979); Macmillan Ltd, London, for data from D. Butler and D. Kavanagh, *The British General Election of 1979* (1980), P. Elias, 'Labour Supply and Opportunities for Women', in R. M. Lindley, *Economic Change and Employment Policy* (1980), and R. Rose *Studies in British Politics*, 2nd edn (1969); Market and Opinion Research International, London, for data from unpublished surveys (1979, 1980, 1981); the *New Statesman*, for data from A. Coote, 'Powerlessness and How to Fight it', *New Statesman* (7 November 1980), and A. Coote and P. Kellner, *Hear This Brother* (1980); Oxford University Press, London, for data from J. G. Francis and G. Peele, 'Reflections on Generational Analysis: Is There a Shared Political Perspective Between Men and Woman?', *Political Studies*, 26 (1978); the editor of *Practitioner*, for data from W. P. T. James, 'Research on Obesity', in I. M. Baird *et al.*, 'Prevalence of Obesity in a London Borough', *Practitioner*, 212 (1974); Routledge & Kegan Paul Ltd, London, for data from C. Smart, *Women, Crime and Criminology* (1976); Social Surveys (Gallup Polls) Ltd., London, for data from R. Rose, *Electoral Behaviour: A Comparative Handbook* (1974); John Wiley & Sons Ltd, London, for data from R. F. Sparks, H. G. Genn and D. J. Dodd, *Surveying Victims* (1977).

1

Sex differences and this book

Ivan Reid and Eileen Wormald

Sex, it would appear, has always been an emotive and difficult word and concept, and, consequently, writing about it has never been a straightforward affair. In the past, taboos, the law and social constraints all but precluded it from serious public consideration. Today, while many of these constraints have been swept away, they have been replaced by much controversy over the definition and implications of the term. This book is about some aspects of the extent and nature of the differences between the sexes – between women and men – in contemporary British society. As such it raises a number of problems, mainly of definition and limitation, and this introductory chapter serves to inform readers of the parameters within which the book has been written.

SEX OR GENDER

There are those who view sex as merely and only a question of physiology, the two sexes having different genitals related to their separate functions in physical reproduction. Many would add other physical differences, such as height, weight, proportion of fat, body hair and number of ribs. Almost all other commonly recognised differences between the sexes are seen as not being intrinsic to sex but rather as the products of society and its way of life – that is, culture. Some people use the term 'gender' to refer to all differences between women and men other than the physical. The value of such a use of terms is that it clearly directs attention to the almost total role of culture in the formation and maintenance of what can be viewed as the separate identities, life chances and experiences of the sexes. For the writers of this book – all social scientists – the social production of the sexes and of the differences between them is

1

transparent. Indeed, we suspect that almost all readers, at least on reflection, will share such a view. Certainly, historical and anthropological evidence fully displays the vast variety of ways in which the roles of women and men and the relationships and differences between the sexes can and do exist. (A good introductory book is Oakley (1972); for anthropology, see Friedl (1975), La Fontaine (1978) and Reiter (1975); for history, Davidoff (1973).)

In any case there are fallacies in the use of the term 'sex' for the physical and 'gender' for the social. In real life the two always coexist, so that sex is never simply a difference of genitals or reproductive function but is inevitably and firmly set within a specific cultural setting. Consequently, sex, like other human attributes including intelligence, becomes meaningful and observable only when overtly expressed, at which point the attribute is so interrelated with culture that it is, for all intents and purposes, inseparable. Similarly the physiological definition of sex is not straightforward: both sexes have male and female chromosomes in their genetic make-up and produce both types of sex hormones – indeed, in relatively rare cases, even genital differentiation is far from clear. Even in the physical sense, then, women and men are somewhat far from separable into two discrete groups. Our understanding and even our recognition of each sex comes from our culture and amounts to generalised stereotypes. In reality all supposed sexual characteristics exist in both sexes, even though their display may be, and usually is, actively discouraged. In everyday life the abusive use of terms like 'effeminate' and 'tomboy' and reactions of shock or humour towards female aggression and assertiveness, or towards male passivity and lack of drive, bear witness to the existence of accepted sex behaviour stereotypes and the mechanisms for their perpetuation. In fact, we can all recognise, in ourselves and in others, that ways of behaving, thinking and feeling are very complex, and not simply divisible into two categories by sex, and yet we can appreciate how society has shaped and affected these aspects of life along sex lines (for an interesting account of how girls learn to be women, see Sharpe 1976). Because of these factors, we have, in writing this book, generally used the term sex to refer to women and men as they are manifested in the culture of our present-day society. However, a further consideration of sex and gender is to be found in Chapter 2.

SEX DIFFERENCES

That there are differences between the sexes in our and all other societies is one of those facts of life that is incontrovertible. Indeed, for some this fact is sufficient for them to believe that such differences are naturally ordained or essential to the existence of society and the wellbeing of individuals. For others they are a constant source of annoyance and dismay. The range of opinions about sex differences is extremely wide. At one extreme such differences are seen as the simple result of the exploitation of women by men, while at the other they are regarded as an entirely justified and reasonable division of rights and duties that allows each sex to enjoy life to the full. For others sex differences are seen as necessary for society to work, since they are assumed essential to the maintenance of society's basic institutions, especially the family. The shades of opinion in between and their variations are too numerous to recount.

The easy recognition of sex differences and the controversy surrounding their existence and persistence have much in common with other forms of social differentiation current in our society. The most obvious of these are other types of social stratification, particularly social class and racial or ethnic groups, although age and geographical differences are also similar. Some people react to social differentiation in terms of indifference or even delight, in that they see them as adding to the rich variety of life. Certainly the differences do not in themselves necessarily present society or its members with a problem. All such differences might well be disregarded, or even enjoyed, if it were not for a consideration of the ideas of equality and equality of opportunity – which are in themselves problematic. Perhaps few people would see the ideal world as one in which everybody was identical, while, hopefully, nearly all would reject one in which groups were denied their basic rights and the wherewithal to exist. Most are probably concerned about the fact that some groups in our society can be shown to be materially deprived through no fault of their own and others disadvantaged in terms of length of life, health and access to services like health and education, which are supposedly provided freely and fully for all. The latter concerns have fuelled and continue to fuel much political debate and some action. However, it appears that typically fights against inequality are not for equality but rather to change the criteria for inequality, and those for equality of opportunity not about access to similarity but rather the expansion of opportunity to be different. Historically, action in the direction of equality has to be seen as piecemeal and incomplete. Equality in voting was effected without disturbing the role of the House of Lords or male dominance in government at all levels. The expansion of educational opportunity took place alongside the continued existence of public schools and private education together with the maintenance of the relationship between social class and educational achievement. The National Health Service has little affected the relationship of social class to health, while private medicine flourishes. Sexual equality in pay, achieved through legislation, has not brought about much change in the imbalance between male and female average earnings.

In each form of social differentiation there appears a clear tendency to highlight the trivial at the expense of the fundamental and to indulge in rhetoric rather than review the evidence. In the case of social class, for example, great play is made of such aspects as snobbery, political views, interests and opinions, with far less, if any, attention being paid to the underlying economic inequalities affecting life chances. A further deflection from serious consideration is the constant claim that things have changed and got better – that we no longer live in a class society, since the classes have merged or become very similar; that equality between the sexes has gone as far as necessary or has almost been achieved. An added gloss to this sort of argument is that those who appear to be disadvantaged, be they the working class or women, either actually enjoy their situation or do not want any change, and would not welcome it or know what to do with it. Such views may sound to readers to be those of the advantaged in the situations – that is, the middle class or men, since they represent those parties' interests in the maintenance of the status quo, or its minimal change. However, it needs to be remembered that ideas do not have such discrete boundaries and that the disadvantaged may also hold such views. Shared general views of social reality, apparently supporting a particular group's interests, are common, particularly in social situations where one party has control or influence over information, knowledge and ideas, or where power in its general sense is ⁓ual between the parties. The importance of values, beliefs or ideologies is almost impossible to overestimate to the extent that they are not necessarily affected or changed through experience or exposure to facts. Hopes that people would realise the injustice or unfairness of social situations merely by being told 'the facts' have often been dashed because of resistance to acceptance caused mainly by participants' 'understandings'. Despite these cautions, it is necessary and valuable that society should have as many facts as possible readily available, to facilitate informed discussion and to provide a basis for social policy. One of the prime motivations in writing this book was the realisation that amid the very considerable discussion about the differences between the sexes in our society there was a general lack of factual evidence informing those debates, probably owing to the lack of readily accessible sources.

So far we have seen that sex differences are similar to other forms of social stratification. At the same time it is necessary to recognise the unusual, if not unique, features of sex. Unlike other social stratifications, there are no real problems of definition, sex being a simple, straightforward dichotomy of society. Similarly, the two sex categories are obviously all-inclusive, involving the entire society. These two factors make sex unlike social class and race or ethnic groups whose operationalisation is, in comparison, both problematic and controversial as well as varied. Of very much greater importance is the way in which the forms of social stratification in our society are interrelated. Clearly there are inherent limitations in using a single form of stratification as if it were in isolation. For example, overall social class patterns of behaviour, unless limited to one sex, are often an amalgam of somewhat different sex patterns within the classes (for some empirical examples of this, see Reid 1981). Differences between middle-class white women and men are demonstrably different from sex differences among the black working class, and this is to ignore probable regional variations. In education the 'pecking order' of achievement and opportunity is transparently one of sex and class – reading, in descending order, middle-class boys, then middle-class girls, working-class boys, followed by working-class girls. At the extremes, boys of professional fathers had, in 1980, a 58 per cent chance of university and an 85 per cent chance of some form of higher education, while similar girls' chances were 38 and 56 per cent. The figures for boys of unskilled manual fathers were 1.4 per cent for university and 2.1 per cent for higher education, with similar girls having the lowest chances of all at 0.8 and 1.2 per cent (Edwards and Roberts 1980). Of course, such interrelationships do not detract from, or deny, the very real differences between the social classes and the sexes. Neither, typically, does the available evidence include more than one or two of the possible variables contributing to the differences. The issue is raised here merely to alert readers to aspects of the complexity of the subject reviewed – a complexity fully recognised by the writers of this book. Just as substantive an issue is how the evidence of differences has been collected, interpreted and represented. Since we live in a society which is clearly stratified, we must expect that the identification of problems and the conduct of research into them, let alone attempts to resolve them, will display at least elements of sexist, social class or other forms of cultural assumptions and imperialism. Some areas of sex differences have a long history of recording and investigation, while others have little or none. In some cases both the classification of information and indeed the very questions asked can be seen to contain sexual or sexist assumptions – predictably, male. These issues are discussed below on pp. 8–9, and specific examples are illustrated in the chapters that follow (see index).

The past two decades have seen a major growth in interest, publicity and action on one front of sex differences, namely on aspects of the apparent disadvantages of women in our society. Although it is impossible to judge with any precision the actual improvement of women's position in society, especially in comparison with that of men, the world of sex differences has certainly changed. While it has often been argued that social legislation is usually retrospective upon social change, the continued controversy, and indeed tribunal cases, over the Sex Discrimination Act, and equal pay legislation, together with the continued need for the work of the Equal Opportunities Commission (EOC), suggests that in this event legislation was to the forefront. The women's or feminist movements have vigorously championed, on a variety of fronts, the cause of female equality and rights and have received considerable, though varied, coverage by the media. Change has taken and is taking place, however limited the achievements to date may be seen by their exponents. Again, there are some parallels with social class, particularly with respect to the trade-union movement – though the legislation in respect of the working class was never as broad or comprehensive as that for women. No real equivalent to the EOC has ever been formally set up. It is also probably true that public opposition to the working-class cause was more vociferous and protracted, though it is too early to make proper comparison or assess outcomes. A further aspect of the present climate around sex differences, of particular importance to this book, is that there is now a fairly large literature on such differences and the rights, opportunities and equality of women, very much of which has been written by women. Much of this writing is understandably and appropriately polemic, and for this as well as other reasons it is difficult to judge the extent of its readership and its effect on opinion and social life.

The purpose of the foregoing brief résumé of some aspects of sex differences in our society is simply to provide something of an overview of the context within which this book was written. Many of the issues raised in it are not pursued in the rest of the book, which was written towards a more specific and confined structure and defined aim. It is to an explanation of these that we now turn.

ABOUT THIS BOOK

At the simplest level the aim of this book is to present a view of sex differences in Britain based on empirical evidence and data. The recognition of the lack of a readily available source of such information was a major motivation in producing this volume. Most existing sources appear to have limitations, tending to be fragmentary, dated, concerned with or including other societies, or written from a specific, if not a polemic, point of view. We have consciously attempted to present as objective (that is, independent of observer's attitudes) picture as is possible, so as to inform the current discussion, debate and political activity concerning sex differences and the relationships between the sexes in our society. In adopting this approach we have followed a long tradition in British social science, that of social arithmetic. The strengths and weaknesses of this tradition, well identified by Halsey (1972), are discussed in relation to our subject below. We expect this book to make a contribution to what has been a neglected topic in academic courses on the social structure of modern Britain.

Using an objective approach does not, of course, mean that the writers of this book are uninterested or uninvolved with their subject. In at least consciously attempting to present data without any

particular sexist, political or philosophical bias, we are preferring
that readers bring their own views to the material and, hopefully,
develop them while in contact with the book. In no way do we
subscribe to the fallacy that the facts speak for themselves. For most
people, their beliefs, feelings and ways of understanding are of
equal or overriding importance to the facts themselves. It is valuable, therefore, to attempt to appreciate the variety of ways in
which the sex differences outlined in this book can be interpreted –
and a start can be made with the range of views given in the previous
section of this chapter (and see below and Chapter 2).

In the same way it has to be fully realised that evidence and data
always have limitations. In the present case these arise from several
sources which need to be appreciated. First, in looking at differences, just these are emphasised, and similarities are overlooked or
underemphasised. Sex differences are rarely total, since, although
the majority of one sex may differ from that of the other, some
members of both are likely to be similar. In turn this raises the
question of within, rather than between, sex differences, which in
some instances may be of the same order and interest. It is valuable,
then, to review the data in this book along such lines, though
explanations of similarity between, and differences within, the
sexes are not treated here in any detail and might, indeed, be more
complex than those for explaining differences between the sexes.
Second, limitations arise because most of the data presented below
were collected for purposes other than exhibiting or exploring sex
differences as such. The implications of using available, mainly
'official' data are that some interesting areas are unexplored and
criticisms can easily be raised about the data's collection, classification and presentation. The EOC have considered the latter in
depth (EOC 1980b) and comment 'the assumptions underlying the
statistical portrayal of women [as contained in official publications]
are, at points, so divorced from reality as to be dangerously misleading'. Third, and perhaps most serious, is that the data are theoretically inadequate. As Halsey (1972) argues in another context,

> A recurring problem is one which arises particularly in interpreting data
> relevant to social policy and the provision of welfare services. This is the
> difficulty of gaining from the statistics any idea of quality or adequacy.
> Obviously any analysis of health or welfare services or of housing should
> include some statement about how far the standard or amount of the
> service supplied meets the need for it. But for the most part the figures

are concerned only with supply; independent measures of need which would be required to judge adequacy are virtually nonexistent.

Ideally the answer to theoretically inadequate data is for research explicitly related to theory to be conducted. Wherever available, such research has been used, though it must be appreciated that, as yet, such work has been piecemeal. In any case it is by no means clear that adequate theories for the research have been developed, and, arguably, it may be some time until they are achieved. This does not mean that this book is atheoretical other than in the formal sense. We see the sexes as cultural products within a societal and historical setting. Consequently, differences between the sexes are clearly related to societal organisation and capable of almost infinite form and change. An aspect of this view is explored at some length in Chapter 2, which argues that the position of women in our society is constrained by, or the result of, their assumed role within the family and particularly in the labour market. By implication, the different position of men, and consequently sex differences, arise from the same factors. Our basic assumption about sex differences is that they are caused and persist because the sexes differ in access to most social resources, to power positions and opportunities. Ideally, perhaps, in a book about sex differences the position of both sexes would be dealt with explicitly and fully, though this would be tedious, given the obvious interrelationship of the sexes in society. So, although this book is explicitly about sex differences, our assumptions, and the cultural setting in which we write, lay emphasis on the aspect of women's penetration into the social structure. This is most obvious, for example, in Chapter 7, which looks at female participation in the sphere of politics, which until comparatively recently was an exclusively male preserve. The emphasis is clearly discernible throughout the book and informs our conclusions in the final chapter. The focus is underlined by the reversal of the traditional mode of presenting data, so that women precede men in all our tables. At the same time, the presentation of data for both sexes allows readers an opportunity to view 'the other side' and to evaluate and possibly reconstruct the portrayal of the sex differences presented.

Even within the limitations imposed by the considerations outlined so far, this book is not a comprehensive view of sex differences in our society. Quite apart from those areas for which there are no or few data, others have been intentionally excluded. Because of the customary assumptions about women's role being primarily within the family, and of sex differences being mainly the result of differing childhood socialisation, there is no direct treatment of either by chapter. Rather, relevant aspects of both appear in our consideration of perhaps less familiar and more important topics (in particular, see Chapters 2, 4, 6 and 8). In any case, the family and socialisation are areas that are best and most fully covered in the existing literature (see, for example, Belotti (1975), Comer (1972), *Half the Story* (1979), Harris (1979), Holter (1970) and Mair (1971)). Within our chosen topics, comprehensiveness, mainly through the necessity to contain the work within a single volume, has not been sought or achieved. Indeed, within general parameters identified here, each chapter is a particular view pursued by its writer.

The remaining general parameters used in this book are as follows. Our concern was only with British sex differences; therefore the data presented are exclusively British, and there is extremely little use, mention or even reference to material from other cultures. While we ourselves were sensitive to the proper meaning of Britain, the vagaries of research and publication in our society, and the limitations of space, have forced this book to follow the 'tradition' of often using English, or English and Welsh, data, rather than those for the whole of Britain. The data presented are, wherever possible, the most up-to-date and large-scale available. The selection was made from available sources up to May 1981; the only previously unpublished data used are those gained from certain public bodies and commercial enterprises to fill some gaps in the published sources. The criteria of data and scale relate to the objective of presenting a general picture of contemporary British sex differences: nearly all the data relate to the decade 1970–80. The criteria have not been entirely rigidly regarded, to the extent that, where historical comparison has been adjudged vital, brief reference has been made. Similarly, where large-scale studies have not existed, or where small-scale studies have made a significant contribution to the aims of the book, small-scale research has been used, or referenced. In the same way, where choice existed, data have been selected for their utility, comprehensiveness or quality and their temporal compatability with other data used, rather than simply for their up-to-dateness.

The data are presented in straightfoward tables to assist use and interpretation. As a general rule, figures and percentages have been rounded to the nearest whole number for the sake of clarity. Wherever available and desirable, base figures (normally sample size) have been provided. Similarly, wherever possible and useful, the average percentages for both sexes (the whole sample) have been included to facilitate comparison. No mention is made of the statistical significance of sex differences reported. This is because the large size of the samples or populations used in the research means that quite small differences are statistically significant. In any case, statistical significance does not tell one much about the importance of an observed difference in real terms. For example, very small numerical differences (which are not statistically significant) are very important in elections, while large differences in other areas may be of extremely limited importance or even interest. It is, then, in 'commonsense' terms that the sex differences presented in the chapters that follow should be viewed and considered. Little attempt has been made to provide a full exposition of the topics dealt with, but rather the text is a commentary on the data. This has been done not only with regard for the aims and limitations of the volume but because it is assumed that readers will have access to other appropriate descriptive and explanatory sources; that they will pursue these by means of the references given; or that their immediate interest centres, like that of this book, on the phenomena of sex differences.

It is also necessary to point out that categorising knowledge in any field is problematic. The following chapters provide cogent accounts of the sex differences to be observed in particular scenarios, and it is therefore possible that an impression of separateness might be deduced. This would be, of course, totally false, since the differences feed into and out of the different areas and should be viewed as a single phenomenon. It is hoped that readers will appreciate these interrelationships, and that the cross-referencing in the text, the index and the last chapter will assist the exploration and understanding of this important point.

2

Sex, gender and society

Andrew Cooper

In popular culture lip service is paid to the idea that there is sexual equality in our society. At the same time contradictory beliefs about women and men are common: first, that women and men are innately different, that they behave differently because they evolved differently, that men are naturally dominant in society and women passive and subordinate, and that this is beneficial and contributes towards the maintenance of social stability; second, that although it might be the case that women and men play different roles and occupy different positions this does not involve inequality, or domination and subordination – women and men simply have different spheres of interest, separate but equal. These two beliefs exist alongside ideas about sexual equality and have proved to be remarkably tenacious. Does this mean that the position of women has not in fact changed very much, or that there have been changes but that these have not been registered in popular culture? In part, of course, this question is bound up with the debate, central to most forms of social theory, about the role that can be accorded to ideology in the explanation of processes of change, and whether ideas are seen as the cause or the effect – or a combination of the two – of social change. Within such a debate it is important to recognise that beliefs and values are never precisely synchronised with objective social and economic conditions. It is the case that beliefs and values express these conditions and relations in complex and mediating ways; so the existence of contrasting beliefs about the position of women underlines the fact that such a position is complex.

It is, of course, possible to advance a number of arguments about the position of women in society. For example, it could be argued that the question is irrelevant, since if there is sexual equality there is no specific sociological problem to explore. Alternatively it could be argued that women are typically subordinate, despite some evidence of self-determination, because of biological influences which generate certain psychological and behavioural traits and which produce dependence on men and an acceptance of passive roles. Or, alternatively again, women's different position might be seen as due to social and cultural influences resulting from the division of labour (see Oakley 1972). What, then, can be regarded as the essential character of the position of women in society? The answer has three main aspects: first, an attempt to rescue women 'hidden from history', to discover the part played by women in relation to social, economic, cultural and political development (see Rowbotham 1973); second, an attempt to understand the nature of sexual divisions, the relations between women and men and the positions they occupy in society; and, third, a concern with the social construction of 'feminity' and what it means to be a woman socially and ideologically (see Sharpe 1976). The first of these aspects demands historical analysis and lies outside the scope of this work, but the second and third aspects provide our focus – namely, the theoretical understanding of the position of women in society. This is best accomplished by examining and attempting to explain the nature and sources of sexual divisions and their dynamic relationship to the general division of labour in society. Above all else it is perhaps vital to recognise that sexual divisions are not only embodied in social ideologies (that is, notions about how women and men should behave, what roles they should appropriately play, what their 'innate' natures are like) but also linked to basic aspects of the organisation of society. The identification of these basic aspects is the most effective way of examining sexual divisions, because these divisions can be seen not simply as 'side-effects' of any particular type of social organisation but as integral to it. The debate about the position of women in society is by no means resolved because of the persistence of fundamental disagreements about the source of sexual divisions. It would be almost impossible to review critically all the social theory and sociological literature in this field. Hence the focus here is to indicate the main aspects of theoretical discussions about the position of women in society and to suggest a particular way of analysing the problem.

SEX AND GENDER

There is a great deal of empirical evidence to suggest that biology plays only a small part in determining the behaviour of women and men (see Mead 1950; Oakley 1972) and that social influences are

much more important. Cross-cultural evidence has shown that
social roles regarded as 'natural' to one sex can easily be associated
with the other, according to social context – thus confirming that
there is no fixed role for either sex (see Mead 1950). Yet the notion
has persisted that women are 'naturally' suited to particular roles
because of their innate biological characteristics. This can be
regarded as an ideological claim more commonly known as 'sexism'
which can be defined as an 'ideology which attributes an unchanging
set of characteristics to a group of people [women] the inferior
position of the whole group and therefore supports and benefits the
group in power, in this case men' (Wilson 1974). And here there
are, of course, echoes of the way in which racist ideology is constructed and operates. Sexist ideology has often reinforced the
socially disadvantaged and socially subordinate position of women
reflected in, among other things, unequal job opportunities, financial and personal dependence upon men, and confinement to certain circumscribed roles (see Barker and Allen 1976a and 1976b).
Moreover, there is much evidence to suggest that the modifications
in the position of women contained in the Equal Pay Act (1970), the
Sex Discrimination Act (1975) and the Employment Protection Act
(1975) have not been very radical in their scope (see Oakley 1981;
Snell 1979). It can be argued, then, that women have remained
socially disadvantaged and subordinate, despite some changes in
job opportunities and legal rights. This is not, of course, to argue
that the position of women has remained historically constant, for
there are some fundamental differences between their position in
contemporary and Victorian Britain. Rather it is to argue that
within the context of different societies women are typically found
in disadvantaged and subordinate positions.

The starting-point of any attempt to understand the complex
relations between sex, gender and society must be a recognition of
the vital distinction that can be drawn between sex and gender. This
distinction is most commonly manifested in the notion that
'women's natural place is in the home'. 'Sex' refers to the biological
differences between men and women mainly in terms of differences
in procreative function. 'Gender', however, is a cultural concept,
relating to the social classification of 'masculine' and 'feminine', and
it refers to the ways in which these are socially constructed and
sustained, and can therefore be changed. The major consequence of
such a recognition is that the roles played by men and women are

seen to be not 'naturally' pre-given, since, if gender roles are seen as socially generated, sustained by socialisation and reflected in, and supported by, institutions, they are specific to, and characteristic of, particular societies. Sex differences may be natural but gender differences have their source in culture, not nature. Sex and gender differences tend to be confused; for example, Oakley (1972) writes:

> the aura of naturalness and inevitability that surrounds gender-differentiation in modern society comes, then, not from biological necessity but simply from the beliefs people hold about it. In particular, most people believe that there are inborn differences between the sexes; that differentiation increases social efficiency; and that differentiation is a natural law.

It is essential to recognise that gender roles are learned, and that the processes of learning are deeply embedded in socialisation and education, and constantly reinforced by the dominant images of popular culture (see Oakley 1972). This remains, though, a necessary but not a sufficient explanation of gender differentiation. While the source of gender differentiation can be located at the level of beliefs or ideologies, it is equally important to see that it has a source in material conditions – that is, in the mode of production and the subsequent social division of labour within which beliefs and ideologies arise.

To understand sex and gender in our society must therefore involve an attempt to disentangle 'sex' from 'gender' and relate gender roles to Britain's culture, polity and economy. One approach is to analyse the theoretical efforts made to understand the position of women. These address a number of key issues: the extent to which women occupy a specific place in the general division of labour; the extent to which women constitute a separate 'sex class'; the extent to which women can be located only in terms of the family; the precise nature of 'female labour'; and the extent to which the position of women is determined by the ideology of patriarchy. Examination of these issues shows how far gender differentiation is produced not by 'biological necessity' or 'inexorable social laws' but by identifiable material and cultural causes.

WOMEN, SOCIAL STRATIFICATION AND THE FAMILY

In attempting to locate women in the overall system of social stratification via the main theoretical contributions, two important qualifications need to be emphasised: first, any such theories are closely related to, and have implications for, the whole question of social inequality and the formation of class; second, the problem of 'locating' women also involves an examination of how their position has been produced both in and by society.

Attempts to produce a theoretical understanding of the location of women and, by implication, to assess the importance of gender as a separate dimension of social stratification have stimulated a great deal of mainly recent research and literature. However, much research into social stratification has failed to consider, in any systematic way, women in relation to the processes of social differentiation and class formation (see Goldthorpe 1980). The position of women has not been regarded as a subject requiring any special or distinctive teatment. Women are subsumed into categories of analysis which are pre-eminently male-oriented, though nominally gender-neutral, and which are 'men's models' (see Acker 1981). The existence of such male-oriented models has produced a feminist critique of conventional sociology in terms of methodological bias (see Acker 1981). It is not true that there is no discussion of sexual divisions within conventional sociology; rather, they are not given any substantial prominence.

It can be said that the dominant form of analysis in social stratification is one in which relations between economic organisation, occupational structure, class, status and power are manipulated to produce different theories of social structure and social inequality, in which problems related to gender are commonly excluded. Such exclusion is frequently taken for granted, though more often it is justified by, and assumes the form of, the thesis of 'marginality': 'Women are ambiguous: they do more than men to sustain the ideology of class, and yet is is clear that they are, even when gainfully employed, less central to social classes than are men' (Macrae 1972). According to this view, because they are marginal to the formation of classes women's position in the social structure is given little theoretical attention. This notion of the marginality of women is expressed elsewhere in the form of a theory of a distinct 'underclass', but this still retains the notions of the marginality and ambiguity of the position of women in the social structure.

Given that women still await their liberation from the family, it remains the case in capitalist societies that female workers are largely peripheral to the class system; or, expressed differently, women are in a sense the underclass of the white-collar sector. They tend to monopolise occupations which not only have a low economic return, but which are lacking in subsidiary economic benefits, have limited security of tenure, and offer little in the way of chances of promotion. (Giddens 1975)

In advancing this notion of an underclass, Giddens considers the overall impact of female employment in terms of the way in which it forms a part of a 'buffer zone' between the manual working class and the white-collar middle class, thus helping to prevent a polarisation of the two major classes. In considering the feminisation of certain white-collar occupations, Giddens says:

the fact that most of the occupations in question have become dominated by women workers probably acts to solidify as much as to dissolve the 'buffer zone' between the working and middle classes, and certainly must lead us to reject any of the more sweeping assertions about the 'proletarianisation' of the lower levels of the white-collar sector. (Giddens 1975)

According to this view, then, although women have been drawn increasingly into routine, lower-level, white-collar occupations, this does not fundamentally explain their place in the overall social structure, since the main conditioners of their position remain domestic labour and their family role. Indeed, the nature of domestic labour and the structure of the family decide the time and point of entry of women into the labour market. Specific patterns of marriage and childbirth are thus seen as the major factors that determine their class positions.

Both the thesis of 'marginality' and the theory of the 'underclass' are based on two interrelated, though tacit, assumptions. First, a claim that the most significant social relations are generated at the levels of production and consumption, which are reflected in the occupational structure in market position and power. And, since women are not as importantly, or as numerically, involved as men in these, they should be accorded a peripheral and inferior role in any analysis. Second, an implicit claim that women's place is in the family and that the family is outside class analysis. This latter is usually argued as an observation about reality and not as a prescriptive comment about what ought to be the role of women. As West (1978) has observed, 'women have been confined chiefly to their position as housewives, and female employment has been theoretically subordinated to the claims of domesticity'. More generally, the family is often seen as the crucial determinant of the position of women in social structure.

Conventional concerns with the role of women in relation to the family have come to occupy an important place in British sociology, especially from the perspective of the social consequences of their greater involvement in the labour market (see Klein 1965; Fogarty, Rapoport and Rapoport 1971; Yudkin and Holme 1963). A common focus of such work has been the examination of the tension between the roles of women in the family and in the occupational structure. This has led to a great deal of empirical work about the 'duality' of the position of women as wife-mother and employee. Over all such investigations have failed to theorise the location of women because the sexual division of labour was not seen as related to the forces and relations of production but rather to the 'changing needs' of 'industry' and 'society' and to changes in female perceptions of their role.

> Sociologists who have looked at the position of women in the labour market have traditionally assumed the general subordination of women in the family and society and have gone on to consider the factors underlying the decisions of women to participate in the labour market. Thus they have stressed the role conflicts that a working wife may experience, the importance of the household structure and the stage of the life cycle, and the family income position. In so doing, they have taken for granted, for example, the facts that men can go out to work without experiencing role conflicts (indeed, men will experience them if they stay at home) and that men will be considered the primary bread-winners. In other words, they have set aside some of the more important sociological puzzles by concentrating on the movement of women into and out of the labour force. By focussing . . . on [this aspect] they have diverted attention from the question of which jobs are filled by men and which by women – and, more importantly, from . . . explaining why . . . there are pronounced differences between men's and women's jobs. (Beechey 1978)

The resolution of these kinds of questions is vital in any attempt to understand theoretically the position of women in society. It must be emphasised that, although such questions can be viewed at the level of beliefs and ideologies (for example, the identification of the cultural reasons behind the general belief that men 'need' to work outside the family while women do not, or the analysis of the ideological construction of 'wife' and 'husband'), ultimately answers must be based on analysis of the forces and relations of production and their effect on social differentiation. Further, because the relations of production are not simply economic but also have political and ideological elements, it can be seen that the position of women in both the family and wider society is shaped by ideas of tradition and human nature, and reinforced by specific forms of social control and state policy (see Barrett 1980), all of which arise from the main productive processes. Conventional concerns about the family, women, and changing roles and perceptions fail to achieve this kind of understanding because they neglect analysis of material forces in favour of concentrating on interchanges between the family and the wider social system. Thus they neglect the question of class, material determination and ideology (see Klein 1965; Fogarty, Rapoport and Rapoport 1971; Yudkin and Holme 1963).

FEMINIST SOCIAL THEORIES

Quite paradoxically, while the domesticity of women has been the principal reason for the relegation of women into 'derivative status', the facts of domesticity have stimulated the emergence of social theories based on feminist social and historical analysis – in particular, feminist-Marxist analysis, which argues for a recognition of the unique location of women (see Barrett 1980; Kuhn and Wolpe 1978). It is important to recognise that these theories pursue two theoretical objectives: first, to identify the complex historical and social processes that generate the specific position of women in society – that is, the processes that operate through, and are mediated by, domesticity, general subordination and dependence, and 'peripheral' economic activity; second, to theorise the location of women in relation to social differentiation. It would be incorrect to characterise feminist analysis as being overtly homogeneous because it contains some methodological pluralism. However, it is possible to identify some of the principal currents within it.

Although there is often a tendency to locate women primarily in terms of the family (as the point of articulation between women and society), it has been argued that

> the family alone does not account for the position of women in the class structure. The sexual division of labour locates women to a particular

place within the structure of labour, that place being itself determined by the forces of capitalist production. . . . If there is no doubt that women manual workers are part of the working class in their own right by virtue of the labour which they perform, there is today much less doubt that most women non-manual workers also are – objectively speaking – part of the proletariat. (West 1978)

The sexual division of labour, then, allocates women to a specific place in a society defined and dominated by men which is, in turn, reflected in, and embedded in, patriarchal ideology, where ultimate anchorage is in the forces of industrial and perhaps capitalist production. This neat schema is able to give the sexual division of labour some priority and yet relate it to both class structure and the forces exerted by economic production. It does not, however, suggest that women occupy a separate position as a 'sex class' but rather that their position results from the way in which the sexual division of labour relates to the formation of classes.

WOMEN: PAID AND DOMESTIC LABOUR

The nature of female wage labour, and its function for the wider labour process, is an important issue for feminist writers mainly in terms of the way in which the sexual division of labour has a concrete impact on the nature of female wage labour. The findings in this field are well known (see Westergaard and Resler 1975). Female wage labour is characterised by low pay, insecurity, low levels of skill and particular susceptibility to recession (see Chapter 6). Clearly an important influence on the nature of this labour is women's acceptance of responsibility for childcare and household maintenance, which means that they are likely to be involved in 'convenient' paid work – for example, part-time and home work. Other categories of women's work are in large part ideologically constructed or at least have ideologically important connotations – for example, caring and serving jobs which are gender-based and for which much anticipatory socialisation occurs both before and during school.

What general reasons could be advanced to understand the nature of female wage labour? It could be argued that women provide an industrial 'reserve army' (see Beechey 1977), that they provide cheap labour and a more 'docile' labour force. There is a temptation to introduce an element of causal circularity into arguments about the nature of women's work: 'Ideological factors are seen as contributing to the preservation of the existing job structure for women, while the job structure is seen as a principal determinant of the inferior status of women as a social group and of the sexist ideology which helps to maintain their position' (Beechey 1978). This might be resolved by identifying particular patterns of female employment and relating them to primary causes – for example, economic expansion, 'rising expectations' or the opening up of certain jobs. Some jobs, while performing important functions in the labour process, have significant ideological elements; for example, nursing performs essential functions in health care but also embodies, reinforces and disseminates gender ideology. In other words, the ideological function is important, since in a crucial sense nursing is both the product of gender ideology as well as its practice. Other jobs do not possess such an obvious ideological element; for example, the employment of women in textile industries is mainly to do with the provision of cheap labour. The ideological element – it is the 'kind of job that women do' – although present, is more difficult to explain.

An important dimension of the nature of female labour is the 'domestic labour debate' (see Gardiner 1975; Molyneux 1979; Secombe 1974). Many conventional discussions of the position of women, although stressing the importance of the family, none the less separate domestic labour from both the wider labour process and the wider social context, thus preventing any serious analysis of the social functions of domestic labour. It has been claimed that domestic labour serves two principal functions, the reproduction of labour power and the reproduction of the relations of production of capitalism (see Secombe 1974). The first is performed by the bearing and rearing of children and by the servicing of male labour, the second by the socialisation and support of male labour. The major difficulty here is whether domestic labour can be regarded as essential to the existence of a given form of production. Some feminist writers are sceptical of this kind of functionalist claim, since it tends to reduce the family to an agent of the reproduction of capitalism (see Barrett 1980). However, this functionalist fallacy can be avoided if domestic labour is seen as a necessary though not sufficient condition of existence. It is clear, however, that domestic labour occurs in the home where gender is constructed, and, since this concept is crucial in understanding the interrelationship of the sexual division of labour and the relations of production, the part played by domestic labour must be emphasised. A much more orthodox view of the nature of domestic labour is to link such labour not to capitalism specifically but more generally to industrial society and to the needs of technologically developed societies, as well as to the influence of biologistic factors.

A major current within feminist writing regards the family as being at the base of women's oppression because it is a prime mechanism for gender socialisation – for example, ideologies of domesticity and maternity for women, and of breadwinning for men (see Zaretsky 1976; Chodorow 1978; Poster 1978). It is sometimes argued that the dichotomy between the 'dependence' of women and the male 'breadwinner' is by no means as dramatic as this, and that the role of women in wage-earning to support the family must be taken seriously (see Land 1976; and Chapter 4). To some extent this seems a rather artificial debate, since in order to show that the present structure of the family is oppressive for women the principal arguments are the existence of a constraining domestic ideology which accords to women the primary role of childcare and other domestic responsibilities. If this can be demonstrated, then some important conditions of oppression are established. What needs to be empirically investigated is the extent to which household structure mirrors the social relations of production (see Barrett 1980). The most significant comment about the family is that, as it is presently constituted, it is simultaneously both the product of gender conditioning and a prime agent of gender conditioning (see Barrett 1980).

WOMEN, MEN AND POWER RELATIONS

In considering the nature of feminist analysis, it is useful to distinguish between those which are pre-eminently concerned with the problem of women's oppression by men, and those which are more informed by various Marxisms which stress how such oppression is related to capitalist political economy. The first is concerned to identify the way in which men control women; the relations between men and women are seen as relations of power. This could be called the 'sexual politics' current within feminist writing (see Millett 1969; Greer 1971; Frankfort 1972; Brownmiller 1975; Smart and Smart 1978). In this view, questions of physical sexuality are regarded as central to the oppression of women, in the sense that the dominant ideology of sexuality creates a relation of domination and subordination between men and women. In turn, these are reflected in a number of diverse areas and practices – for example, in literature and the media, as well as in personal relationships.

A major strength of feminist social analysis lies in its identification of the concrete impact of sexual divisions on all aspects of social life, especially of the way in which relations between men and women tend to be relations of domination and dependence. A further strength resides in the attempt to show how sexual divisions have a material basis in the social relations of production and how such divisions are embodied in, and reinforced by, the family structure, educational processes, state action and the labour market itself. The role of patriarchal ideology in gender conditioning is also underlined, especially the way in which it 'constructs' feminity by stressing 'female characteristics' and propagates a dual image of women as the sexual property of men and chaste mothers of children. The crucial thrust of this kind of social theory is to demonstrate how gender is constructed and how the oppression of women is related to this construction, which is seen as socially engendered and materially anchored.

Within feminist analysis, however, it is clear that some significant theoretical problems remain unresolved – for example, the extent to which sexual divisions tend to distort women's position in the class system and social stratification, and the issue that, although the material basis of sexual divisions can be identified, the way in which these are produced and the needs they satisfy remain unestablished.

SEX, GENDER AND THE ECONOMY

In what way, then, can sex and gender be unravelled from the various attempts to locate women in the social structure? This can be achieved mainly in terms of some theoretical guidelines from the central discussion of this chapter: (1) a recognition that personality and behavioural characteristics are deemed 'masculine' and 'feminine' in relation to, and as a result of, specific cultural and historical situations; (2) a recognition that women occupy a specific position in the general division of labour which is linked to, but not absorbed by, the class system; (3) a recognition that ideology and cultural practice play a central part in the construction of gender – for example, ideologies of domesticity, romantic love and patriarchy operate to produce 'wife', 'mother', 'husband', 'lover', etc. – and that these are ideologically constructed 'subjects'; (4) a recognition that the educational system plays a major part in the maintenance of a gender-divided society through processes of gender conditioning: (5) a recognition that household organisation and female domestic labour, as well as the 'duality' of women's roles, contribute towards the conditions of existence of economic production via childcare, household management, and domestic and wage labour. These guidelines confirm that sexual divisions are not marginal but rather central in understanding modern British society.

The distinction between sex and gender is now widely recognised, though two important problems remain: first, the extent to which recent social and legal changes have transformed or modified the position of women; second, the extent to which sexual divisions can be conceptualised in 'functionalist' terms as necessary for the maintenance of the dominant forms of economic activity. These two problems are clearly interrelated and have been addressed by feminist writers; for example:

> it is inadequate to attempt to grasp the character of women's oppression in contemporary capitalism in terms of the supposed needs of capitalism itself. The reasoning in favour of this analysis has tended to be couched in terms of capital's support for a system of the reproduction of labour power, through domestic labour in the household that operates at the lowest possible cost and provides a cheap and flexible reserve army of married women workers to lower the price of wages in general. Although these are undoubtedly important points in any explanation of capital's support for a household in which a wife and children are assumed to be dependent upon a male breadwinner, the argument leaves unexplained many aspects of women's oppression. The charge that this is a functionalist one is not in my view as important as the fact that it tends towards a reductionist account of women's oppression and denies specific aspects of women's subordination to men in the pre-capitalist period, in socialist societies and within the different classes in contemporary capitalism. (Barrett 1980)

This kind of argument suggests a different, radical, non-functionalist conceptualisation of the position of women.

> A model of women's dependence has become entrenched in the relations of production of capitalism, in the division of labour in wage work and between wage labour and domestic labour. As such, an oppression of

women that is not in any essentialist sense pre-given by the logic of capitalist development has become necessary for the ongoing reproduction of the mode of production in its present form. Hence the oppression of women, although not a functional pre-requisite of capitalism, has acquired a material basis in the relations of production and the reproduction of capitalism today. (Barrett 1980)

If it is accepted that the position of women is causally related in this way to the productive processes of society, then how can social and legal changes in the position be understood – for example, the effects of the Equal Pay Act (1970), the Sex Discrimination Act (1975) and the Employment Protection Act (1975) and the effects of some female entry into professions and occupations previously completely male-dominated? Some of these developments are attributable to changes in the economic system; for example, greater job opportunities for women can be related to economic expansion, the need to exploit the potential 'talent' of a wider population because of the demands of technological development (though economic recession will clearly inhibit this). Other developments must be regarded as the product of struggle or political pressure – for example, the acquisition of abortion rights. It might be suggested that the dominant economic, social and political system can adapt to 'reforms' in relation to the position of women, but its ability to do so in relation to 'radical' transformations in the position of women is doubtful, since such changes would not only have effects on the social system but could only be based on fundamental changes to it.

The liberation of women would require, first, a redivision of the labour and responsibilities of childcare. Whether privatised or collectivised, it would be mandatory that this be shared between men and women. Second, the actual or assumed dependence of women on a male wage (or capital) would need to be done away with. Third, the ideology of gender would need to be transformed. None of these seem to me to be compatible with capitalism as it exists in Britain and the comparable societies today. The widespread and profound job-segregation characterising the social division of labour will prove intractable. Male employment is predicated upon the assumption that domestic and childcare responsibilities are unimportant for them, and this holds true in all classes. State provisions, although not entirely inflexible, constitute a leaden weight of support for the male breadwinner system of household maintenance. The ideology of gender and sexuality is deeply ingrained in our consciousness. These divisions are systematically embedded in the structure and texture of capitalist social relations in Britain and they play an important part in the political and ideological stability of this society . . . and it is impossible to imagine that they could be extracted from the relations of production and reproduction of capitalism without a massive transformation of those relations taking place. (Barrett 1980)

Sexual divisions, then, are profoundly interwoven into the social relations of society. It is clear from this that these social relations and the production system of which they are an intrinsic part could only 'tolerate' certain kinds of change without experiencing fundamental transformations. It can be suggested that there is a shifting 'margin of tolerance' between changes in the position of women that are 'reforms' and those that are 'radical' transformations; and this will depend upon historical circumstances, the balance of social forces and the specific form assumed by the relations of production.

OVERVIEW

A number of conclusions can be stated. First, it is important to acknowledge that sexual divisions appear necessary for British society as it is presently constituted. These divisions are not necessary in any biological or moral sense, but necessary in the sense that there exists a relation of 'dependence' between the position of women and the specific alignments of culture, polity and economy in Britain. The purpose of much empirical inquiry ought to be to describe this relation of 'dependence' and to analyse the part it plays in forming the social structure of Britain. Second, it seems possible that some of the dominant theories about sex, gender and stratification can be challenged – especially, for example, the view that sex differences cannot be usefully thought of as components of stratification

because for the great majority of women the allocation of social and economic rewards is determined primarily by the position of their families – and, in particular, that of the male head . . . only if the disabilities attaching to female status were felt to be so great as to override differences of a class kind would it be realistic to regard sex as an important dimension of stratification. (Parkin 1972)

It is, of course, true that the extent to which gender may cancel out the determining effects of class or any other dimension of stratification remains problematic, and much feminist writing is still grappling with this problem. However, it needs to be recognised that gender does mediate the effects of the other components of stratification, so that

> a new approach to the analysis of class is therefore crucial. We should recognise that women on account of their position in our society as houseworkers, childbearers and dependants of men have a dual relationship to the class structure. On the one hand there is the direct involvement in wage labour which most women now experience throughout the bulk of their adult lives and on the other there is that aspect of their relationship to class which is mediated by the family, dependence on men and domestic labour. (Gardiner 1977)

It therefore follows that

> labour is distributed both horizontally between separate industries or labour processes and vertically within each labour process. Within both the horizontal and vertical distributions of labour, women and men are not evenly spread throughout but are unevenly concentrated in such a way that a large proportion of jobs are predominantly male or female. This uneven concentration is what we mean by the sexual division of labour. (Gardiner 1977)

There remain fundamental disputes about the source of women's position in society. It could be argued that sex–gender relations are primarily generated by patriarchy or by the class system that characterises capitalism, or by the essential nature of 'industrial-technological' society, or by the persistence of 'traditional attitudes'. The extent to which the principle of patriarchy constitutes the most fundamental and compelling principle of social organisation is still open to question:

> When contemporary feminists began to examine the world from a new perspective, bringing their own experience to bear on their understanding of history and modern society, they found it was necessary to distinguish women's subordination as a sex from class oppression. Inequality between men and women was not just a creation of capitalism: it was a feature of all societies for which we had reliable evidence. It was a separate phenomenon, which needed to be observed in connection with, rather than simply as a response to, changes that occurred in the organisation and control of production. So the term 'patriarchy' was pressed into service – as an analytical tool which might help to describe this vital distinction. The term has been used in a great variety of ways. 'Patriarchy' has been discussed as an ideology which arose out of men's power to

exchange women between kinship groups; as a symbolic male principle; and as the power of the father (its literal meaning). It has been used to express men's control over women's sexuality and fertility; and to describe the institutional structure of male domination. Recently the phrase 'capitalist patriarchy' has suggested a form peculiar to capitalism. (Rowbotham 1979)

But the significance of patriarchy in relation to economic structure in determining the position of women remains unestablished. Indeed, it might be argued that the major enduring problem for the social analysis of the position of women in society is the problem of the relation between patriarchy and class domination as the chief principles of social organisation.

3

Vital statistics

Ivan Reid

This chapter is concerned with the literal meaning of its title. It deals with several fundamental aspects of sex differences of life in our society. These aspects are often, though inappropriately, seen as simple biological and intransigent facts of life. The chapter begins with a view of something of the demography of sexes – their sizes, age structures and distribution – leading to a consideration of sex differences in the chances of, and survival at, birth and childhood. There are substantial accounts of various aspects of health, of causes of death and of life expectancy. Finally, the chapter looks at sex differences in that other commonly regarded vital statistic, marital status and experience. Because of the nature of these topics and the concerns of this chapter, there is an almost exclusive use of governmental statistics. While the purpose and manner in which such data were collected do not always coincide with the objectives of this chapter, they are comprehensive in scope and in providing both a national and a historical picture. The topics covered in this chapter are not simply matters of sex. They are clearly related to the culture and development of our society. Of particular importance are the other major forms of social stratification, namely age and social class. While reference to the interrelationships of these factors with the topics covered is made in the text, space has precluded a full treatment. Interested readers will find that the quoted references will usually provide more information on age and often on social class. This last factor is reviewed in respect of birth, health and death in Reid (1981).

As was pointed out in Chapter 1, all data have limitations and have to be viewed from within these limits. These considerations, not rehearsed here, must be borne in mind when reading the present chapter, along with some particular concerns. Most medical data come from the analyses of people seeking or receiving treatment or

29

care and so obviously tell us nothing directly about the health of others. Official health statistics have been accused of being male-biased and therefore relatively uninformative about women (see, for example, Macfarlane 1980). Similarly, studies of some areas of health have not used sex as a variable and are therefore not relevant to this chapter. Indeed, it is perhaps surprising that medical litera-ture does not always use sex as a variable and that in comparison social class appears of greater concern. While some of these con-siderations are specifically illustrated below, this chapter presents the picture of vital sex differences from existing evidence.

THE DEMOGRAPHY OF SEX

A basic biological fact is that the sex ratio at birth is imbalanced in favour of males. In Western societies there are about 105–6 male births to each 100 female births, while worldwide higher variations have been observed – for example, in Korea one of 115.3 males (Noviski 1977). It has been suggested that at fertilisation the figures could be more disproportionate, at around 60 males to 40 females (Penrose 1973). It seems likely that implantation and all subsequent stages of gestation display a higher wastage of male than female foetuses (Teitelbaum 1972).

Despite this fact, women are the majority sex in our society. The figures in table 3.1 reveal that, of the 49,175,400 persons in England and Wales in 1977, 51.2 per cent were females and 48.8 per cent males – the difference amounting to an extra 1,220,800 females. A female majority has been the case historically, though an interesting change has taken place during the present century. Earlier this century there were more females than males in each of the age groups – reflecting the fact that, while more boy babies were born, their chances of survival and their expectation of life were poorer than girls' (see below). By the 1931 census, as the result of improve-ments in medical and health care and consequent enhanced survival at birth, there was a higher percentage of boys than girls in the age group 0–14 years in England and Wales. This change has been maintained, so that by 1977 males were the majority in all age groups up to 40–4 years, the sexes were balanced in the age group 45–9 years, while the older age groups displayed female majorities increasing in size with age (see table 3.1). It seems unlikely, however, that in the future males will become the majority sex in all

TABLE 3.1
THE PERCENTAGES OF EACH SEX IN AGE GROUPS, ENGLAND AND WALES, JUNE 1977 (ESTIMATED)

	% of population	Females	Males	Difference in 1000s	
All ages	100	51.2	48.8	1,220.8	More females
0–4	6.2	48.6	51.4	88.2	
5–9	7.7	48.6	51.4	105.9	
10–14	8.2	48.7	51.3	105.5	
15–19	7.7	48.7	51.3	101.3	
20–4	7.0	48.6	51.4	98.8	More males
25–9	7.2	49.6	50.4	29.9	
30–4	7.0	49.4	50.6	38.2	
35–9	5.8	49.2	50.8	42.3	
40–4	5.6	49.2	50.8	44.8	
45–9	5.8	50.0	50.0	under 1.0	
50–4	6.0	50.6	49.4	38.1	
55–9	5.9	51.8	48.2	103.0	
60–4	5.5	53.0	47.0	162.4	
65–9	5.1	55.2	44.8	259.5	More females
70–4	4.1	58.8	41.2	355.3	
75–9	2.8	64.7	35.3	400.9	
80–4	1.6	70.5	29.5	311.6	
85–9	0.7	74.3	25.7	168.9	
90+	0.3	78.8	21.2	75.4	

	% of population	Females	% of all females	Males	% of all males		
Under 15	22.2	48.6	21.0	51.4	23.4	299.6	
15–44	40.2	49.1	38.5	50.9	42.0	355.3	More males
45 to retirement (male 65, female 60)	20.2	44.4	17.5	55.6	23.1	1,116.7	
Over retirement age	17.4	67.5	22.9	32.5	11.6	2,992.4	More females

(Devised from *OPCS Monitor, PP1 78/2* (1978)

age groups because they have higher mortality rates and consequently lower expectation of life than females (see p. 52 below). As
the lower part of table 3.1 displays, such differences as these,
together with differing retirement ages for the sexes, result in 22.9
per cent of women compared with 11.6 per cent of men being over
the age for retirement. At the same time, 65.4 per cent of males and
59.5 per cent of females were under the age of 45 years. There are
likely to be many social implications arising from the fact that
women remain a majority only in the older age groups. It is of more
than passing interest to note that the heightened interest in women's
rights and position, together with the emergence of women's movements, have occurred at a point in history where for the first time
those women most likely to be actively involved in such concerns are
a sexual minority.

There is some geographical variation in the sexual composition of
our society. This is mainly due to the higher male births and longer
female lives, already mentioned, together with sex-selective migration. Consequently the proportion of males is higher in areas with
high birth rates and lower in areas with high numbers of the elderly.
Major contrasts are to be found only between or within individual
settlements (*People in Britain* 1980). Concentrations of men are
scattered and are to be found in heavily industrialised areas – such as
the West Midlands, South Yorkshire, Slough and Staines, Teesside,
areas on coalfields, and some inner-city areas of the Midlands and
the South. Some of these areas are likely to be affected by the
presence of New Commonwealth immigrant groups, among whom
men predominate. Male concentrations are also to be found in rural
areas as a result of female migration out, in the face of inadequate
employment opportunities. On the other hand, concentrations of
women are most marked in coastal retirement areas – the coasts of
Kent, Sussex, Dorset, Devon, North Wales and West Lancashire.
Older urban areas, like West London, Liverpool, Newcastle and
Scottish cities, also have higher proportions of women, possibly
because of selective migration in by younger women and out by
men, together with higher male mortality rates in deprived areas
(though such concentrations are absent from cities in the Midlands).

BIRTH, INFANCY AND CHILDHOOD

An analysis of the 596,418 live births in England and Wales in 1978
shows that 307,088 were male and 289,330 were female: a sex ratio

of 106.1 to 100 (*Birth Statistics 1978* 1980). This ratio displays some variation over time, being high at 106.5 in 1973 and low at 104.4 in 1930 and lower at 103.5 between 1896 and 1900. Births in 1978 represented a crude birth rate of 12.1 per 1000 population of all ages and a general fertility rate of 60.7 per 1000 women aged 15–44 years. Both these rates are considerably lower than in the previous decade; for example, in 1964 they were 18.6 and 93 respectively.

While still-birth rates are very similar for the two sexes, figures show that infancy and childhood are safer for girls than for boys (see table 3.2). The number of boys' deaths in the first year following birth is almost a third higher than that of girls' – 19.9 compared with 15.3 per 1000 live births – the largest difference being in the first week of life. During childhood the sex difference in death rate increases with age. At ages 1–4 years there are 11.2 more male deaths per 100,000 than female deaths, while at ages 10–14 years the difference is 14. Both infant and child mortality are related to social

TABLE 3.2
STILL-BIRTHS, INFANT DEATHS AND DEATHS TO CHILDREN IN ENGLAND AND WALES 1970–2, BY SEX

	Girls	Boys	
Still-births*	12.7	12.4	Number per 1000 live and still-births§
Early neonatal deaths† (less than a week)	8.6	11.6	Number per 1000 live births§
Late neonatal deaths (1–3 weeks)	1.6	1.8	
Post-neonatal deaths (1–11 months)	5.1	6.5	
All infant mortality	15.3	19.9	
Deaths to children aged:			
1–4 years	67.4	78.6	Rate per 100,000 per year§
5–9 years	28.6	41.6	
10–14 years	22.6	36.6	
Number of deaths	5932	8389	

* Still-births are births beyond the 28th week of pregnancy at which there is no sign of life
† Neonatal deaths and infant mortality are deaths within the year following a live birth
§ All figures are rounded to one decimal place
(Derived from tables 7.7 and 7.8, *Occupational Mortality* 1978)

class, displaying a rise in incidence across the classes from Registrar
General's class I to class V (for a full review, see Butler and Bonham
1963 for deaths under one year, and Adelstein and White 1976 for
children's deaths). Apart from health, childhood appears less
hazardous for girls than for boys; for example, girls have lower rates
of hospital admission, out-patient treatment and deaths because of
accidents (Macfarlane 1979). Finally, though the numbers are relatively low, more boys than girls start life with a malformation, the
rates per 100,000 live births in 1978 being 2117 for boys and 1813 for
girls (*Social Trends No. 10* 1979).

HEALTH AND THE USE OF HEALTH SERVICES

Governmental research provides a number of views of the distribution of sickness, disease and other conditions of ill-health –
normally referred to as morbidity – which, indirectly, provide a view
of the state of health of our society. Of course, there are two related
aspects of health: the subjective – how people feel about, and react
to, their health; and the objective – the diagnosis made by doctors
when consulted. These two aspects are the first concerns of this
section, which also includes considerations of some selected specific
conditions, of health hazards and the use of health services. A
further view of morbidity is provided in the following section on
causes of death.

The *General Household Survey 1977* (1979) contained several
questions designed to elicit people's views of their health, its effects
on their lives and how they coped. A distinction was made between
chronic health problems and health during the fourteen days prior
to interview. For chronic problems, respondents were shown a list
of common conditions (excluding short-term ones like colds, etc.)
described in terms people normally use. Later they were asked to
mention any other health problems. Short-term problems (coughs,
colds, indigestion, and so on) were separately but similarly investigated. Perhaps surprisingly, table 3.3 reveals that only 15 per cent of
women and 23 per cent of men claimed to have no health problems
of either type, and rather similar proportions to have only short-
term ones, while 70 per cent of women and 56 per cent of men
claimed chronic problems, with 43 per cent of women and 31 per
cent of men reporting short-term and chronic problems in combination. Of course, age is a significant factor in health, and as was

TABLE 3.3
SELF-REPORTED HEALTH AND HEALTH BEHAVIOUR OF
PERSONS AGED 16 YEARS AND OVER, BY SEX
(PERCENTAGES)

	Women	Men	
No health problems	15	23	
Short-term problems only	15	21	
Chronic problems only	27	25	
Short-term and chronic problems	43	31	In the 14 days prior to being interviewed
Acted differently because of health problem	53	42	
Took medication*	57	43	
Consulted GP over problem	11	8	
Asked for advice elsewhere	14	12	
% of those with chronic health problem who			
Took constant care	71	67	
Had contact with health services in last year	67	60	
Acted differently because of problem	40	31	In the 14 days prior to being interviewed
Had taken medication*	58	48	
Consulted GP	11	9	
Sought advice elsewhere	9	7	
Reported health in previous year as			
Good	53	65	
Fairly good	34	26	
Not good	14	9	

*Includes medicines, pills, dressings, injections, etc.
N = 12,322 women, 10,731 men
(Derived from tables 6.1–6.7, 6.13, 6.14, 6.16 and 6.18, *General Household Survey 1977* 1979)

seen in table 3.1 the age structures of the sexes are different. With respect to chronic health problems, the percentage reporting these increased with age for both sexes, with more women than men having such problems at all ages, but the difference declined with age. As the second part of table 3.3 shows, of people with chronic problems, over two-thirds of both sexes took constant care – like taking things carefully or slowly, having regard for the weather or taking medication. A slightly higher percentage of women reported having had contact with health services in the past year. Behaviour in the previous fourteen days due to chronic conditions displayed some variation by sex (see last four rows of the second section of the table) but varied little by age. The incidence of short-term health problems showed smaller differences between the sexes, 52 and 58 per cent for men and women respectively; these proportions were similar for all ages, but there was an overall decline of incidence with increasing age (perhaps owing to lower frequency at higher ages and to the more common occurrence of chronic conditions which may mask the short-term ones).

The sample was also asked to rate their health during the previous year. As the last section of table 3.3 shows, almost two-thirds of the men compared with just over a half of the women reported this as 'good', while 14 per cent of women compared with 9 per cent of men chose 'not good'. Obviously such attitudes are related to the incidence of health problems; however, even among those with both types of problem, 47 per cent of men and 38 per cent of women reported their health as 'good'. Over all, women were less likely than men to rate their health as good, this being true for all age groups and even among those with no health problems. It seems probable that this variation may reflect sex differences in attitudes towards health – for example, that men may be less willing to admit problems – as well as to the fact that some common problems apply particularly to women, for example, varicose veins, menstruation and trouble with feet. In all age groups over half the women and about two-fifths of men reported doing something different in the period prior to interview on account of their health. Comparative percentages for women and men were: using medication other than that taken constantly, 57 and 43; consulting a doctor, 11 and 8 (in the age group 16–44 years twice as many women as men did this); consulting somebody other than a doctor, 14 and 12.

Differences in the incidence of particular types of ill-health in the sexes are indicated in a variety of separate sources – from analyses of general practitioner consultations, of absences from work, hospital admissions and the causes of death. The first three are dealt with here and the last in the following section of this chapter. The data in table 3.4 are the results of the careful recording of the consultations undertaken by doctors in forty-three practices in England and Wales during one year, expressed as rates per 1000

TABLE 3.4
RATE PER 1000 POPULATION CONSULTING GPs, BY SELECTED
MAIN DIAGNOSIS; REFERRALS PER 1000 POPULATION; AND
PERCENTAGE OF CONSULTATIONS WHICH WERE HOME
VISITS, BY SEX 1971–2

	Females	*Males*	*Both*
Main diagnosis			
Infective and parasitic disease[1]	82	82	82
Cancer	15	10	12
Endocrine, nutritional and metabolic disease[2]	37	16	27
Diseases of the blood	18	5	12
Mental disorders	149	74	113
Diseases of the nervous system	118	110	114
Diseases of the circulatory system[3]	75	56	66
Diseases of the respiratory system[4]	264	264	264
Diseases of the digestive system[5]	82	81	82
Accidents/poisoning/violence	81	102	91
Prophylactic procedures[6] and medical examination	179	88	135
All diagnoses[7]	700	622	663
Referrals			
In-patient	20	17	18
Out-patient	101	83	92
Investigations	150	79	116
Local authority[8]	7	6	7
Multiple and other[9]	9	6	7
All referrals	286	190	240
% of consultations that were home visits	14.9	13.1	

[1] Includes tuberculosis
[2] Includes diabetes and nutritional deficiencies
[3] Includes heart disease, embolisms and thrombosis
[4] Includes influenza, pneumonia, bronchitis and pneumoconiosis
[5] Includes ulcers and cirrhosis of the liver
[6] e.g. inoculations, vaccinations, contraceptive advice, cervical smears, etc.
[7] Includes causes not specified here
[8] Clinics and social work agencies
[9] Referrals to more than one type or types not identified here
(Derived from tables 9(a), 13 and 15, *Morbidity Statistics from General Practice 1971–72* 1979)

persons on the practices' lists, by sex and diagnosis. Over all there was a larger proportion of female consultations (see row 12). Some grouped, selected diagnoses revealed little sex difference, while others, notably cancer, endocrine, nutritional and metabolic disease, mental disorders, diseases of the circulatory system and of the blood, had much higher rates for females. Accidents, poisoning and violence is the only case in which males have a significantly higher rate. Prophylactic (inoculation, vaccination, contraception, cervical smears, etc.) and medical examination consultations display a female rate over twice that of the male. Similarly, female rates of referral to hospitals and other institutions were higher than those for males, and marginally more consultations with females were conducted in the patient's home.

Consultation with one's local doctor involves not only a very wide range of short-term and chronic conditions but also the whole range of levels of seriousness of such conditions. The first and obviously deeper level of ill-health is incapacity for one's normal activities. For our purposes a useful indicator is absence from work due to sickness or injury certified by a medical practitioner (see table 3.5). While obvious, this indicator is not absolute, since variation can be assumed in both doctor's readiness to certify, and patient's seeking absence from work. Attitudes towards sickness and work, work habits, conditions and demands are clearly involved. Some manual jobs are more hazardous and more demanding of physical fitness than most non-manual ones. The *General Household Survey 1972* (1975) reported higher rates of absence from work due to sickness among manual workers (there was a rising gradient of such absence across the social classes) and among those dissatisfied with their jobs. Further, when looking at the figures in table 3.5, it should be remembered that there is considerable variation not only in the proportion of the sexes at work (see Chapter 6) but also in the age structures of the sexes at work. Women at work are, as a group, younger than men, not only because of differing retirement ages and breaks in, or termination of, employment associated with marriage and child-bearing, but also, in this particular case, because a smaller percentage were insured for sickness or invalidity benefit – the criterion for inclusion (see footnote to table 3.5). With these limitations, the data show that certified spells of incapacity for work were higher per 1000 women at risk than for men in 1975 (536 compared with 449). Some of the observable sex differences in

TABLE 3.5
RATE PER 1000 PERSONS AT RISK* OF NEW SPELLS OF
CERTIFIED INCAPACITY FOR WORK,[†] BY CAUSE OF
INCAPACITY[§] AND SEX, GREAT BRITAIN 1975

	Women	*Men*
Infective and parasitic disease[1]	49	39
Cancer and other neoplasms	1	1
Mental disorders	25	14
Disorders of the nervous system	7	7
Heart disease	3	9
Influenza	50	48
Bronchitis, emphysema	25	34
Other diseases of the respiratory system	125	79
Diseases of the digestive system	29	34
Arthritis, rheumatism (not fever)	15	23
Symptoms and ill-defined conditions	71	45
Accidents,[2] poisoning, violence	22	34
All causes[3]	536	449

* The working population excluding men 65–9 and women 60–4 who were pensioners, all men over 70, all women over 65, the armed forces, mariners at sea, most non-industrial civil servants and Post Office employees, and married women and widows who have chosen not to be insured. Rates have been rounded.
[†] Commenced spells of claims for sickness or invalidity benefits under National Insurance Acts
[§] Selected causes only, classified by diagnosis on last medical certificate
[1]Not including tuberculosis of respiratory system
[2]Excluding fractures, sprains and strains
[3]Including causes not specified here
N = a 2½ per cent sample of claimants whose certified incapacity was recorded at local offices
(Derived from table 11.2, *Health and Personal Social Services Statistics for England 1978* 1980)

particular conditions are probably related to age and employment differences between the sexes – for example, the higher male rates for bronchitis, arthritis and rheumatism. Looking at the seven highest overall rates by cause for each sex reveals that both lists share diseases of the respiratory system, influenza, symptoms and ill-defined conditions, infective and parasitic disease (all of which have higher female rates) and bronchitis and diseases of the digestive system (male higher), but the female list includes mental disorders and the male includes accidents, poisoning, violence. These two sex differences can also be observed in tables 3.4 and 3.6 and are discussed below on pp. 44 and 52.

A further general indicator of the seriousness of ill-health is admission to hospital, though again there will be variation on a host of factors – like availability of beds, referral practice, circumstances of would-be patient and, indeed, choice. Our view is limited to National Health Service hospitals, though the availability and use of private hospitals and beds affects the situation. Note that in table 3.6 the rates are expressed as per 10,000 population (non-psychiatric) and per 100,000 (mental health), whereas tables 3.4 and

TABLE 3.6
IN-PATIENT ADMISSIONS* TO NATIONAL HEALTH SERVICE
HOSPITALS, BY SELECTED DIAGNOSTIC CAUSE AND SEX,
ENGLAND 1975

	Females	*Males*	*Total*
(a) *Non-psychiatric*			
(rate per 10,000 population)			
Tuberculosis, infective, parasitic disease	19	22	20
Cancer	61	62	61
Endocrine, nutritional, metabolic disease[†]	21	15	18
Diseases of the blood	9	7	8
Diseases of the nervous system	19	18	18
Heart disease, rheumatic fever, hypertensive disease	46	65	55
Diseases of the respiratory system[†]	63	86	74
Diseases of the digestive system[†]	83	101	92
Pregnancy, childbirth, puerperium	882* aged 15–44		
Other injuries[§] and reactions	63	86	74
All causes**	1,150	824	991
(b) *Mental health*			
(rate per 100,000 population)			
Mental illness hospitals/units	437	314	377
Mental handicap hospitals/units	23	33	28

* Rates are for all ages, except for pregnancy, childbirth, puerperium, which are for 15–44 only
[†] See relevant footnote to table 3.4 for examples of conditions included
[§] Excluding fractures, dislocations and sprains
** Includes causes not specified here
N = 10 per cent sample of in-patient records
(Derived from (a) table 11.6, *Health and Personal Social Services Statistics for England 1978* 1980; (b) tables A1.1 and B1.1, *In-Patient Statistics from the Mental Health Enquiry for England 1977* 1980)

3.5 used rates per 1000, so direct comparisons of incidence can be made only with appropriate movement of the decimal place. Also, as has been pointed out, such comparisons are limited by the fact that the data arise from separate measures – see below and p. 50. The first section of table 3.6 shows female admission rates to hospital to be much higher than male (1150 compared with 824) – though, clearly, most of this difference is accounted for by the rates for pregnancy and childbirth (see table 3.7 and text below). If that cause of admission is left aside, a comparison of the sexes reveals slightly higher male admission rates for all the listed causes other than endocrine, nutritional and metabolic disease, and diseases of the blood and of the nervous system. With respect to mental health the table reveals an interesting sex difference between mental illness and mental handicap admission. In the first, as might be expected from its incidence in general practitioner consultations and absence from work, the female rate is much higher than the male (437 compared with 314 per 100,000 population). In contrast, admission for mental handicap is higher for males and the proportional difference between the sexes is even greater: males 33 per 100,000 compared to 23 for females.

At this point it is appropriate to reiterate the recognised limitations to the data viewed so far – which were outlined in the introduction to this chapter. The data are only of presented and diagnosed conditions, so that the extent to which they provide a straightforward view of the incidence of ill-health in the population is questionable. To be sure that they did would require knowledge about those not in contact with health services, of any sex difference in willingness to use services, and whether there was sex bias in diagnosis, treatment and admission. For example, Macfarlane (1980) raises the question of whether there is more likelihood that a mentally sick man would be cared for at home than a woman, and whether women run more risk of having their problems diagnosed as mental. Brown and Harris (1979) in a study of only women show there is considerable depressive illness among women who have never consulted a doctor about it.

As was seen in tables 3.3 and 3.4, there is clear evidence that women make greater use of general practitioner services than men. The *General Household Survey 1977* (1979) revealed that the rate per 1000 consulting in the fourteen days prior to interview was women 133, men 104, and that the average number of consultations per person per year was 4.4 for women and 3.3 for men. Similar differences occurred in all adult age groups and were particularly marked among those aged 15–44 years, where consultations by women were 138 per 1000 and 4.4 per year compared with only 79 and 2.5 respectively for men (tables 6.40 (a) and (b), *GHS 1977* 1979). Finally, sex differences were apparent among those in the sample reporting chronic and short-term health problems who went to the doctor about them. However, these sex differences are much smaller if account is taken of conditions confined to females – most obviously those surrounding reproduction (see also table 3.7 and text below). The exclusion of pregnancy and childbirth removes most of the reported sex differences in the use of general practitioners among those aged 15–44 years. What cannot be discovered from present data is the extent to which the long-term effects of child-bearing and, indeed, contraception (particularly the 'pill') affect the health of women and hence their use of health services (for a discussion of the need for a new definition of reproductive mortality, see Beral 1979). Nor, for that matter, can we tell the difference between that and the effects of particular occupations on men and for some women the combination of the two.

These considerations apply equally to the use of hospitals. From the first section of table 3.7 it is apparent that female use of hospital in-patient facilities is greater than male. However, it is clear that much of this difference is due to maternities, since comparison of discharge rates (for definition, see footnote to table) excluding these reveals identical rates for the sexes. At the same time, though, female patients occupy a majority (59 per cent) of the non-maternity beds used daily. Use of hospital in-patient facilities also varies with age and diagnosis (for details of the latter, see *Hospital In-Patient Enquiry* 1980). Discharge rates for all causes other than maternities are highest, and markedly so, for ages 0–4 and 65 years and over, for both sexes. Males have higher rates than females in childhood (0–14 years) and old age (65 years and over), and lower rates between the ages of 15 and 64. It is also noticeable that there is a sex difference in average length of stay in hospital – 12 days for males and 17 for females (excluding maternities). This difference is due to a combination of the factors of age, cause of admission and treatment, together with the standard of home care available to, and role demands upon, discharged patients, which are possibly balanced in favour of men though varying with age and

TABLE 3.7
HOSPITAL IN-PATIENTS: MEAN DURATION OF STAY,
DISCHARGE RATE* PER 10,000 POPULATION, CHILDREN
UNDER 15 YEARS OF AGE, PERCENTAGE OF INJURY CASES,
AND OPERATIONS, BY SEX, ENGLAND AND WALES 1976

	Females	*Males*
All causes		
Mean duration of stay (days)	13.9	12.2
Discharge rate per 10,000*	1,223	886
Average no. beds used daily	116,760	71,125
All causes excluding maternities		
Mean duration of stay (days)	16.7	
Discharge rate per 10,000*	886	
Average no. beds used daily	101,989	
Children under age 15 years		
Mean duration of stay (days)	6.2	5.9
Average no. beds per million population	1,096	1,394
Percentage[†] of injury cases by type		
Road traffic	31	69
Home	60	40
Other and unspecified	43	57
All injuries	46	55
Operations		
Number per 100,000 population	7,034	3,803
Average no. beds used daily per 100,000	166	102

* Discharges (return home, transfer to other hospital/institution, or death) related to home population
† Rounded

N = 10% sample of in-patient records from National Health Service hospitals, excluding those confined to treatment of psychiatric disease
(Devised from tables 9, 13, 18 and 22(i), *Hospital In-Patient Enquiry* 1980)

circumstance. Sex differences in length of stay are particularly pronounced at ages 65–74 (women 23, men 18) and at 75 years and over (women 47, men 27), with 65 per cent of female beds and 47 per cent of male beds being occupied by those over the age of 65. Length of stay is very similar for the sexes among children under the age of 15. The table also reveals a stark difference between the sexes in the number of operations per 100,000 population – the female rate approaching double the male. Finally, the analysis of treatments for injuries shows the majority (55 per cent) to be male and a clear differentiation between the sexes by type, 69 per cent of road traffic injuries being sustained by men and 60 per cent of injuries in the home by women.

So far we have viewed some of the evidence of health differences between the sexes, both in general terms and in relation to generalised types of diagnosis. Because of both the lack of literature and the scope of this chapter, our view of other aspects of sex differences in health is limited and brief. Obviously the sex differences in health outlined so far mask further and subtle differences. For example, as we have seen, women apparently suffer more from mental illness and disorders than do men; indeed, the death rate per million from such causes in 1979 was 45 for men and 84 for women (*Mortality Statistics 1979* 1981). A further view of sex differences in the incidence and diagnosis of mental illness is provided by Grimes (1978). He related all first admissions to mental hospitals and units in 1975 to the estimated populations of each sex, allowing for deaths, and calculated the proportion of each that would be admitted to a hospital for a mental condition during their lives. These calculations show, on the basis of admissions in 1975, that about 10 per cent of the entire population will be admitted during their lifetime. The sex difference is quite stark, at roughly 1 in 12 (8.6 per cent) for men and 1 in 8 (12.4 per cent) for women. Only at ages lower than 17 years is the male probability of admission higher than the female. The only diagnostic group having a higher male than female rate is alcoholism and alcoholic psychosis – the rates being very similar for schizophrenia, drug dependency and personality disorders – while all other diagnoses, including depressive and other psychoses, senile and pre-senile dementia and psychoneuroses, have higher female than male rates. This and similar studies, based as they are on recorded incidence at specific places, also underline the limitations of our knowledge.

A further example is that, like most other forms of ill-health, there are no statistics for the actual incidence of sexually transmitted diseases. The only readily accessible data are for new patients seen at hospital clinics, which reveal that hospital treatment of sexually transmitted diseases is more prevalent among men than among women. Of all new cases in 1977, 70 per cent were men, and the male percentages for differing types were: syphilis, 80; gonorrhoea, 64; non-specific infections, 63; other conditions not requiring treatment, 70. However, for new cases of syphilis and gonorrhoea among young people aged under 20 years there was a female majority of 57 per cent (devised from data in table 8.19, *Social Trends No. 9* 1978). But such data leave unanswered actual incidence – which includes returning patients, those treated elsewhere and, obviously, those untreated.

An alternative strategy is to inquire directly of the population using survey techniques, though these are generally limited to the more general and less serious aspects of health. Dental health has been so investigated and displayed improvement over a decade. A survey in 1968 (Gray, Todd, Slack and Bulman 1970) found 37 per cent of adults to be without any natural teeth, while one in 1978 found the percentage reduced to 29, and noted similar improvements in the condition of natural teeth (Todd and Walker 1980). In 1978 women were more likely to be without any natural teeth than men (32 compared with 24 per cent) and to have lost their teeth at an earlier age (5 per cent more than men being without at ages 35–44 and 15 per cent more at ages 55–64). However, the sex difference closed to only 4 per cent at ages 65–74 and was nearly identical beyond that age. As was seen above, the *General Household Survey* regularly inquires about chronic and short-term health. In 1977 the survey included questions on sight and hearing. People over the age of 16 years were asked whether they wore glasses (spectacles or contact lenses) or a hearing aid, and whether their sight or hearing caused them any difficulties. Over half the men (57 per cent) and two-thirds of women (67 per cent) reported wearing glasses, and a further 3 per cent of both sexes that they did not but had difficulty with their sight. Although there are considerably more registered blind women than blind men in our society, this is largely explained by the facts that women live longer and that many of the causes of blindness are more prevalent among the old (Abell 1976). Two per cent of both sexes said they wore hearing aids, but a larger percentage of men than women reported difficulty with hearing, though not wearing an aid (15 compared with 12 per cent). So, while more women have poor sight than do men, the opposite is marginally the case with hearing.

A further, indirect aspect of health is that some body conditions and habits have been shown to be related to ill-health or identified as health hazards. Obesity and cigarette smoking are two that are topical and for which there is evidence of sex variation. While the figures in table 3.8 are not necessarily representative of the population of Britain, having been collected in the South-East, they do reveal a large proportion of people over the desirable weight. The incidence is greatest among women and increases with age for both sexes, and particularly for women. Men appear to reach their peak weight at an earlier age, since unlike women there is no increase after the age of 50 years. Cigarette smoking is regularly surveyed in the *General Household Survey*, and table 3.9 contains the results for 1976. As will be seen, women were less likely to be smokers than men (38 compared with 46 per cent), much more likely never or only occasionally to smoke, and, if smokers, to use fewer cigarettes. It is of interest to note, however, that, in the face of a general decline in smoking, the sex difference has narrowed. Between 1972 and 1976 the percentage of men who smoked fell from 52 to 46, while the percentage for women decreased from 41 to 38 – only half the proportion. During the same period consumption of cigarettes per male smoker increased by 8 per cent and that of the female by 16 per cent. For both sexes the incidence of smoking is related to social class, with non-manual classes below and manual above the overall average. In each class the percentage of female smokers is lower than male, with the exception of the professional (Registrar General's social class I), where 28 per cent of women and 25 per cent of men smoked.

Finally, our picture of sex differences in health would hardly be complete without a view of the sex structure of those who provide

TABLE 3.8
PERCENTAGE OF MEN AND WOMEN MORE THAN
110 PER CENT AND 120 PER CENT OF THE 'DESIRABLE'* BODY
WEIGHT AT DIFFERENT AGES

	Women		Men	
	110%+	120%+	110%+	120%+
Aged 15–29 years	16	8	14	6
Aged 30–49 years	33	17	45	18
Aged 50–65 years	50	32	43	18

* As defined in Metropolitan Life Insurance tables
(Derived from table 2.1, James 1979, source Baird, Silverstone, Grimshaw and Ashwell 1974)

TABLE 3.9
CIGARETTE SMOKING,* BY SEX (PERCENTAGES)

	Women	Men
Current smokers	38	46
Heavy smokers[†]	14	24
Light smokers[§]	24	22
Ex-regular smokers	12	27
Never or only occasional smokers	50	27
Average number of cigarettes smoked per week per smoker	101	129

* By persons aged over 16 years
[†] 20 or more cigarettes per day
[§] Under 20 cigarettes per day
N = 12,554 women, 10,888 men
(Derived from tables 2.62, 2.63 and 2.65, *General Household Survey 1976* 1978)

the health services. Table 3.10 shows a very large male preponderance among hospital medical and dental staff and among general practitioners. While this situation is changing to the extent that higher proportions of women are now studying medicine than ever before, the current position continues to have implications. While the matter is open to speculation, it is easy to appreciate that the present imbalance of the sexes among the chief, front-line providers of health services is likely to affect sex differences with respect to rates of consulting, type of diagnosis made and treatment received. As in many other arenas reviewed in this book, the medical profession can be characterised as male in definition and operation (see Chapters 6, 7 and 8). The extent to which this may be changed, or affected, by changing sexual composition remains to be seen. Nursing staff display an opposite imbalance, with only 15 per cent of full-time, and only 2 per cent of part-time, nurses being men. Among male nurses the proportion who were registered (SRN, RMN or RNMS) as opposed to enrolled (SEN) was much higher than for female nurses. In stark contrast to the sexual composition of medical staff specialising in gynaecology and birth, hospital midwifery staff were exclusively female in 1977 – though this sexual monopoly has since been broken. Only among community health service staff was there any real balance of the sexes.

TABLE 3.10
MEDICAL PERSONNEL, BY SEX, IN ENGLAND 1977
(PERCENTAGES)

	Women	Men	Number
*Hospital medical staff**			
All staff	18	82	30,520
Consultants	10	90	11,372
Senior registrars	19	81	2,495
*Hospital dental staff**			
All staff	16	84	1,104
Consultants	3	97	445
Senior registrars	12	88	113
*Hospital nursing and midwifery staff**			
All full-time	85	15	222,773
All part-time	98	2	132,987
Registered:			
Full-time	76	24	69,119
Part-time	97	3	37,016
Enrolled:			
Full-time	85	15	34,630
Part-time	99	1	24,181
Hospital midwifery staff	100	0	18,800
General medical practitioners	16	84	22,327
General dental practitioners	11	89	11,784
Community health medical staff	54	46	5,655
Community health dental staff	42	58	1,955

* Excluding hospital practitioners and para. 94/107 appointments
(Devised from tables 3.5, 3.12, 3.16, 3.25, 3.33, 3.36, 3.37, *Health and Personal Social Services
Statistics 1978* 1980)

DEATH

This section looks at sex differences in only two aspects of death:
mortality rates and causes of death. As has been suggested, men
have higher mortality at all ages than women, so that their survival
rates and expectation of life (see next section) are both lower. Table
3.11 provides a straightforward portrayal of this dramatic difference. The number of deaths and the population of each sex at given
ages have been used to compute mortality rates (average number of

TABLE 3.11
MALE MORTALITY RATES FOR 1970–2, EXPRESSED AS
PERCENTAGES OF THOSE FOR FEMALES, BY AGE

Age	Male as % of female	Age	Male as % of female	Age	Male as % of female
0	130	35	144	65	210
5	138	40	141	70	199
10	148	45	148	75	173
15	193	50	165	80	150
20	236	55	185	85	134
25	196	60	202	90	122
30	162				

(Derived from table C, *Life Tables* 1979)

persons in each sex and age group to die in a year); the table shows the male rates expressed as a percentage of the female. The excess of male over female mortality ranges from 30 per cent during infancy to 110 per cent at age 65, with a single peak of 136 per cent at age 20. As the Government Actuary remarks, the mortality rates for women aged 60–75 were, in general, no higher than those for men seven years younger, and male rates were at least 50 per cent higher than the female at all ages from 50 to 80 years (*Life Tables* 1979). The same source reveals considerable improvement in mortality rates at every age and for both sexes through this century. Dramatically, infant mortality in 1970–2 was but a sixth of what it was in 1910–12 (2 compared with 11 of each 100 babies dying before their first birthday). For women, similar reductions have occurred for ages up to 30 years and 50 per cent reductions to the age of 60. For men, other than in infancy, the reductions have not been as great, though the 1970–2 rates for ages up to 50 years are less than 50 per cent of those in 1910–12. At older ages the improvements are quite different for the sexes, women's rates for those over 80 having declined by 35 per cent and those for men over 70 by only 15 per cent.

There are a number of ways in which sex differences in the cause of death might be presented. Space here precludes a demonstration, by sex, of the obvious relationship between age and cause of death (the basic figures but no commentary are to be found in *Mortality*

Statistics 1979 1981), so that here simple overall views must suffice. Table 3.12 shows the sex differences in the number of deaths by selected, grouped causes in 1979, as rates per million population. As would be expected, the overall rate is higher for males. However, a number of causes show higher rates for females than for males: diseases of the blood and the digestive system, mental disorders, and endocrine, nutritional and metabolic disease, together with a marginally higher female rate for diseases of the nervous system. While the causes shown in the table are the same as those used in table 3.4 (for consulting a general practitioner) and in 3.6 (in-patients in NHS hospitals), no real comparisons can be made between the incidence of death and the use of health services by cause, because of the large number of ill-defined, intervening vari-ables involved.

Perhaps a more revealing set of data are contained in table 3.13, which shows deaths in 1976 expressed in numbers and percentages of deaths in each sex and over all. Comparing the percentages for each cause for the population and the sexes reveals some interesting differences. Ischaemic heart disease is responsible for more than a

TABLE 3.12
DEATH RATES PER MILLION POPULATION, FROM
SELECTED, GROUPED CAUSES, BY SEX, ENGLAND AND
WALES 1979

	Females	*Males*
Infective and parasitic diseases[1]	39	53
Cancer	2,365	2,862
Endocrine, nutritional and metabolic disease[2]	156	106
Diseases of the blood	44	26
Mental disorders	84	45
Diseases of the nervous system	143	139
Diseases of the circulatory system[3]	6,014	6,128
Diseases of the respiratory system[4]	1,661	1,838
Diseases of the digestive system[5]	357	303
Injury and poisoning	359	506
All causes of death[6]	11,703	12,437

[1-5] See corresponding footnotes to table 3.4
[6] Includes causes not specified here
(Derived from table 3, *Mortality Statistics 1979* 1981)

TABLE 3.13
DEATHS IN GREAT BRITAIN IN 1976 EXPRESSED IN NUMBERS
AND AS THE PERCENTAGE OF ALL DEATHS, BY SEX

| | Females | | Males | | All |
	No. in 1000s	%	No. in 1000s	%	%
Tuberculosis	0.4	0.1	0.9	0.3	0.2
Cancer					
Digestive system	22.0	6.7	22.8	6.9	6.8
Lung, bronchus, trachea	7.8	2.4	29.6	8.9	5.6
Breast	12.9	3.9	0.1	$\varnothing$	2.0
Cervic uteri	2.4	0.7	0	0	0.4
Diabetes	3.4	1.0	2.3	0.7	0.9
Ischaemic heart disease[1]	76.1	23.0	99.9	30.0	26.5
Other forms of heart, hypertensive disease	26.6	8.0	17.1	5.1	6.6
Cerebrovascular disease[2]	52.6	15.9	32.5	9.8	12.8
Influenza	4.6	1.4	2.9	0.9	1.1
Pneumonia	33.8	10.2	25.4	7.6	8.9
Bronchitis, emphysema,[3] asthma	7.7	2.3	20.5	6.2	4.2
Motor vehicle accidents	2.2	0.7	4.7	1.4	1.0
All other accidents	5.5	1.7	5.0	1.5	1.6
Suicide	1.7	0.5	2.6	0.8	0.6
All other causes	71.1	21.5	66.8	20.1	20.8
All causes	330.7	100	333.0	100	100

$\varnothing$ = less than 0.5 per cent
[1] Inadequate supply of blood to an organ
[2] Relating to blood vessels and blood supply to brain
[3] A condition of the lungs
(Devised from table 8.3, *Social Trends No. 9* 1978)

quarter of all deaths (26.5 per cent), but the male percentage is 30 and the female 23. At the same time, other forms of heart, and cerebrovascular, disease, together accounting for 19.4 per cent of deaths, are more frequent in females. While about 15 per cent of all deaths are from cancer (male 16 per cent, female 14 per cent), those of the lung, bronchus and trachea display a male percentage more than three times greater than the female; the figures for cancer of the digestive system are almost the same for both sexes, while cancers of the breast and cervix (obviously) are almost exclusively female. The higher percentage of female deaths from influenza and pneumonia probably reflects the difference in age structures of the sexes, while higher male figures for bronchitis and other conditions, including cancer of the lung, may be related to sex differences in occupation and smoking habits. More males than females die through accidents – twice the percentage in motor vehicles – but marginally fewer in other types. Suicide, though representing only 0.6 per cent of all deaths, is higher for men than for women (0.8 compared with 0.5 per cent).

EXPECTATION OF LENGTH OF LIFE

It is evident from the differences in age structure and death rates of the sexes that they also enjoy different average lengths of life. The Registrar General, using the actual deaths in the years 1970–2) and the population at the 1971 census, computed life expectancy figures, as displayed in table 3.14. Somewhat similar figures are used by insurance companies for fixing the rates for life insurance. It has to be appreciated that the life expectancies given here do not refer directly to the lives of the current population, since they are based on previously recorded deaths which have been affected by conditions that may now be changed. With this limitation, however,

TABLE 3.14
SEX DIFFERENCES IN THE EXPECTATION OF LIFE AT
VARIOUS AGES

	Females	*Males*
Expectation of life, in years, at age*		
0	75.3	69.0
10	66.7	60.7
20	56.9	51.1
30	47.1	41.5
40	37.5	32.0
50	28.4	23.1
60	20.0	15.4
70	12.6	9.5

* In years of life from age specified (rounded to first decimal place), based on deaths 1970–2 and population at 1971 census (English Life Table 13)
(Derived from table D, *Life Tables* 1979)

they remain as accurate a view of life expectancy as is available. Table 3.14 shows that in our society a girl at birth would, on average, be expected to live some 6.3 years longer than a boy, the expectation of life being 69 for males and 75.3 for females. This difference remains at around five years, though dropping marginally through the ages to 60 years, where it is 4.6, and 70, where it is only 3.1 years. Notice that the age given should be added to the expectancy, so that at the age of 70 men would, on average, expect to live to 79.5 and women to 82.6 years. Over the past sixty years there has been a fairly dramatic increase in life expectancy, though with marked sex differences, women benefiting more than men. Between 1910–12 and 1970–2 expectation at birth increased by 17½ years for boys and 20 years for girls. Much of this change is due to the reduction of infant mortality, though at the age of 20 years life expectancy over the period has increased by nearly 7 years for men and nearly 10 for women. At older ages the proportional improvement in expectation is even greater for women, whose expectation at age 60 displays an increase over the period of 4½ years compared to only 1⅓ for men. As a consequence of this and differing retirement ages, expectation of life in pensionable age is almost 20 years for women (from the age of 60) but only 12 years for men (from the age of 65). And, as we have seen, women are in any case more likely to survive to pensionable age than men. Expectation of life is clearly related to other aspects of life in our society, particularly social class (see *Occupational Mortality* 1978 or Reid 1981). For example, a male subject from birth to the mortality rates of social class I (Registrar General's scale, professional) would be expected to live 7.2 years longer than one subjected to those of class V (unskilled manual).

MARITAL CONDITION

Except for the family and school, marriage is the commonest institution in our society, being experienced by all but a very small minority of people. Statistics reveal, for example, that by the age of 40 some 95 per cent of women and 91 per cent of men in our society had been married (*Social Trends No. 9* 1978). The overall incidence of marriage in the population of England and Wales is shown in table 3.15. Of those over the age of 16 in 1978, two-thirds were married, 22 per cent single, one in ten widowed and 3 per cent divorced.

TABLE 3.15
ESTIMATED PERCENTAGES* OF POPULATION OF ENGLAND
AND WALES AGED 16 YEARS AND OVER, BY MARITAL
CONDITION AND SEX, 1978

	Women	Men	Both	No. in millions
Single	19	25	22	8.3
Married	63	69	66	24.8
Widowed	15	4	10	3.6
Divorced	3	3	3	1.1
Total (millions)	19.6	18.1	37.7	

* Rounded
(Devised from table 1.1(a), *Marriage and Divorce Statistics 1978* 1980)

While the same percentage of each sex was divorced, men were more likely than women to be single (25 compared with 19 per cent) and married (69 per cent compared with 63) and much less likely to be widowed (4 per cent compared with 15). These sex differences are mainly accounted for by three facts: women tend to marry at an earlier age than men, men are somewhat less likely to marry at all (to some extent related to the fact that there are more men than women under the age of 45 and that people of that age account for 90 per cent of all marriages), and women, who live longer, are more likely to outlive their spouses.

Sex differences in age at marriage can be illustrated in a number of ways. For example, of those aged between 16 and 19 years in 1978 it is estimated that 72 in each 1000 women but only 15 per 1000 men were married (*Marriage and Divorce Statistics 1978* 1980). Table 3.16 displays the differences between the sexes and marital conditions in terms of both their average age and the median age at marriage. Median age is the age that splits all brides or grooms into two equal groups, one of which married before the given age and the other after it. Both sets of figures show consistent and marked lower ages for women than for men. Leete (1979a) identifies a growing surplus of single men at the younger marriageable ages which is due to the unequal sex birth ratio, as well as to the fact that men tend to marry women from younger age groups than their own, these

TABLE 3.16
AVERAGE AGE AND MEDIAN AGE* AT MARRIAGE OF
THOSE MARRYING IN 1976, IN ENGLAND AND WALES, BY SEX
AND MARITAL STATUS

	All	*Spinsters*	*Widows*	*Divorced*
Women				
Average age	26.5	22.8	54.2	34.9
Median age	22.7	21.5	55.3	32.5

	All	*Bachelors*	*Widowers*	*Divorced*
Men				
Average age	29.2	25.1	59.4	38.4
Median age	25.2	23.7	60.9	36.0

* That age which divides all into two groups, one marrying younger, the other older, than that age
(Derived from tables 3.5a and 3.5b, *Marriage and Divorce Statistics 1978* 1980)

groups having been affected by declining birth rates. In turn this widens the gap between the marriage rates of the sexes and leads to more men marrying women older than themselves, and in the long term it seems highly likely that the proportion of men who never marry will be much larger than the proportion of women, reversing the pattern established between the wars. The gap between the number of bachelors and spinsters has grown quite dramatically – from 107 bachelors per 100 spinsters in 1961 to 122 per 100 in 1976 (Leete 1977).

Marriages are formally broken either by divorce or by the death of one partner, and, obviously, those divorced and widowed are eligible for marriage. Consequently, marriage opportunities and rates are related not only to the basic demographics of sex and differences in length of life between the sexes but also to the incidence of divorce and changing cultural factors surrounding marriage, divorce, and second and subsequent marriage. In 1978 only 65 per cent of all marriages were the first for both parties, 19 per cent were the first for one party only (with other parties 17 per cent divorced and 2 per cent widowed), and 16 per cent were second marriages for both parties (11 per cent both divorced, 2 per cent both widowed, 3 per cent mixed). The divorce rate in our society has risen from 3.7

per 1000 of the married population in 1968 to 11.6 per 1000 in 1978. Leete (1979a), in analysing recent divorce data, suggests that one in five of the marriages of the early 1970s will end in divorce within fifteen years of the ceremony, and that the figure will increase with length of marriage. Wives are more likely than husbands to be granted a divorce: of divorces in 1978, 69 per cent were granted to wives, 31 per cent to husbands and hardly any (0.2 per cent) to both (*Marriage and Divorce Statistics 1978* 1980). The same source shows a similar sexual bias in petitions for divorce, though a majority were filed by husbands in the period 1901–5 and during and immediately following both world wars.

Remarriage of divorced persons has been interestingly illustrated by Leete (1979b), who surveyed a sample of 1000 couples who were granted divorces in 1973, tracing their remarriages up to 1977. Within four and a half years, about half had remarried, the majority soon after their divorce. Of the 1000 couples, both parties remarried in 268 cases, the wife only in 212 and the husband only in 287, while neither party remarried in 233 cases. The study suggests that divorced men are somewhat more likely to remarry than are divorced women, and that the fact that women generally have care of children after divorce does not explain the sex differences in remarriage.

The differences between the sexes in widowhood are accounted for by two factors we have already viewed – the higher death rates among men and their older average age at marriage. In 1975 the rate of widowhood in each 1000 married persons under the age of 65 years was 2.8 for men and 7.5 for women. Clearly at ages over 65 the longer expectation of life for women makes the difference much more marked. In 1978 there were some 0.7 million widowed men and 2.9 million widowed women, of all ages, while the figures for those over the age of 65 years were men 0.5 million, women 2.2 million. Widowers have higher rates of remarriage than widows (Leete 1977).

One aspect of broken marriages is one-parent families, of which it was estimated there were 750,000 in Great Britain in 1976 (*OPCS Monitor, FM2 78/2* 1978). *General Household Survey* data suggest that by the same year one-parent families were 11 per cent of all families in our society with dependent children – an increase from 8 per cent in 1971. Table 3.17 contains a breakdown of such families by sex and marital status of parent. The majority, 88 per cent, of

TABLE 3.17
ESTIMATED NUMBERS OF ONE-PARENT FAMILIES IN GREAT
BRITAIN, BY SEX AND MARITAL STATUS OF PARENT, 1976

	Number in 1000s	*Percentage*	*Percentage change since 1971*
Mothers			
Single	130	17	+44
Widowed	115	15	−4
Divorced	230	31	+92
Separated (married)	185	25	+9
Total mothers	660	88	+32
Fathers	90	12	+29
Total	750	100	+32

(Derived from table 2.2, EOC 1979, source *OPCS Monitor, FM2 78/2* 1978)

heads of one-parent families are women. Clearly the major causes of one-parent families are divorce and separation, female lone parents of these marital conditions accounting for some 56 per cent of all one-parent families. The table also reveals that the largest increases among female one-parent families between 1971 and 1976 were for divorced (92 per cent, some 110,000 families) and single mothers (44 per cent increase, amounting to 40,000 unmarried mothers). Over all, the number of one-parent families with mothers as heads increased by 32 per cent and, while those with fathers showed a similar increase (29 per cent), the numbers were very much smaller in comparison.

OVERVIEW

With the exception of the first and the last sections, this chapter has been concerned with sex differences in the vital aspects of life – birth, health and death. The illustration of these differences, at least within the limitations of the data, has been straightforward. Their explanation is much more problematic, as are their implications (some of which are taken up in the final chapter). So it is reasonable to conclude with the words of Morris (1975):

Prenatally and during infancy major biological causes are postulated for feminine superiority. Thereafter ways of living may be very different – in occupation, for example, or (still) cigarette smoking – in the behaviour that culture expects. How much is biological, what social, is a continuing debate.

To which it is necessary to add only some elaboration of the concept of culture, particularly in respect of those aspects which bear upon the incidence of disease, sickness and injury, people's reaction to ill-health, and the operation and use of the health services. The whole of this chapter has demonstrated the very real effects of demography on the sex differences observed. In combination the facts of the age structure and proportional differences between the sexes, as well as cultural and economic factors, must be taken into account when viewing empirical data on differences in vital statistics between the sexes. These two factors also affect, or are related to, almost all the topics dealt with in the rest of this book. This chapter has identified one distinct advantage to being a woman in our society: having a longer expectation of life than men. In the face of the extensive illustration of disadvantage for women in the data surveyed throughout this book, and indeed in itself, longer life might well be recognised as a crucial and enviable advantage.

4

Social security and the family

Tony Kidd

It has been said that the United Kingdom lacks a coherent and explicit social policy that is consciously aimed at the family unit (see Kamerman and Kahn 1978). We do not, for instance, possess a government minister whose central concern is the family, as many European nations do, and, partly as a consequence of this, we lack a consciously co-ordinated family policy. One major reason for this, according to Land and Parker (1978), is British suspicion of any substantial intervention in an area considered private and not therefore appropriately exposed to public scrutiny and control.

It would, of course, be an illusion to suppose that social policy takes a neutral or non-interventionist stance towards the family. Indeed, the introduction of many welfare measures has regularly been justified in terms of their assumed impact on various aspects of family life. For example, family allowances, it was said, would encourage a rise in the birth rate, while the low level of many social security benefits is often claimed to be necessary because otherwise parental responsibility or work incentives would be adversely affected. Whatever the consequences, however, social policy reflects certain social values and therefore characteristically makes some clear assumptions about the family. Public-sector housing policy, for instance, has tended to give priority to those living in nuclear families with dependent children, and accordingly has treated less favourably other groups, such as the elderly and the single. The social security system also makes some very clear assumptions about the nature of the family and the roles within it. It will be seen that these assumptions have entailed a conception of the family which has led to differential treatment of the sexes, and that many of these key assumptions can no longer be supported with empirical data.

Much has been written on the modern welfare state but, as

Wilson (1977) notes, little has been said about its impact on women. This chapter explores what we know about the value assumptions underpinning social security provision in relation to certain roles and relationships within the family. In at least one sense these matters are pressing: the EEC Directive (1978) allows member countries six years to ensure equal treatment for men and women in respect of social security programmes, although the ruling applies only to the working population (*Official Journal of the EEC* 1979). Article 2 of the directive states that it shall apply to the working population – including self-employed persons, workers and self-employed persons whose activity is interrupted by illness, accident or involuntary unemployment, and persons seeking employment – and to retired or invalided workers and self-employed persons. This clause may well mean that certain benefits (for example, our non-contributory invalidity pension and invalidity care allowance) will be held not to be included in the text of the directive. The following, however, are specifically included: statutory schemes that relate to sickness, invalidity, old age, accidents at work and occupational diseases, unemployment, and social assistance schemes such as our supplementary benefits.

It will be seen that the British social security system continues to treat marriage partners differentially on the basis of their sex in certain key respects, and much of this has to do with the development of an income maintenance programme which has inherent in it a clear conception of the family in which the husband is the bread-winner and the wife the dependant.

SOCIAL SECURITY AND SEX DIFFERENCES

In respect of pensions, there have been some changes in recent years to ensure a greater equality between the sexes: 'Home Responsibilities Protection' (introduced in 1978), for instance, has reduced the number of contributing years a woman requires in order to obtain a basic retirement pension. Credit is given for years spent caring for a child under 16, or a disabled, sick or elderly person, but such credits are not available for married men. Some further differences remain: for example, a man cannot claim a pension on his wife's contributions, although the reverse is possible; a wife cannot claim a married woman's pension until her husband claims his; and, of course, a woman can receive her pension at 60 whereas a man must wait until he is 65 – she may contribute, therefore, five years less than a man.

Family income supplement is a benefit payable to all parents in full-time work (for a married couple the man must work at least 30 hours a week, for a lone parent 24 hours are sufficient) who have at least one child at home, and whose income falls below a certain level. At present, so far as married couples are concerned, only the man may apply for benefit. This applies also to supplementary benefit, although, in both cases, the EEC Directive will begin to eliminate these discrepancies by 1984.

Until fairly recently, married women received a lower rate of unemployment and sickness benefit compared to men with identical contribution records. Although this difference is being phased out, the conditions needed to satisfy a claim for dependants apply differentially to the sexes. For a wife to claim for her husband as a dependant, he has to be incapable of supporting himself because of physical or mental infirmity as well as not employed. The wife, on the other hand, merely has to be not employed for her husband to be able to claim a dependant's allowance for her.

Non-contributory invalidity pension is a benefit for people of working age who 'have not been able to do paid work for some time and do not qualify for sickness or invalidity benefit because they do not have enough National Insurance contributions'. Men and single women have to demonstrate that they are 'incapable of work' in order to qualify for this benefit. A married or cohabiting woman, on the other hand, has to be incapable of work and 'incapable of performing normal household duties'. The household duties test is based on the following criteria:

> If you live in your own home or another private household you must be incapable of doing BY YOURSELF (even with the use of any aids or appliances) all, or almost all of the tasks normally undertaken by a housewife in her own home. For example, cooking, cleaning, shopping, washing and ironing, etc. You may still be eligible if you are actually doing these tasks but only with great difficulty, much pain, or extremely slowly. (*National Insurance Information Leaflet* 214)

The test effectively denies this benefit to 240,000 women.

Invalid care allowance is a benefit for people under pensionable age who cannot work because they have to stay at home to care for a severely disabled relative. It is not normally possible for a married woman to claim this benefit. The assumption that she might be at home in any event (see *Report of the National Insurance Advisory Committee* 1980) appears sufficient to deny all married women this benefit. A survey conducted for the Equal Opportunities Commission (EOC 1980a) in West Yorkshire has found that of those who are responsible for the care of disabled, sick or elderly relatives 75 per cent are women. Further, table 4.1 demonstrates that this burden is not evenly distributed in relation to the age of the dependant. The care of the disabled, sick and elderly appears largely, then, to be in the hands of women. This has led, according to the same report, to severe restrictions being imposed on the working life of the carer: work had been given up, hours reduced, promotion or training opportunities forgone, and so on. Many women also complained about inadequate help. They felt that there was an assumption on the part of the authorities that, where a female relative is available, dependants are not, for instance, expected to require residential or domiciliary care, that the authorities 'do not wish to know as long as there is somebody who will take the responsibility for the dependant, and that this is particularly the case if that person is a woman' (EOC 1980a). These assumptions made here about the woman's role are also clearly evident in the administration of the invalid care allowance. Social security is thus not the only area of social policy to expect rather more of the married woman than it does of her male counterpart.

TABLE 4.1
MALE AND FEMALE CARERS, BY AGE OF DEPENDANT
(PERCENTAGES)

	Female carer	Male carer
Dependant		
Child	93	7
Adult 65 and under	61	39
Adult over 65	77	23
All	75	25

N = 2500 households
Nearly two-thirds of all male caring is of a wife, and one-fifth of female caring is of a husband.
(Derived from table 5, EOC 1980a)

Social security regulations, then, often treat married men and women differentially and tend not to favour married women in assuming them to be dependent on their husbands and bound to the home. Men's assumed role as breadwinner is reflected in their right to benefit once inability to work has been substantiated. Old assumptions die hard.

BEVERIDGE ASSUMPTIONS

The current system of social security has a long history, but many of the assumptions inherent in current provision are reflected in the Beveridge Report, that is, the *Report of a Committee on Social Insurance and Allied Services*, published in 1942. Beveridge proposed that his scheme should be comprehensive and based substantially on the principle of contributory insurance. The contribution was to be flat-rate and would normally be linked to employment. Thus individuals would earn a contractual right to benefits through their contributions. This seemed an attractive idea, although not a new one, in 1942, after the suspicion and hostility that had often been experienced as a consequence of the scrutiny of means tests. Beveridge was aware that such an insurance scheme would not, at least initially, cover everybody, and he therefore proposed a means-tested assistance scheme to act as a safety net until such time as all would qualify for insurance benefits. The role of the assistance scheme, then, was to be primarily 'residual' until sufficient contributions had been made to ensure that all were entitled, as of right, to benefit. Beveridge had therefore adopted a concept of 'need' which was fundamentally based on interruption of earnings, and the typical insurance contributor was thus considered to be the adult male worker whose income was derived solely from earnings and who needed protection when such earnings were interrupted by unemployment, accident or disease (Harris 1977). One consequence of this assumption has been the difficulty of adequately incorporating into an income maintenance scheme groups who are not experiencing a short-term interruption of earnings, and many one-parent families (discussed below) are an example of this.

Beveridge turned his attention to the question of where women were to stand in his scheme only in 1942, by when the major pillars of his proposal had already been established. Beveridge drew a sharp distinction between the single and married woman and was quite unequivocal in his expectation of the married woman's role in post-war society: 'the attitude of the housewife to gainful employment outside the home is not and should not be the same as that of a single woman. She has other duties . . . in the next 30 years housewives as mothers have vital work to do in ensuring the adequate continuance of the British race and of British ideals in the world' (Beveridge 1942). These duties were to take place within a status that required dependence on her husband:

> all women by marriage acquire a new economic and social status, with risks and rights different from those of the unmarried. On marriage a woman gains a legal right to maintenance by her husband as a first line of defence against risks which fall directly on the solitary woman; she undertakes at the same time to perform vital unpaid services and becomes exposed to new risks, including the risk that her married life may be ended prematurely by widowhood or separation. (Beveridge 1942)

Thus the woman was a dependant of her husband, and her needs were perceived as special and related to that dependency – for example, separation or widowhood. Beveridge's proposals to meet the marriage needs of women included a furnishing grant for setting up home, maternity benefit, separation allowance, provision of domestic help for sick housewives and family allowance. Family allowances and maternity benefit were the only two of these to be successfully implemented, although the latter was operationalised at a cost to women; unemployment and disability benefits were to be paid at a lower rate to the married female contributor to the insurance scheme, partly because 'it is is undeniable that the needs of housewives in general are less than those of single women when unemployed or disabled, because their house is provided either by their husband's earnings or by his benefit' (Beveridge 1942). A second reason for the lower benefit stemmed from the maternity benefit's being 50 per cent higher than the normal unemployment and sickness benefit: it 'must be paid for by someone, it is a benefit additional to other benefits, which will be confined almost wholly to gainfully occupied married women and will reduce the contributions available for supporting their unemployment and disability benefits' (Beveridge 1942). In the event, the high rate of maternity was sustained only until 1953, after which it fell back to the rate of male unemployment and sickness benefit, although the lower allocation of unemployment and sickness benefit to married women remained.

The wife's needs, then, were seen as deriving from her role as a mother and wife. Widows were incorporated into the insurance scheme and treated relatively favourably compared with the deserted, separated or divorced woman. While Beveridge recognised the latter circumstance as a 'risk' of marriage, and had advocated a separation allowance, he was greatly concerned not to be seen to be contributing to family break-up, and a more generous scheme might, he reasoned, produce the result.

Those value assumptions about the nature and role dispositions of the family were symptomatic of attitudes widely held at that time. It should, however, be said that the Beveridge Report removed many of the earlier stark anomalies which had treated men and women differentially, at times in the most grotesque manner (see, for instance, Deacon (1976) on the disallowances for unemployment benefit in the 1920s and 1930s). None the less, Beveridge's projections for the future of the scheme were dependent on key assumptions remaining valid in the future. The focal point for these assumptions was Beveridge's concern to re-establish the unity of the family. Three major assumptions, relevant to a discussion of sex differences, were clearly evident:

1 Beveridge and others had been keen to restore the family's unity after the disruptions of wartime. His proposals accordingly treated the family as a unit, husband and wife regarded as a team. The insurance scheme, remarked Beveridge, 'treats a man's contribution as made on behalf of himself and his wife, as for a team, each of whose partners is equally essential, and it gives benefits as for a team'. This, however, assumes an equitable distribution of income within the family, the verification, or otherwise, of which is an empirical question. The section on pp. 66–74, 'Distribution of income within the family', examines to what extent the evidence supports Beveridge's assumptions.

2 Beveridge considered that the focal point of family unity would be the woman, and therefore that she should be encouraged (expected) to remain within the home, especially where there were children. The breadwinner in the family was the man, and accordingly most of the wife's insurance benefits would accrue to her through her husband's contributions. This was based on the

assumption, however, that the seven-eighths of housewives who, according to the census of 1931, 'made marriage their sole occupation' would not decrease appreciably. Social insurance, commented Beveridge, could not be geared to an untypical minority. The section on pp. 74–8, 'Sources of family income', examines whether the assumption of the male breadwinner has remained valid.

3 The consequences of family break-up, however, were not easily assimilated into a scheme that emphasised the unity of the family. Although Beveridge recommended a separation allowance (in the event not implemented), he was careful to attach a condition to it: that the allowance would be granted to an individual only if the breakdown of marriage was through no fault of their own. The section on pp. 78–83, 'One-parent families', views the incidence and implications of those families that fall outside the concept of the family unit used by Beveridge.

DISTRIBUTION OF INCOME WITHIN THE FAMILY

Unit of analysis

Research into the distribution of income typically uses either 'household' or 'family' as the basic unit of analysis and assumes that income is pooled within these units. A household is defined as 'either one person living alone, or a group of people (who may or may not be related) living at the same address with common housekeeping' (*Social Trends No. 11* 1981). A family is defined as 'a married couple, alone or with their never-married child or children (of any age), or a lone parent together with his or her never-married child or children' (*Social Trends No. 11* 1981). The latter is generally considered to be the smallest unit available for deriving a distribution of income. In both cases, however, there is a clear assumption of the pooling of income within the unit. It may well be, of course, that the inequalities of income that exist between families are only part of the problem, and that disparities within each family are an added and important dimension.

It is possible to demonstrate that the two most common units employed (household and family) can produce quite different statistical results, in terms of which family types bear the weight of poverty most heavily. Table 4.2 indicates the heavy relative burden of poverty carried by women, whichever unit of analysis is taken

TABLE 4.2
THE PERCENTAGE OF VARIOUS FAMILY TYPES WITH
INCOMES OF 100 PER CENT OR LESS OF SUPPLEMENTARY
BENEFIT RATES, USING (a) HOUSEHOLD AND (b) FAMILY
UNIT OF ANALYSIS

	Elderly			Couple with children						Single		Lone parent
Couple	Lone woman	Lone man	0	1	2	3	4	5+	Woman	Man	
(a) Household	16	39	26	2	2	3	5	11	20	7	5	35
(b) Family	18	47	35	2	2	3	5	10	20	16	9	38

Note: These figures refer to the same population sample
(Devised from tables 3.2 and 3.4, Royal Commission on the Distribution of Income and Wealth 1978a)

(household or family) – and it should be remembered that most one-parent families are headed by a woman. The existence of poverty appears less prevalent in certain family types when the household is chosen as the measuring unit. This is because it is implicitly assumed that, where, for instance, more than one family is in the same household, their income is pooled. When, however, the incidence of poverty is measured according to family income, then we assume that each family is self-sufficient, and the results indicate greater poverty among those groups who are more likely to share houses with others – for example, a lone man or woman, the lone elderly, and to some extent the one-parent family. Thus, to illustrate, an elderly woman whose income is 100 per cent or less of the supplementary benefit rates may not necessarily appear in the above statistics if she is living with (say) her daughter and their combined incomes place them above the poverty line, if 'household' is chosen as the measuring rod. If 'family' is used, then provided her income is insufficient to bring her above the poverty line she will appear in the statistics, since now whom she is living with is immaterial. This is why those family types more likely to be living with other families show a greater incidence of poverty when each family unit is assumed to be a self-sufficient unit. Thus table 4.2 indicates that 47 per cent of lone elderly women and 35 per cent of lone elderly men have an income of 100 per cent or less of supplementary benefit rates when 'family income' is taken as the unit of analysis, but these figures drop to 39 and 26 per cent respectively when 'household income' is applied.

In law the husband is required to maintain his wife and children, and this makes the family, to many writers, the most basic of recipient units. Thus one writer has remarked that

> it is implicitly assumed that the 'inner' family is the basic social unit. This is a view propounded by one of the most eminent American economists in this field, Dorothy Brady, who argues that 'a man's obligation to care for his wife and minor children may be viewed as one of the fundamental and unchanging features of our society' . . . this, then, is our definition, which forms the basis of our concept of the income receiver. (Stark 1972)

However, if taking the 'household' as the unit of analysis – thereby assuming income pooling within its boundaries – obscures pockets of poverty, then it could be that the family unit itself may similarly be concealing inequalities between its members. Thus we need to know more about the mechanisms and processes whereby income is distributed between family members.

Mechanisms of income distribution

Studies of the distribution of income among family members have revealed a number of typical arrangements. A significant, though now dated, study is that by Zweig (1961), who found three main types with variations among the manual workers in four firms. These were:

1 *Allowance systems.* The main form, used by 50 per cent of families, consisted of a fixed housekeeping allowance based on basic wage, excluding overtime and shift payments. Less common variations were where the allowance varied according to gross earnings and where the husband dealt with the payment of most bills.

2 *Whole-wage systems.* The whole wage was handed to the wife, who returned an amount to the husband as pocket money. Alternatively, the husband's pocket money was a fixed sum, retained by him, and any excess earnings were spent on the home. Oakley (1974b) found this system practised in thirteen of the twenty working-class families she studied.

3 *Pooled-earnings systems*. Either money was left in a drawer, each spouse helping themselves (this was uncommon), or both spouses budgeted, saved and took money on an 'equal footing'. Zweig saw this latter system as being associated with earning wives.

The effect on the housekeeping arrangement of the wife's earning, however, appears not to be as clear-cut as Zweig had earlier suggested. Leonard (1980), in a study of young couples in South Wales, found that among those with both husband and wife working about 50 per cent operated an allowance system and 20 per cent a whole-wage system.

Gray's (1974) unpublished study of a sample of unskilled and skilled workers indicated two typical types of housekeeping arrangement: one where the husband kept or had returned his own pocket money (similar to Zweig's whole-wage systems) and paid for one or no major item for the household (e.g. rates, rent, coal, gas); another where the wife was given an allowance but the husband paid for one, and usually several, major items of expenditure (similar to Zweig's allowance systems). These two housekeeping systems appear related to certain 'social correlates'. For example, Gray found that the 'allowance' type was more commonly practised in homes where the husband had a skilled occupation, and where the eldest child was under 8 years of age. The 'pocket money' or 'whole wage' system was more common where parents had worked in a traditional primary-sector occupation, and where the children of the marriage were over 14 years old. The 'allowance' system appeared to be associated with a greater flexibility in the housekeeping allowance and the husbands were more prepared to work longer hours. It appears, then, that a housekeeping system that provides an expenditure stake for the husband leads to more frequent changes in the allowance the wife receives and may produce greater incentives at work.

There is some evidence that the type of arrangement may change when the main breadwinner (assumed in these studies to be the husband) is no longer employed. Both Land (1969) and Townsend (1963) found that, prior to retirement, the husband was seen as the family banker who allocated a sum for housekeeping to his wife and held back sufficient for his personal pocket money and to pay for 'family entertainments, holidays, and some household goods'. On retirement, however, 'his wife was no longer mainly dependent on

him for her housekeeping money. Hers became the presiding financial influence in the household. His share of the total income was
cut.'

Pahl (1980) has also suggested that stages in the life cycle may be
associated with particular arrangements: that 'pooling' may be
more common when couples are newly married and both working;
the 'allowance' system more applicable to the period of child-
rearing; a return to 'pooling' once the children have grown up and
the wife is therefore more likely to return to work, or a contribution
to family income is being made by teenage children; and finally the
exigencies of old age may lead to a 'whole wage' system being
adopted. These arrangements are, however, largely hypothetical;
we need to know much more about the effects of the life cycle on
income allocation procedures within the family.

There is also some evidence that the major responsibility for
family expenditure may be related to size of income. Land (1969), in
her study of large families in London during 1965–6, found that the
lower the family income the more likely was responsibility for
household expenditure to be the wife's. She suggests two reasons
for this. First, there was a tendency in all families for the mother to
be responsible for the daily and weekly expenditure, and the father
for the long-term payments, and, since in low-income families most
items of expenditure were of the regular sort, then this would be
normally discharged by the wife. Second, low-income families
usually had sources of income other than the husband's wage (including child allowances and social security benefits) on which the
wife could rely partially to meet household expenses. Table 4.3
indicates the growing importance of the woman as family banker as
the household income declines.

Pahl (1980) considers the possibility of constructing a typology
which might classify the relationship between income level and
allocation mechanism, and provide a suggestive scale which could
be further tested empirically. The whole-wage system appears more
likely to be related to low income levels (such as those families
largely dependent on social security benefits); middle income levels
seem more associated with an allowance system of some kind; while
high income levels and a pooling system seem to be related.

Zweig (1961) had earlier noted that there were regional variations in the allocation mechanism commonly employed. Other
studies confirm this: Todd and Jones (1972), for instance, found

TABLE 4.3
PERCENTAGE OF FAMILIES WITH DIFFERENT LEVELS OF
INCOME, ACCORDING TO RESPONSIBILITY FOR
HOUSEHOLD EXPENDITURE

	*Household income as % of National Assistance scale**		
	Under 100	*100–140*	*140 and over*
Responsibility for household expenditure			
Father and mother jointly	11	35	64
Mother with:			
Part of father's earnings	28	44	19
All of father's earnings	61	19	16

* National Assistance is now known as supplementary benefit
(Derived from table 5.1, Land 1969)

that the proportion of wives who received their husband's whole wage was highest in the North (15 per cent), East Midlands, South-West and Wales (8 per cent each), and lowest in the South-East and London (2 per cent). Why this relationship exists is difficult to ascertain. Pahl (1980) has suggested that one factor may be that, where women are more commonly economically active, a whole-wage or pooling mechanism may be preferred; and, in the more traditional areas where fishing, mining or heavy industry predominate and male dominance is strong, an allowance system may more commonly apply. Again, however, we need to know about this relationship in greater detail.

The distinction between the whole-wage and allowance systems has also been seen in the way young workers contribute to the family budget. Millward (1968), in a study of working-class girls between leaving school and getting married, found two major types of family budget contributions: 'giving in', where the girl gave her total wage packet to her mother and received a fixed amount of pocket money in return; 'on board', where the girl gave her mother an agreed sum of money and retained the remainder herself. The two major types of arrangement, however, subdivided into five stages representing a path along which most girls in Millward's study progressed, although particular stages were sometimes missed out.

1 The unopened wage packet was given straight to the parent (usually the mother) and a fixed amount of pocket money was returned. Some items of expenditure were paid for by the parent, such as clothes, lunches and fares.

2 As 1, but the girl opened her own wage packet.

3 As 2, but the girl kept her own bonus and/or overtime earnings in place of pocket money from parents.

4 The girl paid an agreed fixed sum for board and lodging, and the parent continued to provide money for fares and lunch.

5 As 4, except that the girl was now entirely self-supporting.

The first three subdivisions represent the status of 'giving in', while the fourth and fifth represent 'on board' arrangements. The transition from 'giving in' to 'on board' status was commonly marked by a major event, such as engagement and the start of saving for marriage, 18th birthday, change in job, or increase in wages. This study is confirmed by Gray's (1974) findings that the type of arrangement for handling and distributing income within the family may have an impact on incentives at work. Millward suggested that there was some evidence that those 'on board' had a greater incentive to earn bonuses, since they would keep the additional earnings themselves.

Process of income distribution

The mechanisms for distributing money within the family, then, vary considerably. The actual process of distributing that money is, however, also of considerable importance. It is, of course, difficult to assess the degree of equitability of a given distribution of funds. It may, on the subjective level, be difficult for some wives to make a judgement of this sort, since a number of women do not know what their husbands bring home in their wage packet. Oakley (1974b), for instance, found that 25 per cent of her sample of working-class wives did not know what their husbands earned, and in Townsend's (1963) study the figure was 27 out of 45 wives. In Gorer's (1971) study, over one in six wives who received a housekeeping allowance did not know their husband's income.

The most usual method of judging equitability, however, is to examine the wife's share of income over a period of time. Thus Young (1952) concluded that 'there may be a tendency for wives to suffer, relatively to their husbands, in any period of inflation . . .

like other unorganised workers, their money income may not advance as fast as prices'. Young and Syson (1974) have confirmed this more recently. They studied 50 households where the wife was not working: 20 wives had not received any increase in their allowance during the previous year; in 4 cases the allowance had decreased; and in 26 it had increased. During that year the pound had fallen in value by at least 25p. In about 50 per cent of these cases, then, the housewives' and the children's standard of living had declined in relation to their husbands'. *Woman's Own* (1975) conducted a survey from a representative sample of 4000 readers who replied to a questionnaire. The average housekeeping allowance had increased between July 1974 and July 1975 by £2.40 when a rise of £3.63 (a third more) would have been necessary to keep pace with inflation. One in five received no increase in housekeeping allowance at all, and the worse-off were the most likely to have had no increase.

Thus it seems that income accruing to the wife decreases in value most in those families who are in any case most vulnerable to inflationary pressure. The amount of income allocated to the wife from husband and even working child may, in any case, be determined more by local tradition than by the real needs of the family. Both Land (1969) and Millward (1968) found evidence of this. Since the arrival of an extra child is likely to be an added drain on the wife's funds, pressure on her housekeeping is likely to be further exacerbated. Since the overwhelming function of the wife's share of income is to cover expenditure on food (see table 4.4), then it is reasonable to assume that economies may often be made in nutrition, particularly in poorer families. Land (1969), in her study of large families, found that the mother was the most likely to sacrifice food for herself, that over half had no cooked meal in the middle of the day, a quarter had no breakfast and nothing more than a sandwich for lunch, and 1 in 12 never had a cooked meal. Her study indicated that the mother considered the needs of the father to come first, the children's second, and her own third. Marsden's (1969) study of lone mothers showed that between a quarter and a third were missing meals every day or were regularly eating either very little or food lacking in nutritional content. They were particularly concerned that their children should be seen not to be unduly suffering, and were prepared to make sacrifices themselves to that end.

TABLE 4.4

RESPONSIBILITY FOR EXPENDITURE ON HOUSEHOLD ITEMS

| | Buying food | Who usually dealt with | | |
		Paying for gas and electricity	Paying for rent, rates and mortgage	Dealing with any surplus
Wife	89	49	45	36
Husband	3	38	45	20
Either or both	7	10	8	43
Other answer	1	3	2	1

N = 1977
(Derived from section 4.1, Todd and Jones 1972)

There is some evidence that financial difficulties that stem from inequitable income distribution may be a contributory factor in marital breakdowns. In a study of 25 women whose marriages had broken down through violence, Pahl (1980) found that 15 had attributed their marital problems in part to financial difficulties. One-half of the women whose husbands kept control of the money coming into the house received either no money for housekeeping or only irregular amounts.

The evidence suggests, therefore, that the use of the family as the unit of analysis obscures inequalities within those families least able to cope with a relatively declining income. We need to know more about the mechanisms and the process of income distribution between members of the family, but the evidence so far indicates that the assumption made of 'pooled income' by the social security system needs careful and critical examination.

SOURCES OF FAMILY INCOME

When the social security system assumes the woman to be dependent on the man, it recognises the legal obligation of a man to support his wife and children. Beveridge had constructed his social security framework on the assumption that women would remain at home and so be dependent. What has happened since is that women have made a contribution to family income far above that envisaged by Beveridge. There are various ways of assessing that contribution statistically.

The first section of table 4.5 shows the proportion of married women who work full-time, part-time, or are self-employed, and indicates that the proportion of married women so employed has more than doubled since 1951. These figures, however, obscure the differential involvement of the various age groups. As can be seen from the second section of the table, something like 6 out of 10 married women who are most likely to be raising, or have recently raised, children are engaged in economic activity. This is a very substantial figure for a group assumed by the social security system to be dependent on their husbands. It is clear, therefore, that many more women are 'gainfully employed' than Beveridge had envisaged. Indeed, the above statistics are limited by the time period they are based on: Hunt (1968) found that some 85 per cent of wives had been employed at some time during their marriage. However, none of these statistics enables us to assess the extent of the contribution of working women to the family income. What impact, then, do working wives have on family funds?

Hamill (1978a) has shown the increasing numbers of women acting as sole or joint breadwinners. She estimated that in 1974 there were about 300,000 'role reversal' cases – that is, where the husband was not working and the wife was – and about 360,000 cases of 'breadwinner' wives – where the wife's earnings represent

TABLE 4.5
PERCENTAGE OF MARRIED WOMEN ECONOMICALLY
ACTIVE, 1951–1979, AND BY AGE GROUP, 1979

1951	*1961*	*1971*	*1973*	*1976*	*1979*
22	30	42	46	49	50

		Age groups		
19–19	*20–4*	*25–44*	*45–59/64*	*60/65+*
51	58	59	61	10

(Devised from table 5.2, *Social Trends No. 11* 1980)

at least half of the gross family income. Hamill suggests that the average working wife was responsible for around 25 per cent of the gross family income. In this respect it must be borne in mind that female earnings are lower than male and a greater percentage of women work part-time (see Chapter 6, pp. 127–37). Table 4.6 shows the distribution of wife's contribution to family income. A relatively small minority, 5 per cent of wives, were 'breadwinners' (earning more than 50 per cent of family income), though just over a third earned between 30 and 50 per cent. The table indicates the impact on family income of the wife's contribution in relation to all families. Greater insight into the impact of the wife's income is achieved by measuring her contribution against the husband's income, as table 4.7 shows. Thus, of those wives contributing more than 50 per cent of family income in 1974, 75 per cent had husbands earning £40 per week and under, whereas of those wives contributing between 1 and 20 per cent nearly 70 per cent had husbands earning over £50 per week.

The evidence suggests, then, that a negative relationship exists between the husband's earnings and the wife's contribution to the total family income. For lower-paid families, in particular, the wife's income may well be an indispensable part of the family budget. Indeed, the Royal Commission on the Distribution of Income and Wealth (1978b) showed that, but for the wife's income, there would be three times as many families living on an income level below that of supplementary benefit – see table 4.8. That table demonstrates that the proportion of those with income below 140 per cent of supplementary benefits increases markedly when wife's income is excluded from the calculation. Thus a little over 17

TABLE 4.6
ESTIMATED DISTRIBUTION OF THE EARNING WIFE'S
CONTRIBUTION TO FAMILY INCOME, GREAT BRITAIN 1974
(PERCENTAGES)

		% contribution			
10 and under	*10–22*	*20–30*	*30–40*	*40–50*	*Over 50*
18	22	21	21	13	5

(Devised from table 2, Hamill 1978a)

TABLE 4.7
THE PERCENTAGE CONTRIBUTION OF EARNING WIVES TO
TOTAL FAMILY INCOME IN RELATION TO HUSBANDS'
EARNINGS, 1974 (PERCENTAGES)

| | *Wife's contribution as % of family income* | | | | |
	0	*1–20*	*21–35*	*36–50*	*Over 50*
Husband's gross earnings (£ per week)					
0	9	2	*	2	29
40 and under	19	12	17	31	46
40–50	21	19	27	30	18
50–60	17	24	26	19	*
60–80	19	27	22	14	*
Over 80	15	18	7	3	0

* Not calculated owing to smallness of number
(Devised from table 8, Hamill 1978a)

TABLE 4.8
PERCENTAGE OF FAMILIES* WITH INCOMES, RELATED TO
SUPPLEMENTARY BENEFIT, BY TOTAL FAMILY INCOME,
AND EXCLUDING WIFE'S INCOME

| | *Total income* | *Income excluding wife's gross earnings* | |
	All couples	*All couples*	*Couples where wife is currently working*
% of supplementary benefit			
100 or less	3	10	13
100–19	6	12	13
120–39	9	17	20
140–99	39	40	37
200–49	23	13	11
250–499	20	8	6
Over 500	1	0.5	1

* Couples with children and earning man
(Derived from table 7.9, Royal Commission on the Distribution of Income and Wealth 1978a)

per cent of all couples have incomes below 140 per cent of sup-plementary benefit, but this figure increases to nearly 39 per cent of couples if the wife's income is excluded. If we consider only those couples in which the wife was currrently working, then the exclusion of her income places 46 per cent of couples below 140 per cent of supplementary benefit rates.

The wife's income, then, prevents real hardship for many fami-lies. It will not be surprising to discover, therefore, that a substantial proportion of her income is spent on basic household expenses. Hunt's (1968) study, for instance, found a negative relationship between household income and the proportion of the wife's income that was devoted to housekeeping expenses. Where total household income was low, 84 per cent of housekeeping expenses (including rent) were met from income earned by the wife; in contrast, where household income was relatively high, only 50 per cent of housekeeping came from the wife's income. In the same survey the sample were asked 'How would you say the money you earn is mostly spent?' Their answers confirmed that a substantial propor-tion of the wife's income was spent on essential family items; 58 per cent indicated contribution to housekeeping and/or rent.

The social security system was constructed on the assumption that women would not be gainfully employed. This section has clearly demonstrated that growing numbers of married women have en-tered the labour market, and made a substantial contribution to family income, a contribution that, for many families, is an in-dispensable part of the family budget. As Hamill (1978a) concludes, there may be, at the present time, relatively few cases of women being the main breadwinner, or relatively few instances of 'role reversals', but there is plenty of evidence that many wives are operating as 'joint breadwinners'.

ONE-PARENT FAMILIES

Beveridge's concern to emphasise the unity of the nuclear family, and his proposals for social security provision which were, in part, dependent on this, did not readily incorporate one-parent families into the main insurance benefits. He had anticipated that such families would remain relatively small in number and their needs adequately dealt with through the family allowance and separation allowance scheme, with the 'National Assistance net' (now supplementary benefit) operating as a back-up. Beveridge had in any case expected that those dependent on assistance would be a declining group as more and more of the population qualified for insurance benefits. In fact, rising numbers of people have been drawn into the 'assistance net' since the last war, and something like two-thirds of these are women – that is, single women not eligible for National Insurance, unsupported mothers, wives of men claiming supplementary benefit, prisoners' wives, divorced and separated women, widows and women pensioners. A significant feature of these figures has been the growing numbers of one-parent families, 89 per cent of which are headed by a woman. Something like one in eight families now are one-parent, and two-thirds of families with children who are receiving supplementary benefit are one-parent.

It is impossible to be sure about the precise number of one-parent families; it is not possible, for instance, to know precisely how many separated men and women there are, since there is no documentary evidence for this. However, estimated figures by the Office of Population Censuses and Surveys and the National Council for One-Parent Families (1980) show an increase in one-parent families from 474,000 in 1961, to 570,000 in 1971 and 920,000 in 1980. So, since 1971, there has been an increase of 61 per cent in one-parent families, many of which are dependent on means-tested benefits. In April 1980, 49,000 lone mothers and 1000 lone fathers were receiving family income supplement and, in 1979, 320,000 one-parent families received supplementary benefit. The most dramatic increase in numbers, however, is to be found among divorced women (see table 3.17 and p. 57).

Of the groups classified as one-parent families, the single, divorced and separated women are the most in need. A survey conducted for the Royal Commission on the Distribution of Income and Wealth (1978a) indicated the relatively disadvantaged position of one-parent families, and the large proportion of the single, divorced and separated living below the official poverty line, as can be seen in table 4.9. The low figure for 'lone men' is because 86 per cent of them worked and so would not be eligible for supplementary benefit; only 44 per cent of single women were employed (see table 4.12). The position of widows is eased by the existence of an insurance benefit for them and the possibility of their earning in addition to that without its affecting the benefit. It seems fairly clear 'that the problem of poverty in one-parent families relates mainly to those where the parent is a woman' (Royal Commission on the Distribution of Income and Wealth 1978a).

The number of one-parent families that have been recipients of supplementary benefit has been increasing steadily during the last decade. However, this increase has been relatively greater than the increase in one-parent numbers. Table 4.10 shows the steady increase in one-parent recipients of supplementary benefit, the number of whom rose by some 50 per cent between 1971 and 1978; this contrasts with an increase of 45 per cent in one-parent numbers during that period. The reasons for this are disputed. Finer (1974) had suggested that the increase was due to generous benefit levels and encouragement to claim benefit as of right. Hamill (1978b) has pointed, however, to 'demographic factors' – in particular, the

TABLE 4.9
THE PERCENTAGE OF ONE-PARENT FAMILIES WITH INCOME
LESS THAN 100 PER CENT OF SUPPLEMENTARY BENEFIT, BY
TYPE OF PARENT

Single woman	58
Widow	18
Separated woman	43
Divorced woman	51
Lone man	12
All one-parent families	38
All two-parent families	4

(Devised from table 8.1, Royal Commission on the Distribution of Income and Wealth 1978a)

TABLE 4.10
NUMBER OF ONE-PARENT FAMILIES RECEIVING WEEKLY
PAYMENT OF SUPPLEMENTARY BENEFIT (1000s)

	1969	1970	1971	1972	1973	1974	1975	1976	1977	1978	1979
One-parent families	180	195	217	231	233	250	283	310	317	330	320

(Devised from table 3.25, *Annual Abstract of Statistics* 1979)

increase in divorce since 1971. She also produces evidence of declining rates of economic activity among single and divorced women, and considers that this may be partly due to the increase in lone parents with children under 5; see table 4.11. Possible additional reasons adduced are the steady rise in unemployment during this period, and that it had become less attractive for women to work because it would entail a loss of benefit.

Table 4.12 contains more recent figures produced by the Royal Commission on the Distribution of Income and Wealth (1978a) and displays the continuing decline in economic activity for single and divorced mothers. About one-half of lone mothers work but receive low wages in relation to men and in many cases have to engage in

TABLE 4.11
PERCENTAGE OF ECONOMICALLY ACTIVE
LONE MOTHERS AND LONE MOTHERS WITH CHILDREN
UNDER 5 IN 1966 AND 1971

	Lone mothers		Lone mothers with children under 5	
	1966	*1971*	*1966*	*1971*
Single	56	45	57	66
Separated	48	47	48	46
Widowed	56	56	14	12
Divorced	64	57	26	28
All	54	52	32	35

(Derived from tables 6 and 7, Hamill 1978b)

TABLE 4.12
PERCENTAGE OF ECONOMICALLY ACTIVE ONE-PARENT
FAMILIES, BY TYPE OF PARENT

Single woman	44
Widow	56
Separated woman	57
Divorced woman	50
Lone man	86

(Devised from table 8.8, Royal Commission on the Distribution of Income and Wealth 1978a)

part-time work. Many also rely, at least in part, on supplementary benefit. It is not surprising, therefore, that the major reason for lone parents' contacting the National Council for One-Parent Families is financial: in 1979 33 per cent of initial contacts were made for this reason, and this represented a 3 per cent increase over the previous year – reflecting, perhaps, reduced employment opportunities.

The level of lone-parent dependence on the various social security benefits is well illustrated by table 4.13, which assesses the major sources of family income. The greater part of income for the lone parent comes from social security benefits and other sources, whereas by far the most significant source of income for the two-parent family with two children is wages and salaries. The lone parent, of either sex, is very likely to be faced with considerable financial hardship. There is little question, however, that these hardships bear particularly heavily on women. Most one-parent families are headed by a woman, she is much more likely to be living in poverty, has fewer opportunities to be economically active, and is very likely to find herself dependent, at least in part, on means-tested benefits such as supplementary benefit and family income supplement. Beveridge had not envisaged family break-up as a major problem, and in any case in the event his proposal for a

TABLE 4.13
SOURCES OF AGGREGATE INCOME FOR TWO FAMILY TYPES
(PERCENTAGES)

	Lone parent with one or more children	Couple with two children
Wages/salaries	42	79
Self-employment	2	8
Investment	0.7	1.3
Annuities and pensions	0.4	0.3
Social security benefits	26	6
Subletting and imputed income from owner/rent-free occupancy	5	5
Other sources	24	0.5

(Devised from table 46, *Family Expenditure Survey* 1979)

separation allowance was not implemented. Thus one-parent families have emerged as a major group dealt with substantially by the safety net of selective benefits, with their attendant problems of stigma and often poor take-up.

OVERVIEW

The social security system in this country is imbued with certain value assumptions about the nature of the modern family and its members' roles. These assumptions include the notion that the focal point of the family is the wife, and her role therefore continues to be seen as dependent on a breadwinner husband. Because the married woman is often assumed not to be engaged in economic activity, her qualification to benefit is sometimes treated differently from that of men. These assumptions about the dependency of women were clearly evident in the Beveridge Report (1942). That dependency was enshrined in a concept of family unity which assumed women's minimal involvement in economic activity, a pooling of income within the family, and a relatively insignificant amount of family break-up.

Women's involvement in economic activity since the last war has been marked. Although the average involvement of married women is currently around 50 per cent, for most ages between 20 and the normal retirement age that figure increases to nearly 60 per cent. Women's stake in the economy, then, is considerable, and their importance is particularly evident among those family groups who, without the woman's income, would be officially operating below the poverty line. Beveridge's projection has, therefore, proved inaccurate. The implicit assumption of the pooling of income within the family has, as a consequence, often hidden from view inequalities within that unit. We need to know much more about how income is distributed within the family, but, from what we do know, women's share of family income is disproportionately affected during periods of inflation, and this is particularly the case among the least well-off.

Finally, the Beveridge conception of family unity has had to contend with a steady increase in divorce since the last war. One product of this has, in part, been the growth of one-parent families, and this development has had important implications for women. Almost 90 per cent of lone parents are women. Moreover, they are between four and five times more likely to be living in poverty than their male equivalents. They have been subject to the prevailing assumption that men are the breadwinners and to the suspicion of a social security system which has never dared to be over-generous to the consequences of family break-up for fear of encouraging those who are still seen as transgressing the indivisibility of the institution of marriage. The original assumptions behind social security provision remain deeply ingrained in the present system, despite social change.

5

Educational opportunity and achievement

Margaret Wilkin

It might be assumed that in the 1980s the educational opportunities, experiences and attainments of girls and boys in Britain are not too dissimilar. Since the 1944 Education Act all children have been entitled to a free education according to age, ability and aptitude. There are no prescribed or formal sex-based distinctions concerning the length of schooling or the curriculum. The Sex Discrimination Act of 1975 prohibits preference being given to one sex at the expense of the other, specifies that all children should have equal access to the different subjects of the curriculum, and requires that the distribution of funds should be equitable between the sexes. By 1978, 86 per cent of schools for pupils aged 11–16 were comprehensive (though the percentage depends on the definition) (*Statistics of Education 1978* 1981). In much the same fashion, most children now attend mixed schools. While some 49 per cent of schools in the private sector are single-sex, in the maintained sector such schools amount to only 4 per cent. In both sectors there are more boys' than girls' schools and single-sex schools are predominantly secondary. It might, then, be claimed that a very large proportion of children now attend schools that should be capable of providing pupils of either sex with an equal chance to sample a wide range of curricular activities and attain school-leaving qualifications.

Yet recent evidence shows that the final educational attainment of women continues to fall behind that of men. Although girls are seen to exhibit more learning-appropriate behaviour and attitudes in their early years (Barker Lunn 1972; Ingleby and Cooper 1974; Hartley 1980), and show superiority in a number of educational skills, they leave school less well qualified than their male counter-

85

parts, having entered for, and obtained, fewer A-levels, and they have a poorer record of access to higher education and careers in education. In general, the participation rate of qualified women in higher education has, in fact, fallen relative to that of men (Roweth 1981). Although the cumulative attainment of girls may be lower than that of boys, girls have persistent success in one or two subject areas, notably those of languages and biology. Their subject-specific attainment may therefore be high, but their cumulative attainment begins to fall off at the end of their school career.

This situation may be contrasted with that found in the early years of schooling. Large-scale surveys in the 1960s reported that on average girls did better than boys in the primary school (e.g. Douglas 1964). Recent evidence suggests that the picture is somewhat complex. In some skills girls show superiority, in others, boys. It cannot be said that either sex has a total educational advantage in the first year or two at school, though girls have less difficulty in learning to read. Girls do well in CSE and GCE O-levels, both entering for more exams and obtaining more passes than boys. But thereafter they are more likely to move sideways than upwards in the educational network, choosing to go into further rather than higher education. From the age of 18, the number of women engaged in the higher levels of the educational system, whether as students or as employees, is lower than the number of men. Women are less likely than men to go to university or to do postgraduate work; fewer go into higher or further education as teachers, and, of those who do, fewer are appointed to senior posts. Although women have always entered schoolteaching in large numbers, they are less likely than men to hold positions of responsibility. While their early success rates imply that they are capable of the same levels of achievement as men, women seem progressively to withdraw from competitive participation in the educational system.

There is no evidence to indicate that women are by nature less intelligent than men, or are differentially less intellectually competent as they get older – for example, that at O-level a higher proportion of them are reaching their intellectual limits. The latter seems unlikely, and would require an explanation of why this did not also happen to men. Alternatively, the reasons for women's comparative lack of attainment could be social or psychological – for example, that women fail to see the relevance of further qualifications for their future lives, that they are discriminated against, that they lack the motivation or attitudes to apply for promotion, or that the demands of home and family are such that women are discouraged from investing more time and effort in their occupational role (see Chapter 6).

The main concern of this chapter is to outline and account for some of the differences between the sexes in educational performance and involvement. The explanation of such differences, which are clearly complex, could be approached in two distinct ways: either to account for the relatively superior educational achievement of men, or to explain the relatively inferior achievement of women. This is not to suggest that the two approaches are mutually exclusive or that they do not share several fundamental common elements – such as questions about who defines and operates the educational system, what is educational success, what differences are causally related to achievement, and so on. However, the confines of this chapter – and, indeed, of the literature – preclude a comprehensive treatment; hence what follows is addressed to the basic question: why is it that girls, who display promise initially, fail to maintain their position *vis-à-vis* boys in terms of educational success, when there are few formal sex barriers in education?

ATTAINMENT IN YOUNGER CHILDREN

The evidence suggests that girls and boys may have an approximately equal start in the educational race, or that girls may enjoy a slight advantage. An early survey by Douglas (1964) provided data from a large national sample on the academic attainment of children in Britain up to the age of 11 years. According to teachers' judgements of reading, more boys than girls were found to be outstandingly bad, and fewer outstandingly good. When tested at both 8 and 11 years, girls were the more advanced readers – although at 11 their superiority was less marked. The boys, however, had a larger vocabulary throughout. Fourteen years later, the survey *Primary Education in England* (1978) echoed these findings, showing girls in a superior position initially, and the reading abilities of the sexes diverging less as age increased. Tests were administered to over 5000 children in more than 370 schools, and the conclusion reached was that, although at 9 years of age girls obtained slightly higher scores on the reading test, at age 11 the difference was smaller. A study by Maxwell (1977), with a sample of about 2500 pupils drawn from Scottish primary schools, produced similar results. At age 9 girls had reached a higher level of reading and language attainment than boys, though two years later this difference had disappeared. Since 'boys and girls at the same stage were taught in the same class', it was 'possible to make a direct comparison between the reading attainment of boys and girls who received the same teaching and took the same test'. A further study (Start and Wells 1972) used a test which 'had shown no consistent bias in favour of one sex or the other' and found that boys, on average, were marginally better readers than girls at the age of 11, although this difference was very small.

In mathematics the respective attainments of the sexes are less straightforward. At 11 years old, boys have been shown to do better on items concerned with graphical presentation, though the overall scores of girls and boys displayed no statistical difference (*Primary Education in England* 1978). Elsewhere it has been found that girls do better at computation (Ward 1979). The data produced by Ward have been further analysed by Schuard (1981), who concludes that boys are better at items that involve spatial perception, place value and problem-solving, whereas girls have higher scores on verbal items such as naming shapes. It seems, then, that in mathematics girls have strengths principally in a single aspect, that of computation, while boys have strengths elsewhere, and appear to have a wide-ranging mathematical ability. The mean scores of 11-year-old boys were found to be significantly higher than those of girls in the sub-categories of length, volume and capacity, rate and ratio (*APU Mathematical Development Primary Survey* 1980). By halfway through their schooling, then, there are no outstanding differences between the sexes in overall attainment in these two basic subjects.

ATTAINMENT IN OLDER CHILDREN

By the time pupils sit their first public examinations, the specific subject specialisation hinted at in the primary school has become firmly established. Table 5.1 shows the attainment by subject of girls and boys at higher-grade Certificate of Secondary Education and General Certificate of Education O-level (that is, CSE grade 1 and GCE grades A, B and C), during the academic year 1977–8. More girls than boys were successful in English (42 compared with 32 per cent). In mathematics the position was reversed: girls 21 and boys

TABLE 5.1
PERCENTAGE OF SCHOOL LEAVERS OBTAINING HIGHER-
GRADE* GCE O-LEVEL OR CSE, BY SEX AND SUBJECT,
ENGLAND AND WALES, 1977–1978

	Girls	*Boys*	*All*
English	42	32	37
French	17	11	14
Music/drama/visual arts	15	10	13
Mathematics	21	29	25
Physics	6	18	12
Chemistry	6	13	10
Biology	18	12	15
Any subject	54	49	51

* Grades A–C in GCE and grade 1 in CSE
(Derived from table iii, *Statistics of Education 1978* 1981, vol. 2)

29 per cent. Boys were likely to gain more passes in the sciences and girls in the arts.

In examinations at 16, girls did well over all; table 5.2 indicates that they were more likely to gain CSE and GCE O-level passes. Fewer girls (only 12 per cent) than boys (14 per cent) attempted no public examination at this level, or attempted but did not pass. At this stage, by these measures girls are rather more successful than boys, though the interests of both sexes lie within specific subject ranges. This pattern represents what might be expected as a development of the situation found in primary school, where girls generally showed a more positive attitude than boys towards school and a tendency towards competence in language, though limited skill in mathematics.

There is little difference in the proportion of the sexes staying on at school for either one year (girls 28 per cent, boys 27 per cent) or two years (girls 18 per cent, boys 19 per cent) beyond the minimum school-leaving age (*Social Trends No. 11* 1981), but it is at A-level that boys begin to outperform girls. Although boys are only marginally more likely to enter for A-levels (girls 17 per cent, boys 18 per cent) – as table 5.2 shows – and, although an approximately equivalent percentage of boys and girls obtain one or two A-level passes, a higher overall percentage of boys gain A-levels because they are

TABLE 5.2
PERCENTAGE OF SCHOOL LEAVERS WITH QUALIFICATIONS,
BY SEX, ENGLAND AND WALES, 1977–1978

	Girls	Boys	All
A-level GCE passes			
3 or more subjects	7	10	9
2 subjects	4	4	4
1 subject	3	3	3
Any subject	14	17	16
Higher-grade* GCE O-level or CSE passes			
5 or more subjects	10	8	9
1–4 subjects	29	24	27
Any subject	39	32	36
Lower-grade† GCE O-level or CSE passes	33	36	34
School leavers sitting			
CSE examinations	74	71	73
GCE O-level examinations	57	54	55
GCE A-level examinations	17	18	18
No examinations	12	14	13
Examinations but with no passes	1	1	1

* Grades A–C in GCE and grade 1 in CSE
† All grades other than those specified as higher*
(Derived from table D, *Statistics of Education 1978* 1981, vol. 2)

more successful at the three-or-more pass level. There is, then, a reversal of the situation at the O-level stage, when more girls gained passes. At A-level too differences in subject choice by the sexes are very pronounced. On the basis of their O-level qualifications, it might be expected that a higher proportion of girls than boys would enter for A-level examinations. However, they participate less – a tendency also evident at entry into higher education. Recently, qualified women's participation in higher education has decreased more rapidly than that of men; 'out of those qualified to enter higher education, currently around one in nine men and one in four women . . . do not take up that option' (Roweth 1981).

Just over 3 per cent more men than women enter degree courses at universities, polytechnics or other establishments (table 5.3). In universities the percentage of female undergraduates has increased over the past decade (from 32 to 37 per cent) but still represents only just over a third of the total undergraduate population (table 5.4). The percentage of women reading science degrees (which has always been lower than that of men) shows a slight decrease of 2 per cent, while male decrease is 4 per cent, suggesting a reaction to social or cultural pressures or influences of a general nature, probably unrelated to the sex of the student (table 5.5). Once at university, however, women progress very similarly to men, though they gain proportionately fewer first-class honours degrees.

TABLE 5.3
THE DESTINATIONS OF SCHOOL LEAVERS IN ENGLAND AND
WALES, 1977–1978, BY SEX (PERCENTAGES)

	Girls	Boys	All
Degree courses	5.7	8.8	7.3
Teacher-training courses	0.9	0.2	0.5
GCE A- and O-level courses	4.1	3.4	3.7
Secretarial courses	5.2	*	2.5
Nursing courses	1.4	*	0.7
Other courses[†]	8.4	5.4	6.9
Employment	65.3	73.8	69.7
Unknown	9.0	8.4	8.7

* Extremely small numbers, around 100
[†] Includes catering courses, which girls are twice as likely to enter as boys
(Derived from table ii, *Statistics of Education 1978* 1981, vol. 2)

TABLE 5.4
THE SEX COMPOSITION OF
BRITISH UNIVERSITY UNDERGRADUATES,
1971–1972 TO 1977–1978 (PERCENTAGES)

	1971–2	1972–3	1973–4	1974–5	1975–6	1976–7	1977–8
Women	32	33	34	35	36	36	37
Men	68	67	66	65	64	64	63

Note: In 1971–2 there were 182,678 undergraduates and in 1977–8 214,540
(Derived from table C(i), *Statistics of Education 1977* 1980, vol. 6)

TABLE 5.5
PERCENTAGE OF BRITISH UNIVERSITY UNDERGRADUATES
READING SCIENCES, 1972–1973 TO 1977–1978, BY SEX

	1972–3	*1973–4*	*1974–5*	*1975–6*	*1976–7*	*1977–8*
Women	37	37	37	36	35	35
Men	64	63	62	61	60	60
All	55	54	53	52	51	51

(Derived from table C(ii), *Statistics of Education 1977* 1980, vol. 6)

There are problems of comparing the educational achievement of
the sexes, which arise from the question of how comparable the sex
groups are. It might be argued that, since female university students
are a smaller proportion of their sex than male students, they are a
more exclusive group on certain criteria. They are so in respect of
social class: women undergraduates are more likely to be from the
middle class and less likely to be from the working class than men
(Kelsall, Poole and Kuhn 1972; Edwards and Roberts 1980). Claims
of differences between the sexes in terms of ability are confused by
our lack of knowledge about the extent to which the most able of
either sex apply and/or are chosen for university and other higher-
education courses.

So far, there has been no evidence to suggest that the discrepancy
between the sexes in university entrance is due to innate differences
in intelligence. Up to GCE O-level, girls do better in school than
boys. Unless some extraordinary characteristic of female intelligence is hypothesised – namely, that the intellectual competence of women suddenly starts to decrease after the age of 16,
but that the minds of men are not affected by ageing in this way – this
cannot be regarded as a biologically developmental process. Nor is
there any evidence from comparative testing to suggest that women
and men differ fundamentally in their biologically inherited degree
of intelligence. Wittig and Petersen (1979) conclude that the
amount of variance in intelligence accounted for by sex is generally
quite small. And while there are demonstrable differences between
the sexes in some areas of cognitive functioning – that is, differences
of kind – even this is not assured, since by the time children are
capable of taking a test they have acquired a vast array of cultural

assumptions about sex roles, attitudes and values, which affect their responses, perhaps explaining why tests discriminate between the sexes on some items. So, while it has been established that the sexes differ – for example, in spatial awareness and verbal functioning – it cannot be properly concluded that these are either innate or acquired traits, since social influence can be neither eliminated nor accounted for.

Women, then, are less likely to attend university, and fewer embark on any degree course. Those who do show a very marginal preference over men for polytechnics, but are more than twice as likely as men to enter other establishments (*Statistics of Education 1977* 1980, vol. 2). Why women apparently choose to attend degree-awarding institutions that are, irrespective of the quality of the courses or teaching, of lower status than universities is interesting. It is not because women are academically less well qualified, since entry requirements are, with some exceptions, nominally the same for degree courses. It could be because their limited subject interests result in a shortage of places at universities and polytechnics – but this would also be true for men. It may be that many of these institutions have evolved from teacher-education colleges which were always heavily populated with women students. Possibly it could be argued that women may elect to enter non-university degree courses because they perceive them as less demanding.

Table 5.3 gives the destination of all school leavers aged 16–18 for 1977–8. Women were four times more likely than men to enter teacher training, wherever it was located. However, the cutbacks in student numbers in this area, together with declining job prospects in teaching, invite speculation about women's future entry into higher education. For example, the previously discussed trends suggest that women may not enter other degree courses in very large numbers in lieu.

It is worth noting that, since nearly all teacher-training and some nursing courses are, in fact, now degree courses, the distinction made in the official statistics between these and degree courses is misleading. Thus the gap between the numbers of women and men entering degree courses is not so great as at first appears, since the data mask the true situation. The separation of the courses in this way is, however, useful in indicating where women's preferences for type of degree courses lie. Women entering post-school education show a greater tendency than men to enter courses that incorporate an obvious training element, whether of degree level or not.

Fewer women than men participate in higher education, and women are also less likely to enter employment on leaving school (table 5.3). A higher proportion remain in the education system on further-education courses, for GCE O- or A-levels, secretarial, nursing or catering qualifications, and on other unspecified courses. The different destinations of women and men after school invites speculation. Women might be seen to be underselling their abilities in choosing lower-level courses, when they should be capable of acquiring GCE A-levels and higher qualifications. The data may be seen as suggesting that women take a more instrumental view of their education after school. Although they enter employment later than men, it can be argued that they make up their minds on their occupational role earlier. Taking a degree may postpone occupational choice; taking a nursing or teacher-training course confirms it – and, for women, also confirms the female role. It might be that women feel the need to establish themselves in an occupational role as soon as possible, knowing that their job expectancy is limited by the future demands of marriage and child-bearing. Such occupations may be perceived as conducive to, or accommodating of, the female family role. Further, it can be seen that women's tendency to prefer teaching, nursing and catering reflects and utilises traditional feminine attitudes and skills, those of caring, nurturing and responsibility for the welfare of others: these jobs are extensions of a generalised feminine image. Thus it is hardly surprising that a large proportion of women elect for traditional areas of female employment. Obviously a similar situation operates with respect to men and jobs that involve aspects of the culturally defined masculine image. How and why they may arrive at these choices must now be considered.

SOCIALISATION

To question the inevitability of the variations between the sexes in educational attainment and destination is to direct attention towards what determines them. There are considerable difficulties in determining any biological base to sex or gender differences as displayed in social life. Sharpe (1976) and Delamont (1980a) take a strongly social view, regarding most of our sex-related characteristics as being socially conditioned, and using comparative examples to show that there are very few forms of behaviour defined as sex-specific in our culture which, in other cultures, are not performed by members of the opposite sex. It is not claimed that female and male roles are solely the products of intensive, long-term and consistent socialisation; but the social transmission of gender stereotypes is an undeniable force in creating our sexual identities.

Gender identity is initially shaped through interaction within the family. From birth the sexes are treated differently (Belotti 1975). Girls and boys are given different toys, different standards and rules apply to their behaviour, and they are assumed to have different interests (see Sharpe 1976; Deem 1978; Delamont 1980a). While some parents may tolerate a wide range of behaviour in their young children, most parents are both consciously and unconsciously conservative in shaping their children's sexual identity. Hence most children enter primary school with a clear-cut understanding of sexually appropriate behaviour, which is reinforced by the school through both the overt and the hidden curriculum; and the school is a very powerful socialising agent, particularly because of the impressionability of young pupils, and the length and intensity of school experience.

OVERT AND HIDDEN CURRICULA

Schooling is often regarded as a timetable comprising lessons – the overt curriculum, a daily round of mathematics, history, craft and games. The hidden curriculum, operating largely at the level of sub-awareness, is also a potent force for learning. It pervades school life – in classroom, corridor and playground – and is the network of cultural assumptions, values and attitudes, including sexually specific behaviour, which we confirm by re-enacting it daily. The child starting school is subject to a pattern of routines of organisation which for convenience are likely to be based on, or related to, sexual distinction.

Besides being used as an organising principle, sexual distinctiveness may be used to enforce discipline (Delamont 1980a). Boys, for example, may be reprimanded for behaving like girls, and vice versa. As a child progresses through school, so sexual distinctions increasingly become established, polarised and immutable. Girls learn to be girls – to be quiet and studious, anxious to please and to help, being praised for being neat and careful workers. Boys are encouraged to be aggressive and tough and are expected to acquire technical knowledge with ease. Girls are expected to acquire technical knowledge with difficulty if at all. Boys are encouraged to be confident and fearless, girls to be sensitive and meek. The school constrains, controls and shapes its pupils' behaviour, echoing the social codes of conventional and acceptable norms and values for women and men.

Many writers see children's books as a particularly influential vehicle for transmitting sex roles, since learning to read is a fundamental skill, the acquisition of which assumes crucial importance in young pupils' early years at school. In her analysis of seven popular reading schemes, Lobban (1975) concluded that the world represented in these texts was one in which 'the sexes are consistently different, and where females are consistently inferior in all spheres that are ascribed high status in our society.' There was 'a predominance of male central characters and a rigid separation of the activities, possessions and aspirations of female and male children . . . an almost exclusive concentration on the wife and mother role of females . . . the world outside the home reserved almost entirely for males.' All the reading schemes analysed were shown to be strongly sexist, hence reinforcing traditional sex stereotyping. Women were seen to be heavily engaged in domesticity. Men were active, dominant, decisive. Lobban makes the point that such extreme sex typing does not reflect the actual reality of today's world, where there is greater flexibility in the interpretation of sex roles. But, by representing sex-differentiated behaviour in such a clear-cut manner, these reading books may be all the more effective socialisers.

Another way in which the overt curriculum embodies the hidden curriculum is through the differential availability of subjects for boys and girls, particularly in the secondary school. A large-scale curriculum survey investigating fourth- and fifth-formers' subject options in single-sex and mixed schools commented that, taking into account the differences in facilities available (laboratories, etc.), schools ought to satisfy themselves 'that differences in the curriculum as between the sexes do not unfairly and unnecessarily militate against the personal development or the careers prospects of girls. There is evidence in the survey that some differences do have this effect' (*Curricular Differences for Boys and Girls* 1975). This survey also noted that although girls and boys are expected to behave differently in nursery and infant classes, 'in many instances schools begin to formalise their different expectations of boys and girls when the children enter the junior classes at about seven years of age and that this becomes widespread for the 9–11 year olds.' It found that the headteachers of the 98 per cent of the 302 mixed secondary schools which separated the sexes for some of their work gave organisational reasons for this arrangement. Convenience and the availability of facilities may generate a sexually differentiated timetable, which in turn is likely to have consequences for the development and maintenance of beliefs about the appropriateness of certain curricular activities for girls or boys (Sutherland 1981).

The separation of the sexes for craft subjects was also noted by a later survey investigating curriculum choice in secondary schools (*Aspects of Secondary Education in England* 1979). This survey concluded:

> differentiation by sex in the craft subjects occurred, in practice if not design, in something over 65 per cent of the 365 schools. This situation obtained in schools of all types, although to a markedly lesser extent in full range comprehensive schools, and applied to pupils of all abilities. Nevertheless, traditional attitudes were observed to be changing during the survey . . .

When, at age 13 or 14, children choose 'under guidance' what subjects they are to take, their choice may be partially constrained by what they have already done. Past choices may eliminate alternatives in the future, because certain subjects are grouped together, either for organisational reasons or because it is assumed that there is a useful degree of continuity or overlap of knowledge or skills between certain subject areas. For example, Sharma and Meighan (1980) found that some of the differential attainment of boys and girls in mathematics could be attributed to different previous experience in mathematically related subject areas. Thus the formal curriculum may operate to limit both the choice and the success of pupils, by maintaining traditional sex roles. The counselling of pupils may also confirm sex stereotypes, since teachers tend to direct children towards what they believe to be suitable future employment. Parents also play their part by being 'realistic' in their advice. To many, traditional female careers must seem the obvious and most convenient jobs to aim for.

> Teachers like parents acquire attitudes. It is as natural for them as it is for the parents of those whom they teach to accept assumptions about inherent characteristics of boys and girls . . . . It is still probable that assumptions about expected preference and capabilities are in many schools handed down undisturbed from one generation of teachers to the next. (*Curricular Differences for Boys and Girls* 1975)

Therefore, even if a full range of school subjects is nominally available to pupils of both sexes, there may be a number of constraints that reduce choice for either sex.

Also noteworthy is the influence that mixed or single-sex schools have on both pupil choice and pupil success. Table 5.6 shows that, although 75 per cent of girls in mixed schools were offered physics, only 11 per cent of girls took it, and girls in single-sex schools were more likely to take physics than girls in mixed schools where it is more readily available. A similar pattern was found for chemistry. However, it was not true for boys in the case of more 'female' subjects, such as art and music, although fewer boys took biology in mixed than in single-sex schools. It seems possible that, in mixed schools, traditional attitudes towards subjects as being either 'female' or 'male' have a stronger influence. The presence of both sexes may emphasise the polarisation of sex roles. Staff may assume that girls will wish to do needlework and boys physics, irrespective of individual choice, and the pupils themselves may well conform, since they may not wish to detract from their gender image by choosing certain gender-related subjects. The pressures to act in accordance with sex stereotypes will be less in single-sex schools. Harding (1979) studied the performance, rather than the choice, of pupils in 16-plus public examinations. In mixed schools boys were more successful than girls in science examinations, while girls in girls' schools were more successful than girls in mixed schools. Harding's conclusion was that 'girls may be particularly disadvantaged in the study of science in the mixed comprehensive school'. It can be suggested that coeducational schools, whatever they do for social relations – and Dale (1974) suggests that they have a lot to recommend them in this respect – perpetuate female educational and social characteristics. Preece (1979), investigating second-year pupils in five comprehensive schools, found that on most arithmetic test items 'the overall ratings did not differ initially for the boys and girls although the profiles differed in detail'. Girls' ability fell off sharply, however (see also Sharma and Meighan

TABLE 5.6
THE AVAILABILITY AND CHOICE OF SUBJECTS BY FOURTH-
AND FIFTH-FORMERS IN SINGLE-SEX AND MIXED
SECONDARY SCHOOLS, BY SEX

	% of pupils being offered subject		% of those offered who chose subject		% of all pupils taking subject	
	Single-sex	Mixed	Single-sex	Mixed	Single-sex	Mixed
Physics						
Girls	62	75	23	15	14	11
Boys	85	91	60	52	51	47
Chemistry						
Girls	75	78	27	22	20	17
Boys	81	79	36	35	29	28
Biology						
Girls	96	96	49	53	47	51
Boys	79	91	39	30	31	27
French						
Girls	92	90	49	43	45	39
Boys	75	87	37	28	28	24
German						
Girls	44	38	18	21	8	8
Boys	33	36	21	11	7	4
Geography						
Girls	72	61	53	46	38	28
Boys	91	61	55	54	50	33
History						
Girls	69	61	46	48	32	29
Boys	92	57	45	40	41	23
Art						
Girls	98	98	39	37	38	36
Boys	97	98	36	38	35	37
Music						
Girls	94	81	16	16	15	13
Boys	55	75	11	13	6	10

(Derived from p. 13, *Curricular Differences for Boys and Girls* 1975)

1980), as 'the female attitude to mathematics developed. Girls did
not expect to succeed, they felt that no-one else expected them to
succeed, therefore there was no point in trying.' The key to the
problem is seen as one of attitude not ability, and this is supported
by Isaacson and Freeman (1980) in replying to Preece:

Girls turn away from mathematics primarily because their careers are not terribly important to them. There is reason to believe that girls' attitudes and achievements in their school subjects are more influenced by images of themselves as future home-makers and parents, and less by images of themselves as future wage-earners. . . . If girls develop negative attitudes towards mathematics . . . their freedom to participate on equal terms in the world of work in adulthood will be impaired . . .

The importance of self-image was also demonstrated in an experiment in which first-year pupils in a secondary school were placed in mixed and single-sex sets for mathematics (Smith 1980). All children were of the same ability range and were taught by the same teacher. Initially, there was little difference between the test scores of girls in either set. After a year the average score of girls in the mixed set had fallen well behind that of the boys. The girls in the single-sex set achieved much higher scores, only marginally below those of the corresponding group of boys. The few O-level GCE mathematics girls in the school were quoted as saying that they felt uncomfortable in the strongly masculine environment of the mixed-sex group. They tended to adopt 'a deliberately passive role in the class'. It is, then, a question of acquired attitudes – such as that girls are no good at mathematics, since it is a boys' subject. The belief that women may be excused for relatively poor performance in a masculine activity was illustrated by Rogers's (1980) finding that 15-year-old boys tended to excuse girls for failure at mathematics, while rewarding other boys for their success. We might not be surprised, then, that the sexes vary in their estimates of their achievements. The DES survey *Curricular Differences for Boys and Girls* (1975) concludes:

the prevailing picture is of traditional assumptions being worked out through the curricular patterns of secondary schools, and of support for and acceptance of these patterns by the majority of teachers, parents and pupils. . . . It is likely that a society which needs to develop to the full the talents and skills of all its people will find the discrepancies in subjects studied by boys and girls disturbing.

Investigating the subject preferences of 1204 pupils in secondary schools, Ormerod (1975) found that sex-linked polarisation of subject preferences were more marked in coeducational than in single-sex schools. The author points out that research indicates that in science boys and girls have different learning styles and respond differently to variations in teachers' behaviour and strategies, and that teaching style may be partially responsible for the greater popularity of the sciences at girls' schools. Ormerod argues that teaching mixed classes is therefore difficult and unlikely to favour girls, since in mixed schools the science teachers are likely to be men. Be this as it may, in single-sex schools the teachers are more likely to be of the same sex as the pupils, irrespective of the 'gender' of the subject. The polarisation of subjects is then challenged, and models are offered to the pupils that contradict the usual sexist assumptions about subject choice.

In a study of the relationships between subject preference and perceived subject easiness, in a sample of 348 14-year-olds from a range of schools, Keys and Ormerod (1977) found not only that 'male' subjects such as physics and chemistry were considered difficult, but that 'female' subjects such as music and religious instruction were regarded as easy. Both sexes agreed on the rank order of subject easiness, but disagreed in their preference – boys tending to prefer the most 'difficult' subjects, girls the 'easiest'. The authors conclude that perceived difficulty is an important factor affecting subject choice. Why is this the case? Two possible reasons come to mind. First, that it is a practical expression of girls' relative lack of confidence in themselves (Barker Lunn 1972). Second, it could be interpreted as an unwillingness to challenge a traditionally male area. Having internalised gender prescriptions from family, peers and the media, a girl may believe that such things are not for her: such subjects are seen as part of the male world, unfeminine and threatening. Hence many girls express little interest in so-called 'male' subjects.

The internalisation of gender roles may have consequences for a pupil's success in examinations. Examiners in English, for example, may unwittingly select passages or items that appeal more to the interests and feelings of one of the sexes. Wood (1978) analysed the questions and marking of O-level GCE English language papers. He found that boys did better than girls on items relating to a man reminiscing about his childhood near a railway, and that girls did better on a passage about a girl's ordeal at a dinner-dance. It is argued that this association may unwittingly favour one sex. Careful scrutiny of examination questions would be required to ensure a balance of gender-specific items. Discriminatory situations such as these – a measurable structural 'event' – are comparatively easy to diagnose.

Another potential source of discrimination between the sexes is the provision of resources. Byrne (1975) is at pains to assure the reader that discrimination found in the allocation of resources in her survey areas was

> less a case of negative conscious discriminal allowance than implicit acceptance of inherited and unexamined social and educational assumptions that girls were destined for different, mainly subsidiary, marriage based roles in society and needed therefore different routes and less sophisticated equipment and education for a terminal occupation of wife and mother.

Her research involved 133 mixed and single-sex schools. Almost all the girls' schools were found to be deficient in science laboratories. Elsewhere boys had the use of laboratories while girls studied biology in the classrooms. One local education authority consistently awarded higher capitation and financial allocations per capita to its boys' schools than to its girls' schools. In all but four schools the distribution of material resources for options reflected assumptions about the adult roles of the sexes: that girls do not have to earn their living; that girls become shop assistants, typists and computer programmers, whereas boys become accountants, managers and doctors. The organisation of pupils according to these assumptions was explained in terms of what the pupils wanted, what local employers wanted, and so on. Byrne saw such a situation as a continuing cycle of deprivation, and much consciousness raising and self-reflection would be required to alter such well-established traditions.

When discussing the socialising influence of education, it is convenient to make an analytic distinction between the acquisition of personality characteristics and preparation for the expected events of adult life. As has been noted, these two dimensions are, of course, interrelated. Women, typically, are discouraged from being outgoing and aggressive, and they are also less likely either to attempt or to be successful in a career. Schooling for many girls involves tension between these two aspects of the female role and the demands of education. Delamont (1980a) gives numerous examples of the ways in which gender is transmitted through subject content, teaching methods and organisation in the school. Across the subject range, texts stress the feats and achievements of men, with women generally in supportive and caring roles, when featured at all; while the hierarchy of school staff from the headteacher (male) to the cleaners and administrative staff (female) emphasises women's relative lack of status and success. On the other hand, education in our society is deemed to be something worth striving for. The successful examinee is lauded, irrespective of sex. Girls are thus caught in a double bind. They are subjected to pressures to conform to their gender role, yet at the same time the official ideology of education promotes academic achievement. But doing well at school, being clever, 'involves losing an important ingredient of feminity' (Sharpe 1976). The majority of her sample of indigenous and immigrant girls from four Ealing schools supported the belief that boys feel threatened by girls who are too clever. A girl may therefore tend to feel she cannot be too academically successful or she will not be attractive to boys, and she may seek competence only in traditionally female areas. Deem (1978) suggests that how a girl resolves this tension depends largely on her social class expectations and on parental influence. The lower the social class, the more rigid is gender stereotyping likely to be. Working-class girls will thus be more likely to reject any involvement with school beyond the minimum leaving age, since their immediate destiny is perceived as that of wife and mother. Middle-class girls, though, are more likely to regard motherhood as their *ultimate* destiny before which there is time for acquiring further qualifications and perhaps embarking on a career. Most of the girls in Sharpe's study regarded school as boring, trivial and petty, but above all irrelevant for their future lives. As she points out, though, to make education more 'relevant' would be to increase the domestic component still further, thus reverting to the days when government reports (for example, Hadow Committee 1927; Norwood Committee 1941) recommended that for girls the curriculum should include preparation for their life's career of wife and mother.

Sharpe suggests that elimination of formal barriers of sexual discrimination does not seem to have resulted in greater freedom for women to be individuals, since, to compensate, more pressure has been laid on informal beliefs and sanctions. This hidden curriculum of life outside the school is of considerable influence, owing to its repetitious, pervasive and, above all, unrecognised nature. Even young schoolchildren are not immune from its influence. The reinforcement of gender images through the media (see Goffman 1979) starts with young children's comics, which Sharpe (1976) character-ises as follows. Boys' comics are full of action and adventure, while the girls' stress emotions and the nurturant role of women. The scenarios in girls' comics are limited to the home, the family and the school; boys' heroes venture into outer space. Men feature in girls' comics, rarely vice versa, and girls who show a tendency to be independent are led by the sequence of events to see the error of their ways. In adolescent magazines, girls are portrayed as preoccu-pied with finding the right man and with the idealisation of romance. As Delamont (1980a) comments:

> Girls do not seem to realise that they will have to work for most of their lives in badly paid unskilled jobs unless they leave school with qualifica-tions even if they marry. Adolescents seem to be blinded to the reality of the labour market by the rosy glow of romance, in ways that boys are not, and schools seem to be failing totally to dispel that rosy glow.

Undoubtedly the media contribute to the image that girls and boys have of themselves and their future adult life, which in turn may affect what subjects they choose at school and their level of success. But the school itself also contributes to the differential achieve-ments of the sexes. Discrimination in favour of one sex or the other may be overt and measurable, as in the case of resources. It may also be more subtle, as in the structuring of curriculum choice. Attitudes of staff, parents and fellow pupils generate or constrain motivation and career expectation.

That the characteristics and inclination of both sexes have ele-ments of both the biological and the social is a sound hypothesis. What is important for the development of individual talent and interests is that both sexes should feel able to step outside the shackles of social stereotypes if they so wish. Education may have an important part to play in contributing to this greater freedom.

SUCCESS AND OPPORTUNITIES

There are, of course, a number of girls and women who succeed in the educational system, despite the matrix of constraints confront-ing them. Two further points need to be considered. First, what happens to these, the 'survivors', who reach higher education, when they enter the occupational system as qualified adults? Our view here is limited, considering only those 'survivors' who enter educational professions (though see Chapter 6, pp. 127–37, for a more general review). Second, what opportunities are there to make up the educational deficits of the school and post-school years, and what use is made of these opportunities? In the university sector, over the past decade, the percentage of women postgraduates has risen slowly but remains at just less than one-third of the total (table 5.7). In the non-university sector, between 1974 and 1977, 516 men but only 84 women obtained higher degrees from the Council for National Academic Awards (CNAA) (*Statistics of Education 1977* 1980, vol. 3). The differential rates of participation within the categories of type of postgraduate study at universities show a familiar pattern (table 5.8). Women are proportionately much more likely to take non-higher-degree courses than men, though it will be recalled that women are more likely than men to enter teaching, for which a postgraduate certificate of education is required. Men far outnumber women on courses leading to higher degrees by research. Perhaps gender personality plays a part here. Independence of thought and self-confidence, as well as a certain amount of aggression, are all useful qualities in research work, and are perhaps more usually exhibited by men.

One of the criteria for appointments to the staff of a higher-education institution is often the possession of a higher degree. Men are clearly in the more favourable position here, and they far outnumber women on the staffs of such institutions. In 1977 women

TABLE 5.7
THE SEX COMPOSITION OF BRITISH UNIVERSITY
POSTGRADUATES, 1970–1971 TO 1977–1978 (PERCENTAGES)

	1970–1/71–2	*1972–3*	*1973–4*	*1974–5*	*1975–6*	*1976–7/77–8*
Women	25	26	28	30	30	32
Men	75	74	72	70	70	68

Note: Female postgraduates numbered 7847 in 1970–1 and 9905 in 1977–8, the respective figures for male postgraduates being 23,447 and 20,889
(Derived from table E(i), *Statistics of Education 1977* 1980, vol. 6)

TABLE 5.8
FULL-TIME UNIVERSITY POSTGRADUATES, BY TYPE OF
COURSE AND SEX, GREAT BRITAIN, 1977 (PERCENTAGES)

	Women	Men	Both	Sex composition of each course Women	Men
Research for higher degree or other qualification	11	39	50	22	78
Taught course for higher degree	6	20	26	24	76
Taught course for other qualification	11	14	25	44	56
All postgraduates	38	72	100		

N = 48,871
(Derived from table 11, *Statistics of Education 1977* 1980, vol. 6)

formed only 12 per cent of all teaching and research staff at universities (table 5.9). Even in education, which attracts more women at undergraduate and postgraduate levels, women do not occupy the positions of authority (female professors 2, male professors 112). Women are most likely to fall into the 'other' category, which subsumes those staff whose remuneration and status are lowest, and where women are proportionately overrepresented. In the public sector there were, in 1977, approximately five times more male than female academics. Taking into account the supposed nature of the job – that members have academic freedom, that promotion is assumed to be dependent on merit rather than ascribed characteristics that there exists a sense of vocation in the transmission of knowledge – it might be expected that women would be found in relatively large numbers (Blackstone 1975). But that this is not so does not necessarily constitute discrimination against women. The author showed that women were less well qualified than men and, though no less experienced in years of service, had less experience in terms of numbers of posts held previously. Women were found to be less ambitious, expressing satisfaction with their salaries and less often seeking promotion than men. These attitudes can be seen as reasonable, reflecting as they do women's place in the wider society.

TABLE 5.9
THE PERCENTAGE OF FEMALE AND MALE FULL-TIME
BRITISH UNIVERSITY STAFF, BY LEVEL OF POST AND SEX
COMPOSITION OF THOSE LEVELS, 1977

	Women	Men	All	Sex composition Women	Men
Professor	∅	12	11	2	98
Reader/Senior Lecturer	9	22	21	6	94
Lecturer/Assistant Lecturer	68	60	61	14	86
Other	19	6	8	32	68
All posts	100	100	100	12	88

∅ = less than 1
N = 33,490
(Devised from table 31, *Statistics of Education 1977* 1980, vol. 6)

Job and salary satisfaction are relative. The salary a woman receives as an academic, whether she is single or married, is seen as quite adequate, and, compared with other women and in the historical development of women's employment, her position has status and is well regarded.

Although the case that women are discriminated against seems to be a weak one here, Bradley and Silverleaf (1979) suggest that there is none the less indirect discrimination against women in higher and further education. Women are much more likely to be staffing low-level courses, and there is a high percentage of women in part-time work. University women themselves experience little sense of discrimination – which does not mean, of course, that it does not occur. They attribute their lack of status to qualities in themselves, though this perception of self, with all its consequences for inhibited ambition and unrealised potential, may have its roots in early socialisation. In this sense women can be seen as authors of their own 'discrimination'. By their attitudes and actions they invite being passed over for promotion. Thus, if a criterion for promotion in higher education is publication and women do not publish, they are not suffering from discriminatory tactics (though it could be argued that the criterion has been chosen by men). Actual discrimination, however, requires some active choice against women which lacks a 'rational' base.

> It seems clear that we must seek to explain [women's position here] by reference to more fundamental issues pertaining to the position of women in the wider society . . . The main reasons they gave were first subjective role conflict – women's expectations are not geared towards a career, the social pressure on them is to marry and eventually drop out of the serious pursuit of a career, and associated with this they lack the sustained interest and ambition necessary to do so. . . . Objective role conflict is also present in that most women are unable to devote all their energies to careers because of domestic commitments . . . (Blackstone 1975)

Crucial, then, is how women and men themselves feel about their commitments and roles, and this could go some way to explaining why there is a low level of publication among single female academics (Blackstone 1975). The fact that the single woman has not married does not result in an automatic transfer of attitude to the ambitious careerism of men. Role socialisation remains, and the single professional woman can experience considerable role conflict, since she does not have the 'excuse' of a family for not assuming the traditional male attitude towards her career.

Acker's comments (1980) follow up this theme of role conflict, making the point that men can be helped by having the services of a wife to run the home. She also suggests that women academics' role is difficult because they are a minority group. Further she considers the domination of knowledge and practice by men. These are all problems 'embedded in everyday life', the world of education being influenced and coloured by social norms and values outside the educational system. Thus Acker contradicts the notion that superficial structural adjustments, such as positive discrimination in favour of women at entry into higher-education courses, would result in women's attaining parity with men in occupational roles. Objective role conflict can be overcome, but subjective role conflict is a much deeper problem. The evidence 'provides strong support for the argument that a more radical programme involving a revaluation of our values and in consequence a fundamental change in the way children are socialised is necessary if women are to participate in professional careers on equal terms with men' (Blackstone 1975).

The situation in schoolteaching is not dissimilar to that found in higher and further education. Although women enter schoolteaching in very much larger numbers than men – in 1978 they outnumbered men by over 78,000 (*Statistics of Education 1978* 1981, vol. 4) – it is men who hold positions of authority. Male teachers are more likely be graduates (men 41 per cent, women 23 per cent in March 1978), and this may partly explain their position in schools, particularly secondary ones. Tables 5.10 and 5.11 show the distribution of

TABLE 5.10
PERCENTAGES* OF FEMALE AND MALE NURSERY AND
PRIMARY SCHOOL TEACHERS, ENGLAND AND WALES, 1978

	Women	Men	All
Headteachers	7	29	12
Deputy headteachers	8	17	10
Senior teachers/second masters and mistresses	0.3	0.5	0.3
Assistant teachers on scales 3 and 4	5	10	6
Assistant teachers on scales 1 and 2	80	44	72
All teachers	77	23	100

* Percentages over 1 rounded
(Devised from table 12, *Statistics of Education 1978* 1981, vol. 4)

TABLE 5.11
PERCENTAGES* OF FEMALE AND MALE SECONDARY
SCHOOL TEACHERS, ENGLAND AND WALES, 1978

	Women	Men	All
Headteachers	0.8	3	2
Deputy headteachers	2	4	2
Senior teachers/second masters and mistresses	3	4	4
Assistant teachers on scales 3 and 4	22	40	32
Assistant teachers on scales 1 and 2	72	49	43
All teachers	44	56	100

* Percentages over 1 rounded
(Devised from table 12, *Statistics of Education 1978* 1981, vol. 4)

men and women in scaled posts in primary and secondary schools in 1978, and the higher positions of men are very evident. In primary schools, men holding headships outnumbered women by more than four to one, and they held twice as many deputy headships; almost twice as many women as men were on the lowest scales (1 and 2). At the secondary level, the imbalance between the sexes was not so great, though less than 14 per cent of headteachers in secondary schools were women. In all schools, the average salary of women in 1978 was £4290, that of men £4936. The minority argument of Acker (see above) does not, of course, apply here, but the effects of role conflict might be seen to be just as applicable.

It remains to discuss the extent to which women can and do redress both the actual discrimination and self-discrimination that have been discussed. A distinction can be made between the entirely voluntary renewal or extension of education – that is, through the Open University or attendance at evening classes – and that which is at the discretion of a higher authority – that is, release from employment. This is a theoretical distinction to the extent that it is impossible to assess motivation.

Men are four times more likely than women to obtain day release, and, for every woman, twenty men attend block-release courses (*Statistics of Education 1977* 1980, vol. 3). These figures are for all types of industry, and no account is taken of the total numbers of women and men in the different types of employment (see Chapter 6, pp. 127–39). But even in those industries in which women outnumber men, such as the service industries, women clearly have less opportunity than men to extend their education, albeit of this narrowly specific kind. The distribution of enrolment for evening-only classes confirms the trend, evident in further and higher education, for men to opt for advanced courses to a greater extent than women (table 5.12). Women's participation in the non-advanced courses far outnumbers that of men.

The Open University was established to 'provide opportunities at both undergraduate and postgraduate level of higher education to all those who for any reason have been or are being precluded from achieving their aim through an existing institution of higher education' (McIntosh 1979). Initially the proportion of women applying to the Open University was low in relation to men, though it has steadily increased (table 5.13). Analysis of the class and occupational background of female and male applicants showed that a

TABLE 5.12
ENROLMENTS ON EVENING-ONLY COURSES IN FURTHER
EDUCATION, ENGLAND AND WALES, BY SEX (THOUSANDS*)

| | Advanced courses[†] | | | Non-advanced courses[§] | | |
	1973	1975	1977	1973	1975	1977
Women	5	5	9	453	477	404
Men	31	32	32	294	287	242

* Rounded
[†] Including first degrees, HND, HNC and higher TEC and BEC courses
[§] Including OND, ONC, GCE, CSE and City and Guilds courses
(Derived from table 16, *Statistics of Education 1977* 1980, vol. 3)

TABLE 5.13
SEX COMPOSITION OF APPLICANTS TO THE
OPEN UNIVERSITY, 1970–1978 (PERCENTAGES)

	1970	1971	1972	1973	1974	1975	1976	1977	1978
Women	30	33	37	43	42	42	42	44	51
Men	70	67	63	57	58	58	58	56	49

(Derived from McIntosh 1979)

majority of both were teachers, or clerical or professional workers, with very few from manual occupations. However, compared with the men, female applicants had not educationally under-achieved at school. Male students were more likely than women to cite work-related reasons for undertaking an Open University degree – for example, improving promotion prospects and changing careers. Working women, particularly, gave non-work-related reasons more frequently. That women, whether working or not, did not mention 'to make up for missed opportunities' as often as 'generally to learn' can come as no surprise in the context of the earlier discussions on women's relative lack of career orientation. It is interesting to note that, while women take longer to graduate, in time they outnumber male graduates at the Open University (McIntosh 1979).

OVERVIEW

The preceding discussion has shown that cumulatively women have not realised in their post-school education the potential they showed during their early school years. In the profession of education they tend to hold minor positions, both in schools and in universities. Men are more likely to further their formal qualifications, whereas women prefer to take lower-level courses which as a base for career advancement are either limited or irrelevant.

It is difficult to establish the extent to which women's limited educational success relative to that of men is a consequence of overt discrimination. That there is a lower proportion of any social group in a given area of employment does not necessarily imply discrimination. Direct discrimination occurs when there is equivalence between applicants. Even more difficult to monitor and present systematically are the effects of assumptions about sex-role behaviour, because these assumptions are so internalised by members of both sexes and are so pervasive and well established in our social life. Women and men may fail to recognise the extent to which their behaviour, attitudes and values are socially constructed and maintained, and the extent to which these are sexist.

The wastage of talent and opportunity among both sexes in education is undeniable. It is difficult to challenge the prevailing orthodoxy. It can take courage for a boy to show a serious commitment in home economics at school, just as it does for a girl to insist on becoming an engineer. If girls are discouraged in a variety of ways from developing an interest in mathematics, it is also true that boys may be denied the opportunity to become interested in literature and the arts. Change in expectations about social roles can be threatening and unwelcome. There are, however, signs that women are participating more in education (for example, the rise in female GCE A-level and Open University students), although their involvement still remains below that of men. The effects of recent legislation to ensure that all children, whatever their sex, undergo the same curricular experiences in schools will not be felt for some time, and it is difficult to estimate whether the benefits will accrue equally to women and men, since the elimination of formal barriers to sexual equality may not result in equivalent diminutions of informal distinctions. The extent to which education can promote individual freedom from sexual stereotyping remains to be seen. But, by providing opportunities for children of both sexes to exercise choice and to follow personal interests, the school may be able to assist the development of greater sexual equality in society at large.

6

The labour market

Michael Webb

Work occupies a very significant proportion of adult life and accounts for a number of differences and inequalities within society. A feature of sex inequality in work is that women are poorly represented in the higher-paid and higher-status jobs. Ironically, two of the high-status professions that men have monopolised more than most have been economics and industrial sociology, and perhaps, as a result, women's work and gender inequalities in the labour force have in the past been all but ignored in the literature (Delamont 1980b).

The recent increase in research into sex differences in the labour market has been helped by the availability of a mass of official data. Using the decennial *Census of Population*, the biannual *EEC Labour Force Survey* or the annual *General Household Survey*, it is possible to determine which segments of the population are in paid work. The annual survey of employees, the *New Earnings Survey*, gives details of particular jobs and the pay that attaches to them. It is more difficult to relate incomes to particular segments of the population, since the British official surveys of the population such as the census do not contain details of income, but it is possible to use *Inland Revenue Statistics* and the analyses of the Royal Commission on the Distribution of Income and Wealth. However, it is important to remember that official data on employment have usually been collected so that the government may manage the economy. Data collected for this purpose concentrate on the 'mainstream' economy, and may not give a full picture of the differences between the sexes. For example, the *New Earnings Survey* covers only employees with sufficient pay to be in a PAYE scheme, so that there are no reliable official data on the part-time work done by millions (mainly women), nor on work done for firms at home. Moreover, since official unemployment figures record only demands for work

114

registered at employment offices, many women who would like work are not reported. And, of course, neither the government nor society as a whole counts unpaid labour in the home, such as housework or child-minding, as 'work' at all, so that the researcher hoping to present a full picture of the contribution of women to the economy must look elsewhere for information in this area.

Some researchers have been successful in using statistical material to show what inequalities in work are like and how they come about. For example, one study of clerical workers was able to demonstrate that women received 20–50 per cent less office space than men doing roughly the same work in the same office, and that, the higher the concentration of women in a particular area of the office, the lower the standard of décor (Benet 1972). None the less it must be remembered that statistics cannot carry the flavour of what it is like to be a woman attempting to enter or undertake a high-status job traditionally done by men, nor how difficult it is for a woman trying to work full-time and cope with domestic responsibilities also to participate in a male-dominated trade union to better her position at work. Sociological analysis can attempt to account for changes in the supply of women workers, but economic analysis is necessary to show where the demand for those workers comes from, and how they are used in the economy by comparison with male workers. The two disciplines together show a depressing picture of what has been called 'industrial apartheid between men and women' (Wainwright 1978), with the two sexes occupying very different roles not only within society but within the world of work, in which the roles allocated to women involve low status, low power and low rewards. Numerically, women play a much larger part in the workforce than is commonly realised, but any impression of apparent equality between the sexes is destroyed by a closer examination of the work that each does and the pay that each receives.

During the late Victorian period, women were to a large degree excluded from paid work; however, the twentieth century has seen a return to the situation where women are engaged in large numbers in paid economic activity. During the 1960s and 1970s there was an increase of over two million in the total number of people in the 'working population' (those officially recorded as being either in paid work or looking for such work). As table 6.1 shows, this overall increase in the workforce was made up of a slight reduction in the male labour force and a large increase in the female labour force.

TABLE 6.1
WORKING POPULATION, BY SEX AND MARITAL STATUS,
1911–1980

| | Working population (1000s) | | | Women as % of working population | |
	Women	Men	All	Married	Non-married*
1911	5,424	12,927	30	NA	NA
1921	5,701	13,656	30	4	26
1931	6,265	14,790	30	NA	NA
1951	7,419	16,007	31	NA	NA
1961	8,407	16,366	33	16	16
1971	8,708	15,837	36	23	14
1975	9,506	15,698	38	26	13
1977	9,814	15,854	38	26	13
1979	10,054	15,678	39	26	14

*Single, divorced and widowed
NA = not available
Note: column 3 = column 4 + 5 except for rounding approximations
(Devised from: table 6.1, *Annual Abstract of Statistics* 1981; table 5.1, *Social Trends No. 11*
1980; 1911–71 based on census data, 1975–9 based on *Labour Force Survey*)

The result is that the proportion of women in the workforce, which during the first half of the century had increased only in wartime (and then only temporarily), rose dramatically during the 1960s and 1970s.

The rise in the female labour force during recent decades was due not principally to 'population effects', such as an increase in the numbers in the working age groups, but rather to an increase in the female 'activity rate' – the proportion of women in the relevant age group who are in the labour force (see table 6.2). As male activity rates fell, partly because of a tendency to stay in education longer or retire earlier, so women's rates rose, though women are still less 'active' in the labour market than men. However, it is important to distinguish between women of different marital status, since in all but the 'retirement' age groups the tendency of women who are not married to participate in employment is much closer to that of men than that of married women. Indeed, activity rates of non-married women have been falling in most age groups, like those of the men. Similar reasons probably apply, though in addition, because of the

TABLE 6.2
PERCENTAGE ECONOMICALLY ACTIVE,* BY AGE AND SEX,
1951–1979

	Aged 15–19[†]	Aged 20–4	Aged 25–44	Aged 45–59(W) 45–64(M)	Aged 60+(W) 65+(M)	All ages
Married women						
1951	38	37	25	22	5	22
1961	41	41	33	33	7	30
1971	42	46	46	53	14	42
1975	52	54	55	60	13	48
1979	51	58	59	61	10	50
Non-married women[§]						
1951	NA	NA	81	61	11	55
1961	73	89	85	71	12	51
1971	57	81	81	73	11	44
1975	60	77	79	73	9	42
1979	63	79	78	71	5	43
All women						
1951	79	65	36	NA	NA	35
1961	71	62	40	41	10	37
1971	56	60	51	57	12	43
1975	59	64	58	62	11	46
1979	62	68	62	63	7	47
All men						
1951	84	95	98	95	31	88
1961	75	92	98	97	25	86
1971	61	90	98	94	19	81
1975	66	89	98	94	15	81
1979	69	90	97	91	10	79

* Those in employment or actively seeking it, excluding students in full-time education
[†] Figures for 1975 and 1979 relate to 16–19-year-olds, because of the raising of the
school-leaving age in 1973
[§] Single, widowed or divorced
NA = not available.
(Derived from table 5.2, *Social Trends No. 11* 1980)

growth in divorce and lone-parenthood, non-married women are caring for dependent children more than in the past. By contrast, married women have shown an increasing tendency to take up paid work, though the female activity rate may have ceased to rise at the end of the 1970s.

In dealing with changes in economic activity, it is important to distinguish between those working full-time and those who work part-time, following the traditional distinction that the latter are those who perform 30 hours a week or less. Such a breakdown can be found in table 6.3, which reveals that part-time work is very much the province of women. During the period 1971–8 part-time work accounted for almost all of the one-million increase in the numbers of women in paid employment, so that by 1978 two-fifths of women with jobs worked part-time.

Since the increase in employment involved mainly married women and consisted of part-time jobs, it is obvious that married women do much of the part-time work available. Indeed, the *General Household Survey 1980* (1981) reveals that 60 per cent of the married women in employment had part-time jobs, compared with only 6 per cent of single women, 39 per cent of other non-married women, and a very small percentage of men. The small number of

TABLE 6.3
FULL-TIME AND PART-TIME EMPLOYEES, BY SEX, IN GREAT
BRITAIN 1971 AND 1978

| | *Number in 1000s* | | *% change* |
	June 1971	*June 1978*	*1971–8*
Female employees	8,224	9,158	+11
Full-time	5,468	5,478	+0.2
Part-time	2,757	3,679	+33
Male employees	13,424	13,096	−2
Full-time	12,840	12,392	−4
Part-time	584	704	+21
Female part-time as % of all female workers	34	40	
Male part-time as % of all male workers	4	5	

(Devised from p. 61, *Employment Gazette* (February 1981))

men (and of some non-married women) who do have part-time jobs tend to use them to ease the transition into retirement, whereas married women mostly work part-time during their middle years, when there are likely to be heavy demands on them at home (Trades Union Congress 1980). Married women generally turn to part-time work when their children are young, and return to full-time work as the children grow older (table 6.4), though non-married women with young children remain in full-time employment to a much greater degree than their married counterparts. Clearly, though, whether married or not, the involvement of mothers with full-time work is not nearly as great as that of women without children: between the ages of 25 and 34 the full-time activity rate of the latter is 76 per cent, with only a further 9 per cent involved in part-time work (which provides a strong contrast with the picture for mothers – see table 6.4).

Having established the importance of part-time work for married women, we are now in a position to assess the causes of the rise in female employment in the 1960s and 1970s. This phenomenon was

TABLE 6.4
PERCENTAGE OF WOMEN AGED 16–59, WITH DEPENDENT CHILDREN, WHO WORK, BY MARITAL STATUS, AGE, AND AGE OF YOUNGEST CHILD IN THE HOUSEHOLD 1978

| | *Married women* | | | *Non-married women** | | |
	Working full-time	*Working part-time*	*All working*	*Working full-time*	*Working part-time*	*All working*
Women aged 16–34	10	29	39	20	18	39
Women aged 35–59	22	43	66	21	28	50
With youngest child in household aged:						
0–4	5	22	28	15	12	29
5–9	14	45	60	17	29	46
10 or over	29	44	74	28	28	55
Total	16	37	53	20	23	44

* Single, widowed, divorced and separated
(Derived from table 5.6, *General Household Survey 1978* 1980)

connected with the decision to defer child-bearing and for women to remain in gainful employment for longer before having a child. Such an explanation for women's entry into work might be supported by the fact that in the late 1970s there was an upturn in the birth rate and the increase in employment ceased. However, it is important not to underestimate economic factors – for example, the impact of the recession on job opportunities after 1979. Changes in fertility do not explain the whole range of variations in activity rates of women (see table 6.2), which took place at all stages in the life cycle, including the period of child-rearing. The *General Household Survey 1980* (1981) shows a rise in the proportion of women with dependent children who work part-time from 26 per cent in 1971 to 35 per cent in 1975, with a further small rise to 36 per cent by 1980. Since the proportion of mothers working full-time remained constant at about 16 per cent, it seems likely that the explanation for the rise in activity rates lies in the availability in the economy of suitable part-time work.

INEQUALITIES IN PAY AND HOURS

A glance at any pay statistics that give data separately by sex shows that on average women earn substantially less than men. Table 6.5 demonstrates this clearly in terms of hourly earnings. Women fare particularly badly in comparison with men in non-manual work (women's work is concentrated in the non-manual area – see pp. 127–37). Within each category, part-time workers earn less per hour than their full-time counterparts, and as we have already seen married women are concentrated in part-time work (and in part-time non-manual work, where the gap between women's pay and that of the full-time male is the greatest of all). Indeed, the Low Pay Unit (*The Part Time Trap* 1978), in a survey of 351 part-time workers of both sexes, found low pay much more prevalent than suggested by official figures.

Differences in pay between the sexes – quite large in the case of hourly earnings – is greater in the case of weekly or annual earnings, because men tend to work longer hours. The Royal Commission on the Distribution of Income and Wealth (1978a) showed that, among couples with children, mothers worked much shorter hours than fathers. In general, in families with more children, it was the mother rather than the father who worked shorter hours, though there was a tendency for women with more than four children to work longer than those with smaller families, presumably because of financial necessity. The different roles within the family probably explain the fact that married men work slightly longer hours than single men, whereas married women work much shorter hours than single women (see table 6.6). However, marital division of labour cannot explain all the differences in hours worked: for example, single men work longer hours than single women; and within the full-time

TABLE 6.5

AVERAGE GROSS HOURLY EARNINGS* OF MANUAL AND NON-MANUAL, FULL-TIME AND PART-TIME EMPLOYEES, BY SEX, GREAT BRITAIN 1980

	Manual workers	*Non-manual workers*
Female part-time workers	154	183
Female full-time workers	170	221
Male full-time workers	241	361
As % of male full-time hourly earnings		
Female part-time earnings	64	51
Female full-time earnings	71	61

* In pence per hour
(Derived from tables 86, 178, *New Earnings Survey* 1980)

TABLE 6.6

NORMAL HOURS OF WORK* AND ANNUAL EARNINGS, BY SEX AND MARITAL STATUS, GREAT BRITAIN 1975

	Wives	*Husbands*	*Single Women*	*Single Men*
Normal weekly hours	26.8	40.6	36.0	39.9
Overtime weekly hours	0.4	3.7	0.7	2.1
Weeks worked	47.7	50.8	50.4	49.8
Annual earnings (£)	1222	3193	2427	2685

* Rounded to 1 decimal place
(Derived from table 1, Greenhalgh 1980; based on data from the *General Household Survey*)

The Labour Market

category (not shown in the table) older women work shorter hours than younger ones, whereas this is not true for men. These differences are probably mainly due to the different jobs done by these various groups of workers, since major variations in hours worked are found when comparing different jobs, but not when comparing the sexes doing the same job.

One major difference between jobs is the amount of overtime involved, for hours in excess of the basic working week command a premium payment. Table 6.7 shows that, for full-time work, women's relative exclusion from the manual occupations is a major cause of differences in the length of the working week and in earnings between the sexes, since manual occupations have marked

TABLE 6.7
COMPOSITION OF EARNINGS AND HOURS WORKED OF
MANUAL AND NON-MANUAL FULL-TIME WORKERS, BY SEX,
GREAT BRITAIN 1980

| | *Women (aged 18+)* | | | *Men (aged 21+)* | | |
	Manual	*Non-manual*	*All*	*Manual*	*Non-manual*	*All*
As % of average gross weekly earnings						
Overtime payments	3.6	1.2	1.8	14.1	3.5	8.9
Payment by results, etc.	8.8	0.9	2.7	8.7	2.6	5.7
Shift premium payments, etc.	2.1	1.1	1.4	3.3	0.6	2.0
% of employees who receive						
Overtime payments	17.0	10.7	12.4	54.3	19.6	39.3
Payment by results, etc.	32.2	6.5	13.3	42.3	12.0	29.2
Shift premium payments, etc.	11.5	9.3	9.9	23.0	5.7	15.5
Average weekly hours worked						
Total hours	39.6	36.7	37.5	45.4	38.7	42.7
Overtime hours	1.1	0.4	0.6	5.7	1.6	4.0

(Derived from table 1, *New Earnings Survey* (1980), vol. A)

differences between the sexes in work hours and overtime. However, even within these categories of work, men tend to do more
overtime than women. Nor do women restore their position relative
to men by earning the other additional payments listed in the table
(payment by results and shift payments), since women are relatively
excluded from such payments by virtue of their concentration into
non-manual work where additional payments are unusual, and
since they are excluded by law from working most night shifts.

While the current situation shows women at a disadvantage in
terms of hours and additional payments, there was a slight change
during the 1970s. Between 1973 and 1980, the hours of full-time
work of manual men fell by 1.3 hours, compared to a fall of only 0.3
hours for women. However, there was no equivalent change among
non-manual employees and, more significantly, any reductions
took place in the basic working week, there being very little change
in the amount or distribution of overtime. The fact that there has
been little variation in hours or overtime during the 1970s means
that, in examining changes in the earnings differential between
women and men, it is immaterial whether one uses data for hourly
earnings or for weekly earnings, since each gives the same year-to-
year pattern. Weekly earnings are therefore used, since in any one
year the absolute level of the female/male weekly earnings differential gives a truer picture of inequality than would its hourly equivalent.

Until the advent of the *New Earnings Survey* in 1968 and 1970, the
only comprehensive data on earnings were for manual workers.
Those data showed that the female/male earnings differential had
remained remarkably constant over a very long period of time,
female weekly earnings being 50.2 per cent of those of males in 1906
and 50 per cent in 1970, with only minor variations in between
(Chiplin and Sloane 1974). From 1970 onwards the data cover all
full-time employees; the figures are presented in table 6.8. Between
1970 and 1977 there was a substantial improvement in the relative
position of women, this improvement being particularly marked
during the years 1974–6 – clearly the effect of the Equal Pay Act,
which came into full operation in 1975. The table also contains data
indicating levels of earnings in terms of their real value in 1981. The
figures show that between 1975 and 1976 the real value of women's
earnings rose at a time when male earnings were not keeping pace
with inflation. However, it is apparent that since 1977 improve-

TABLE 6.8
AVERAGE GROSS WEEKLY EARNINGS* OF FULL-TIME
MANUAL AND NON-MANUAL EMPLOYEES, BY SEX, GREAT
BRITAIN 1970–1980

	1970	1974	1975	1976	1977	1978	1979	1980
Female wages as % of male								
All employees	55	56	62	64	65	65	64	65
Manual employees	50	54	58	61	61	61	59	61
Non-manual employees	50	53	58	60	61	59	58	59
Real earnings (in 1981 £):*								
Female manual employees		65	73	75	71	74	75	76
Male manual employees		120	126	124	116	121	127	125

* Money earnings have been corrected to remove the effects of inflation and are expressed at price levels ruling in April 1981.

(Devised from *British Labour Statistics 1970* (1971); *Employment Gazette* (1974–80 wages data); *Monthly Digest of Statistics* (1974–80 price indices))

ments in women's earnings have ceased, and it looks likely that a new stable differential has emerged, with women's earnings being just under two-thirds of those of men. However, the non-manual ratio is generally below that for manual workers (though it exceeded it in 1975), and of course it is important to remember that all these figures relate only to full-time employment. The omission of part-time work gives an unrealistically favourable impression of women's position.

So far we have viewed the dispersion of earnings using averages. An alternative view is given in table 6.9, which shows median weekly earnings – that is, the earning that splits all earners into two equal groups, one earning more, the other less, than the figure. The figures in that table relate only to full-time work, and show that in 1980 the lowest-paid tenth of women earned below £49.50 and one-quarter earned below £58.80, whereas men earned much more. As seen above, women's average earnings have crept closer to those of men; however, the 1980:1970 ratios in the table show that the biggest gains were made by those in the lower earnings ranges – higher-paid women did not gain nearly as much. This change has

TABLE 6.9
DISPERSION OF GROSS WEEKLY EARNINGS* OF FULL-TIME
ADULT WORKERS, BY SEX, GREAT BRITAIN 1970 AND 1980

	Lowest decile[1]	Lower quartile[2]	Median[3]	Upper quartile[2]	Highest decile[1]
1970 weekly earnings					
Women	9.7	11.6	14.6	18.8	24.8
Men	17.8	21.7	27.2	34.5	43.7
1980 weekly earnings					
Women	49.5	58.8	72.4	91.2	116.7
Men	74.7	90.7	113.3	143.4	183.1
1980 as ratio to 1970					
Women	5.1	5.1	5.0	4.9	4.7
Men	4.2	4.2	4.2	4.2	4.2
Female earnings as % of male earnings					
1970	54.5	53.5	53.7	54.5	56.8
1980	66.3	64.8	63.9	63.6	63.7

* In pounds sterling, rounded to first decimal place, not corrected for the effects of inflation
[1] *Decile* is 10%; *lowest* means that 10% of workers earned less than sums shown, *highest* that 90% earned less than sums
[2] *Quartile* is 25%; *lowest* means that 25% of workers earned less than sums shown, *highest* that 75% earned less than sums
[3] *Median* splits workers into two equal-sized groups, one of which (i.e. 50% of workers) earned less than sums shown.
  (Devised from table 7, *Employment Gazette* (October 1980))

now reversed the 1970 situation, when the higher-paid women could expect to have earnings relatively closer to their male counterparts than was true for the lower cohorts. Other figures suggest, however, that in terms of total earnings per year, including holiday pay and bonuses, the upper deciles for the two sexes are still (1979 data) closer together than the lower deciles (*Employment Gazette* (June 1980)).

A further view of the earnings differential between the sexes can be obtained by comparing proportions earning given levels. From table 6.9 we know that the median earnings for males were £113.30 in 1980. *Employment Gazette* (1980) data show that somewhere between 82 and 91 per cent of female workers fail to earn that much. Low pay may be defined as whatever amount was earned by the lowest decile of male workers (Royal Commission on the Distribution of Income and Wealth 1980a). On this definition, well over half of women are low-paid, and in most years they constitute up to three-quarters of all low-paid workers. At the other extreme, the Royal Commission on the Distribution of Income and Wealth (1976) was concerned about the small number of women in the higher-income tax ranges, quoting figures for the 1973–4 tax year in which women comprised only 2 per cent of people with employment incomes of at least £10,000. Because women tend not to figure in the higher earnings range, the spread of earnings is less wide for women than for men (described in statistical terms by Chiplin, Curran and Parsley 1980). Women's incomes tend to be bunched in the lower ranges; hence the peak of the distribution for women is well below the median.

The picture so far painted, of inequality in remuneration between the sexes, is incomplete because it ignores fringe benefits such as company pensions, sick pay, life assurance, cheap mortgages, school fees, company cars and holiday entitlements. The Royal Commission on the Distribution of Income and Wealth (1978b) showed that fringe benefits are of particular importance in the case of higher-salary earners, and therefore widen the gap between men and women's earnings. For example, in 1979, according to the *General Household Survey*, only 55 per cent of full-time women employees were covered by private pension schemes, compared with 68 per cent of men, though the growth in such schemes during the 1970s narrowed the gap somewhat. In the case of full-time non-manual workers, women and men are equally well covered by sick pay arrangements, though female manual workers fare less well than men. These two examples are based on full-time work, yet women suffer further because many of them work part-time, and are often excluded from fringe benefits available to full-timers. A major survey of employers by the Equal Opportunities Commission (McIntosh 1980) found that, although 72 per cent of establishments offered benefits beyond the state pension scheme, in only 14 per cent were part-time workers eligible. Similarly, the exclusion of women is implicit in many fringe benefits schemes that are provided for particular categories of employees in which few, if any, women are found. For example, although the same provisions for paid holidays apply to men and women, entitlements often increase with length of service and grade, so that the general level tends to be higher for men than for women.

PATTERNS OF EMPLOYMENT AND PAY

The underlying assumptions of the previous section can now be spelt out. Direct discrimination is not the central reason for the unequal distribution of earnings and fringe benefits between men and women. This is confirmed by a survey of employers (McIntosh 1980) which found that, in almost all jobs done by both sexes, scale rates of basic pay were the same for both sexes, and, indeed, part-timers were usually paid the same hourly rates as full-timers. Nor can the differences in hours of work between the sexes fully explain why women are not paid as much as men. Women are, in fact, remunerated badly for three principal reasons. First, where a woman and a man are doing what is classified as the same job, the man may be on higher rates of pay – for example, because he has been employed longer and so qualifies for a length-of-service award, or because he holds a position of seniority (has reached a higher grade), which may mean that his job is effectively different from that of the woman. Second, women and men tend to have very different occupations, and women predominate in those that have low pay. Third, women tend to be employed in industries or establishments where pay is low; and, while it is true that the low pay of some industries or establishments may simply reflect the low-paid occupations within them, in others there may be independent effects reducing the level of pay in each job.

This section describes the way the sexes are distributed between high- and low-paying trades, occupations and industries, and it attempts to establish which of the three causes of inequality in pay are the most crucial. Later sections discuss whether or not this unequal distribution between jobs is evidence of employment discrimination, and whether or not the low pay that attaches to female jobs is the result of wage discrimination.

In terms of occupation, a not wholly inaccurate caricature of women's work is provided by the list of the 'ten deadly Cs': catering, cleaning, clerking, cashiering, counter-minding, clothes-making, clothes-washing, coiffure, child-minding and care of the sick. Many of the jobs women are expected to do involve the direct servicing of people's immediate needs, and are often extensions of the types of jobs associated with domestic tasks (Baxandall, Ewen and Gordon 1976). Often women work in trades where the physical attributes fostered by traditional female upbringing (such as manual dexterity) are a significant advantage. Part-time work is of the same kind, and Hunt (1975) suggests that there is an important category of part-time workers who are confined to establishments which otherwise employ very few part-timers, and who do work, such as cleaning or catering, and the like, which has little or no relationship to the main processes of the establishment.

Table 6.10 shows which occupations are effectively 'women's jobs' and which are 'men's jobs'. Many of the former are those of low skill and status. It is, of course, important to be aware of the possibility that jobs are defined as skilled according to criteria that give weight to skills that are traditionally male. None the less the pattern of unskilled work being performed mainly by women is unmistakable. This pattern is reinforced by the part-time nature of many women's jobs; for example, within most establishments, non-manual part-timers are usually found among clerical and office staff rather than in managerial and professional occupations.

Table 6.11 shows the proportion of women in different categories of occupations at different times this century. Between 1951 and 1971 women's share of total employment rose by about 6 per cent, but this was associated with large increases in the share of the unskilled categories (for example, clerks and unskilled manual workers) and an actual fall in the share of some more skilled jobs (particularly skilled manual jobs). Such developments took place against a background of a general shift in employment away from manual work and into white-collar work. It is therefore important to look at how the total workforce is distributed between the occupation categories, and particularly at recent changes in the balance between skilled and unskilled work (see table 6.12). Clearly the emphasis in employment as a whole has shifted towards jobs of higher status and skill, but women still tend not to occupy these positions; for example, only one woman in ten has a skilled manual occupation, whereas three men in ten do.

The influence of women's domestic role shows in the pattern of female penetration of those professions that have in the past been regarded as the preserve of males (table 6.13). In many cases the occupations women are entering have a work pattern and flexibility of hours that particularly suit women with demanding domestic duties. This is, for example, true of accountancy, and by 1978 women had come to comprise over one-fifth of newly qualified graduates entering this field (*EOC Annual Report 1978* 1979), so

TABLE 6.10
OCCUPATIONAL GROUPS* LISTED ACCORDING TO THE
DEGREE TO WHICH THEY ARE DOMINATED BY ONE SEX

Predominantly female occupations	*Predominantly male occupations and groupings of occupations*
90 per cent or over	*90 per cent or over*
Hand and machine sewers and embroiderers	Miners and quarrymen
Nurses	Furnace, forge, foundries, etc.
Maids, valets, etc.	Electrical and electronic (excluding assemblers)
Canteen assistants	Engineering trades (excluding inspectors)
Typists, shorthand writers, secretaries	Woodworkers
	Butchers and meat cutters
75 and under 90 per cent	Construction workers
Shop salesmen and assistants	Painters and decorators
Charwomen, cleaners and sweepers	Drivers of stationary engines, cranes, etc.
Kitchen hands	Building and contracting labourers
Office machine operators	Drivers: road-passenger service and goods vehicles
Hairdressers, manicurists and beauticians	Postmen and mail sorters
Telephone operators	Commercial travellers, etc.
	Police
60 and under 75 per cent	Administrators and managers
Clerks and cashiers	Engineers
Waiters and waitresses	Technical and related workers
Primary and secondary schoolteachers	Armed forces
Packers, labellers and related workers	Groundsmen and gardeners
Cooks	
Bartenders	

* These are traditional and standard occupational titles; those including 'men' or 'women' do
not imply sex-exclusiveness
(Derived from p. 17, *Social Trends No. 5* 1974)

that in future the profession may well be less dominated by men
than in the past. Whatever the limitations on the extent to which
women are beginning to follow professional careers, the trend
towards greater participation clearly exists and is important within

TABLE 6.11
FEMALE WORKERS AS A PERCENTAGE OF ALL WORKERS IN
EACH OF THE MAJOR OCCUPATIONAL GROUPS 1911–1971

	1911	1951	1961	1971
*Occupational groups**				
Employers and proprietors	18.8	20.0	20.4	24.9
White-collar workers	29.8	42.3	44.5	47.9
Managers and administrators	19.8	15.2	15.5	21.6
Higher professionals	6.0	8.3	9.7	9.9
Lower professionals and technicians	62.9	53.5	50.8	52.1
Foremen and inspectors	4.2	13.4	10.3	13.1
Clerks	21.4	60.2	65.2	73.2
Salesmen and shop assistants	35.2	51.6	54.9	59.8
All manual workers	30.5	26.1	26.0	29.4
Skilled	24.0	15.7	13.8	13.5
Semi-skilled	40.4	38.1	39.3	46.5
Unskilled	15.5	20.3	22.4	37.2
Total occupied population	29.6	30.8	32.4	36.5

* See footnote to table 6.10
(Derived from table 16, Hakim 1980a)

an occupational structure that generally confines women to jobs of low skill, low status and low pay.

There have been a number of attempts to measure the extent to which the pay levels of occupations are associated with the proportions of females within them, but most have failed to find such a relationship (Chiplin and Sloane 1974; Chiplin and Sloane 1976a; Sloane and Siebert 1980). The last of these researches did, however, show that female part-time workers were unfavourably distributed by occupation, in that they comprised a higher percentage of those in occupations in which pay was low. Our understanding is not advanced much further by switching attention to a comparison of the female:male wage ratios within occupations. It is true that

TABLE 6.12
NUMBERS IN PARTICULAR OCCUPATIONAL GROUPS AS A
PERCENTAGE OF THE WORKFORCE, BY SEX, 1961 AND 1978

| | *Women in the occupational group as % of women in the workforce* | | *Men in the occupational group as % of men in the workforce* | |
	1961	*1978*	*1961*	*1978*
Managerial and professional	16	26	18	32
Clerical and other non-manual	31	30	7	5
Foremen and supervisors	2	5	5	8
Skilled manual	12	10	36	32
Unskilled and semi-skilled manual	39	29	34	23

(Derived from table 6.12, Royal Commission on the Distribution of Income and Wealth 1980)

women do well in relation to men's pay in some occupations where they are only a small percentage of the workers, such as professional management and administration, or transport and storage. However, women also do relatively well in some occupations in which they are in a majority, such as clerical work or in education, welfare and health. The most that can be said (Chiplin, Curran and Parsley 1980) is that women earn a high proportion of men's pay in those occupations (such as the professional categories) where the two sexes tend to work similar hours or to earn equally high shift or overtime payments.

It seems, then, that to understand pay inequalities we must examine the differences between men and women within the same occupation. Chiplin, Curran and Parsley (1980) argue that, of the differences in pay between the sexes, only 7 per cent can be accounted for by the effects of their distribution among occupations, a further 13 per cent by differences in hours worked, and a

TABLE 6.13
PERCENTAGE* OF FEMALE MEMBERS OF PROFESSIONAL
BODIES IN 1971–1972 AND 1980

	1971–2	*1980*
Chartered Insurance Institute	4	10
Institute of Bankers	1	13
Institute of Chartered Accountants of England and Wales	2	4
Institute of Mechanical Engineers	0.1	0.3
Law Society	3	12
Royal Institution of Chartered Surveyors	0.4	1
Royal Town Planning Institute	6	7
British Medical Association	18	22
Institute of Building	0	0.4

* Percentages over 1 rounded
(Derived from table 3.4, *EOC Annual Report 1980* 1981, and *Women and Work: A Review* 1975)

total of almost 80 per cent by differences that occur within occupational groups. In the same way Sloane argued before the Royal Commission on the Distribution of Income and Wealth (1978b) that 'unequal pay given existing occupations is roughly twice as important as unequal occupational distribution given pay'. In other words, the key to earnings inequality lies not in 'horizontal segregation', which exists when different types of jobs are performed by women and men, but in 'vertical segregation', which exists when both women and men work in the same general job categories, but within these men perform the work that is more skilled, responsible or better paid. It could be that the effects of 'vertical segregation' would have been apparent in the research described above if the occupational categories used had been less general (Hakim 1978 and 1980a, describing census data).

Within an occupation, men are more likely than women to have the higher-status and higher-skill grades: as an illustration, 'on the buses' women are more likely to be conductors than drivers. Where the grading system involves responsibility for the work of others, men are more likely to have the senior positions: only 4 per cent of women in clerical work can be classified as supervisors, compared with 12 per cent of men *(New Earnings Survey* 1976). The disproportionate representation of men in the upper reaches of career structures is illustrated in tables 3.10, 5.9, 5.10 and 5.11.

To understand women's underrepresentation in the hierarchy of a particular occupation it is important to know its full background: for example, the women in the occupation may be unrepresentatively young, particularly if women have only just started to enter the job; hence the fact that in 1981 only 2 per cent of sergeants in the Metropolitan Police were women may reflect the recruitment pattern of some years ago, rather than the current picture, where a quarter of the intake are women. None the less, women do not appear to be promoted as much as men. In order to rise in the hierarchy of the medical profession, women tend to have to be in less fashionable (and therefore probably less competitive) fields such as specialities relating to children or mental disorder (Oakley 1981). McNally's survey of female temporary clerical workers (McNally 1979) showed that, in the world of the secretary, promotion usually involves working for a 'boss' of higher status, rather than having responsibility for others.

Whether analysed in terms of occupations or in terms of grades within occupations, women are excluded from the positions of power and influence at work. As Marsh (1979) comments: 'Women work with women, but are supervised more often than not by a man.' Women are almost entirely absent from management which does not involve the supervision of women workers. In 1979 they accounted for only 1 per cent of the British Institute of Management (*EOC Annual Report 1979* 1980). Only 2 per cent of the members of the Institute of Directors were women, and these seem to have come from the less prestigious companies, since in the late 1970s there were no women directors on the boards of the twenty largest firms in Britain (Labour Research Department 1978).

Once the position of the two sexes in terms of occupation and grade has been examined, it is important to analyse jobs in terms of the industries in which they take place. There are a number of industries whose business requires very few of the occupations in which women are found and which therefore predominantly employ male workers. In the industrial classification in table 6.14, examples of 'male' industries are 'mining and quarrying' and 'construction', though a more detailed classification of industries would show that some, such as 'shipbuilding', are even more exclusively male. Because women are outnumbered by men in the labour force, and

TABLE 6.14
INDUSTRIAL DISTRIBUTION OF EMPLOYEES IN
EMPLOYMENT, BY SEX

	(1980) Women as a % of industrial group	*(1980)* % of total of each sex in employment		*(1974–1980)* % change in numbers in employment	
		Women	Men	Women	Men
All manufacturing industries	29	21	37	−22	−14
All service industries	54	76	48	+8	+1
Agriculture, forestry, fishing	25	1	2	−6	−4
Mining and quarrying	5	—	3	+9	−5
Construction	9	1	9	+9	−7
Gas, electricity, water	20	1	2	+7	0
Manufacturing industries					
Food, drink, tobacco	40	3	3	−16	−10
Petroleum, chemicals	26	3	3	−12	−2
Metal manufacture	12	0.5	3	−26	−24
Engineering	24	5	11	−24	−13
Vehicles	24	1	5	−17	−11
Textiles	46	2	2	−30	−31
Clothing	77	3	0.5	−18	−22
Other manufacturing	28	6	10	−22	−15
Service industries					
Transport, communications	20	3	9	+7	−5
Distributive trades	56	17	10	−2	0
Insurance, banking, financial	54	7	5	+13	+8
Professional, scientific services	69	27	9	+8	+1
Leisure and personal services	58	16	8	+21	+10
Public administration	39	7	8	+2	−2

(Devised from p. 20 and table 1.4, *Employment Gazette* (January 1976 and January 1981))

are often absent from crucial skilled occupations and positions of responsibility, there are no industries with predominantly female labour forces, though there are several where women are in a clear majority. It is not possible to say definitely that women are concentrated into a narrower range of industries than men, since this depends on the classification of industries used. However, women's work takes place to a large degree in service industries, whereas men's work is spread more evenly through service and manufacturing industries. An even higher concentration in service industries is found in the case of female part-time work. The distribution, education and health industries, for example, together employ almost two million part-timers. Much of this part-time work in service industries is manual work, such as cooking and cleaning.

The effect of recent changes has been to reinforce the extent to which women are employed in service rather than manufacturing industries. While employment of both sexes in manufacturing has declined in recent years, the reduction of the employment of women has been more rapid than that of men, partly because semi-skilled manual jobs have been dispensed with, and partly because industries traditionally employing female labour (such as clothing and textiles) have been in decline. However, the female labour force in service industries has grown more rapidly than the male. Part-time employment has reflected these changes, but to a more marked degree, with a larger percentage fall than for full-time jobs in manufacturing, and a larger percentage rise than for full-time jobs in service industries.

The statistical analysis of Chiplin, Curran and Parsley (1980) suggests that changes in the industrial distribution of the workforce in the 1970s had little to do with the improvement in the female:male earnings ratio during that period. This is surprising, since the ratio is clearly higher in service industries than it is in manufacturing industries, and one might have expected a shift into services to be the cause of a relative improvement in women's earnings. Similarly, one might expect the position of women to be affected by their relative share of jobs in the public and private sectors, since in the former in 1980 the average female wage was almost 70 per cent of the male, compared with less than 60 per cent in the latter (though the difference was more marked in the previous decade).

An alternative way of showing the possible effect on women's pay of the industrial distribution of employment is to relate the percentage of women in industrial groups to average earnings for the group. With such data, Chiplin and Sloane (1976a) found that, for manual workers, the higher the proportion of females in an industry's workforce, the lower was the male earnings level. It appears that in industries where wages are high (such as vehicle manufacture) women get jobs only in small numbers, and in industries where women form a large percentage of the workforce (such as clothing and footwear) pay is lower. However, a later piece of research (Sloane and Siebert 1980) did not find, with another set of data, the effect demonstrated by Chiplin and Sloane.

None the less, the hypothesis that female earnings are depressed not by the occupations they enter but by where they work is not entirely implausible. Some firms will inevitably be more prosperous and some will offer better promotion and training prospects than others, even to people in the same occupation. One particularly important feature of women's employment is that it takes place disproportionately in smaller industrial establishments and firms which pay less and have fewer positions of responsibility (*Bolton Committee of Enquiry into Small Firms* 1971).

In the context of this argument – namely, that women's poor relative earnings position is at least partly attributable to the types of industries and firms that employ them – one should not forget those industries that rely on home work for the manufacture of their products. In manufacturing, the typical business delivers materials to the worker's home, and then collects and sells the finished product. One survey found that over half of homeworking involved knitting or machine sewing (Crine 1979), though the researchers deliberately excluded child-minding, which could be considered home work. Because the worker is often officially self-employed, there are no reliable statistics on this type of work. Townsend estimated that there were some 250,000 homeworkers, plus 130,000 child-minders (Trades Union Congress 1978), while Hakim (1980b) considers that the number of homeworkers lies between 200,000 and 400,000. The people involved are almost entirely women, and because they have little alternative work they are very poorly paid. The Low Pay Unit survey (Crine 1979) found that most homeworkers were paid on a piece-work basis, and under this sytem 30 per cent of its sample earned below 20 pence an hour. A survey of people working from home for the toy industry found that only 2 out of a sample of 178 got holiday pay, and none got sick pay (Advisory Conciliation and Arbitration Service 1978).

PROMOTION AND TRAINING

The general impression given so far is that women are confined to the less-skilled, low-status and low-pay occupations in the labour market. The next few paragraphs show how the employment potential of women is under-utilised in comparison with that of men.

One indicator of potential for employment is a person's educational qualifications. Table 6.15 shows that, for both sexes, there is a relationship between educational level and earnings – but also that women are likely to earn less than men with similar qualifications. For example, of those with degrees, 48 per cent of men but only 21 per cent of women earned £6000 or more, though the women surveyed were likely to have a lower average age than the men. Williamson's (1981) survey in 1977 of graduates found that, when differences between the sexes (such as hours of work and length of

TABLE 6.15
HIGHEST QUALIFICATION LEVEL ATTAINED, BY ANNUAL
EARNINGS AND BY SEX: CUMULATIVE PERCENTAGES OF
PERSONS AGES 20–69 IN FULL-TIME EMPLOYMENT, GREAT
BRITAIN 1978

	Degree or equivalent		*Higher education below degree*		*GCE A-level or equivalent*	
	Women	*Men*	*Women*	*Men*	*Women*	*Men*
Gross annual earnings (£)						
2000+	86	96	88	97	80	96
2500+	84	94	79	95	58	91
3000+	79	89	66	90	33	79
3500+	73	85	51	82	16	69
4000+	61	83	33	71	8	52
4500+	49	74	19	57	5	38
5000+	38	66	11	42	2	26
6000+	21	48	3	20	0	14

(Derived from table 6.7, *General Household Survey 1978* 1980)

work experience) had been taken into account, female graduates' salaries were more than 10 per cent below those of men. It has been suggested that the limited pool of opportunities for graduates is illustrated by the very existence of graduate secretarial courses (McNally 1979).

An alternative way of showing how the potential of women is not realised is to look at the profile of earnings of people of different ages, which should give an indication of whether or not people 'make progress' through a career structure. Women's earnings seem to peak much earlier than those of men, and subsequently remain stable, whereas men's earnings rise faster and peak much later (Royal Commission on the Distribution of Income and Wealth 1980, table 8.1). This may indicate that promotion structures are organised so that for women a break in employment for child-rearing acts as a significant handicap; however, it is also possible that women are excluded in other ways from opportunities for advancement (Davidson and Cooper 1980; Greenhalgh 1980).

One major factor leading to the failure to realise the potential of women in the labour market is the way in which training schemes fit them for certain limited roles. On the Youth Opportunities Programme (table 6.16) women tend to be gaining experience of cleaning, clerical work or selling ('work experience on employers' premises') or in community service, rather than in making or farming ('project-based work experience' and 'training workshops'). Similarly, TOPS courses (table 6.17) reinforce the traditional occupa-

TABLE 6.16
THE SEX COMPOSITION OF CATEGORIES OF YOUTH
OPPORTUNITIES PROGRAMME SCHEMES, 1980
(PERCENTAGES)

	Women	*Men*
Work experience on employers' premises	53	47
Project-based work experience	24	76
Training workshops	26	74
Community service	61	39
Short training courses	44	56
All	49	51

(Derived from table 1, Bedeman and Harvey 1981)

TABLE 6.17
THE SEX COMPOSITION OF ADULT 'TOPS' COMPLETIONS
FOR SELECTED COURSE GROUPS, GREAT BRITAIN 1978–1979
(PERCENTAGES)

	Women	Men
Shorthand and typing	98	2
Clerical	84	16
Office machine operating	70	30
Food preparation and serving	68	32
Hairdressing and cleaning	65	35
Management	16	84
Science and technology	10	90
Heavy Goods Vehicle driving	2	98
Construction	1	99
Carpentry and joinery	1	99
Welding	*	100

*Approximately zero
(Derived from figure 2.16, *EOC Annual Report 1979* 1980)

tional patterns of the sexes; very few women train at skill centres or employers' establishments, which is where the majority of craft courses are taken. The pattern differs between men and women not simply in the type of training but in its amount. Table 6.18 shows that women take part as much as men in training 'on the job' but receive much less training away from work; the latter is, of course, often crucial to promotion prospects.

Many traditionally female jobs do in fact require skill, but because they are undervalued inadequate training is given. This lack of training means that women are further confined to low-paying jobs, grades and industries.

EMPLOYMENT AND UNEMPLOYMENT

The failure of the economy to make full use of women's work potential can also be seen by examining trends in employment and unemployment during periods of prosperity and periods of recession. In the context of the argument that women are undervalued as part of the labour force, it is significant that the figures the state uses

TABLE 6.18
PERCENTAGE OF EMPLOYEES TAKING ADVANTAGE OF
TYPES OF IN-SERVICE TRAINING, BY SEX, 1980

	Women	*Men*
On-site		
On the job	16	16
Off the job	2	5
Off-site		
Ad hoc	3	4
Day release	1	3
Block release	1	3
Other further education	∅	2
Employees taking advantage		
of any type of training	23	33

∅ = less than 0.5 per cent
(Derived from *Employment Gazette* (November 1980))

to indicate the level of unemployment fail to record fully the number of women who are out of work. Official unemployment figures are based on the numbers who are registered as able and willing to work. The incentive to register is that doing so is a prerequisite of drawing unemployment or supplementary benefit. Many women, however, are not entitled to unemployment benefit, either because they have not worked long enough to pay sufficient National Insurance contributions, or because they are married and exercised their former right to opt out of the full contributions. If these women, married or not, are living with a man, they also lose their right to supplementary benefit. Having therefore no financial incentive to register as unemployed, many fail to do so.

The extent of this 'hidden unemployment' can be seen in survey results (such as those shown in table 6.19). The 1971 *Census of Population* showed that there were 1.4 million unemployed people, at a time when only 0.8 million were registered as unemployed. The *General Household Survey* reveals how hidden unemployment changes year by year, and how it is distributed between the sexes. Between 1976 and 1980 the proportion of unemployed men who were unregistered remained relatively constant at around 10 per cent. The proportion of unemployed married women who were not

TABLE 6.19
FEMALE UNEMPLOYMENT, BY SEX AND MARITAL STATUS,
GREAT BRITAIN 1951, 1971 AND 1978

	April 1951	*June 1971*	*June 1978*
Female % of labour force	31	36	39
Female % of registered unemployed	35	14	29
Female % of total unemployed	29	32	45
Female registered unemployed as % of total unemployed	63	23	58
Married female % of labour force	12	23	25
Married female % of registered unemployed	NA	5	11
Female registered unemployment rate	1.2	1.2	4.2

NA = not available
(Devised from table 6.4, Elias 1980, and tables 1.1 and 2.2, *Employment Gazette* (June 1981))

registered was much higher, but fell steadily from 70 per cent in 1975 to 43 per cent in 1980. This change is partly due to the 1977 legislation's phasing out of the married women's National Insurance option.

Because registered unemployment is a misleading indicator, it is important to examine whether recessions bring unemployment disproportionately to one sex by looking at 'true' or 'total' unemployment figures. These suggest that during periods of prosperity such as the 1950s or early 1970s men suffered more from unemployment (relative to their participation in the workforce); however, during periods of recession, women bore the brunt of unemployment. This picture of women's employment being more volatile than that of men can also be seen from figures showing changes in employment over a number of decades, particularly in the manufacturing sector (Counter-Information Services 1981). This volatility may be associated with the jobs women do, or may arise because more of them work part-time. In addition to changes in the numbers employed, the hours of work of women seem to vary more from period to period than those of men.

A recent statistical study by the OECD (*Recession 1974–*

75 and the Employment of Women 1976) found that in the recession
of 1974–5 women experienced greater employment losses than men
in manufacturing, but over all women fared better than men
because layoffs struck most lightly in service industries, where
women predominate. However, there is no certainty that in future
recessions the disproportionate loss of women's jobs in manufacturing will be counterbalanced by their more favourable experience in
the service industries. It is noteworthy that from 1974 to 1976
industry was taking on part-time while shedding full-time labour
(*Employment Gazette* (February 1981))), perhaps partly in the hope
that part-time jobs could be shed more easily should the need arise.
In the years since 1976 (table 6.20) it is difficult to decide which sex
has been harder hit by the recession. It seems that women bore the
initial brunt of the slump, but as it deepened in 1980–1 male jobs
were eventually badly affected.

Given the different nature of their employment, it might be
expected that the experience of married women in recessions would
be different from that of other workers. In a study of the 1961–74
period (Joshi 1978), cyclical movements in employment were found
to be strong among the younger age ranges of married women; older
married women, however, were affected not so much by the trade
cycle as by a seasonal cycle. In the light of this, it is interesting to
note that younger married women seem to have the most difficulty
in finding work (table 6.21). This does not necessarily imply that
older married women do not suffer from unemployment, since it is

TABLE 6.20
PERCENTAGE CHANGES IN EMPLOYMENT AND REGISTERED
UNEMPLOYMENT 1977–1981, BY SEX,
GREAT BRITAIN

| | Registered unemployed | | | In employment | |
	All women	Married women	All men	All women	All men
1977–8	+13.0	+16.9	−0.8	+1.1	+0.1
1978–9	−6.2	+5.3	−8.4	+1.5	+0.1
1979–80	+22.0	+21.6	+10.4	−2.0	−1.3
1980–1	+52.6	+52.6	+73.0	−4.8	−5.7
1977–81	+97.3	+128.3	+76.3	−2.5	−6.8

(Devised from tables 1.1 and 2.2, *Employment Gazette* (August 1981))

TABLE 6.21
PERCENTAGE UNEMPLOYED,* BY SEX, MARITAL STATUS
AND AGE, GREAT BRITAIN 1977

	Married women	Other women	Men
Age			
16–19	18	10	10
20–4	11	7	8
25–34	10	8	5
35–49	5	7	4
50–9	4	6	4
60–4	3	5	7
65+	2	4	4
All ages	6.5	7.4	5.1

* Includes unregistered unemployed; study was a sample of the general population
(Derived from table 5.31, *Labour Force Survey 1973, 1975, 1977* 1980)

possible that married women eventually give up hope of finding work and stop looking, or find a part-time job instead of a full-time one, thus 'disguising' unemployment. Older married women's employment problems are demonstrated in official unemployment figures (*Employment Gazette*), which for January 1981 reported that the average woman aged 55 and over, registered as unemployed, had spent marginally longer out of work than her male counterpart.

So far, this discussion has focused mainly on those already in the workforce. However, researchers have also been much interested in the question of whether or not the general level of demand in an economy (as indicated by unemployment levels) influences the decision of women, particularly married women, to enter the workforce at all. There is the possibility that a recession actually encourages married women to look for work if their husbands are laid off, thus increasing the female economic activity rate. However, most research has found that this 'added worker effect' is swamped by the 'discouraged worker effect', in which the general difficulty of finding work discourages women from looking for it (Berg and Dalton 1977; Greenhalgh 1977; McNabb 1977). This conclusion accords with the historical process by which women have been drawn into the labour market since the war; the government stimulated demand in the economy and, because labour was therefore in short supply, employers made every effort to attract women into the workforce.

If the willingness of women to do paid work is sensitive to the kind and amount of work available, this ought to be apparent in comparing data from parts of the country that have different job oportunities. Economic activity probably does vary with employment opportunities. For women, the variation in activity between regions is more pronounced than for men, and female activity rates are lowest in the less urban areas such as Wales, the South-West and East Anglia where there is likely to be a more restricted range of jobs available (*Regional Trends*, table 8.5). None the less, high activity rates for women are sometimes associated with low earnings in relation to men (*Regional Trends*, table 13.6) and a high share of total unemployment (*Employment Gazette*), as is the case in Scotland.

CHOOSING EMPLOYMENT

So far we have seen that women now participate in the labour market in large numbers, and increasingly register as 'able and willing to work' rather than remaining among the 'invisible unemployed'. Even if she marries and stays at home to look after children while they are young, a woman can still expect to spend the majority of her adult years in paid employment; only 5 per cent of women aged 25–44 who are not in the workforce have not previously worked (*General Household Survey 1978* 1980). However, far more women than men work part-time, and the sexes also have very different jobs. It is therefore appropriate to examine whether there are differences between the sexes in the demand for work, or whether work inequalities are imposed by the structure of the labour market and by their domestic circumstances.

Housework as a whole forms a very large part of the unpaid work performed each year. It is difficult to put a monetary value on housework, but the figure of about two-fifths of the value of the country's entire production is most widely quoted (Oakley 1980; Wickham and Young 1973). The vast majority of those for whom 'keeping house' is their major activity are women, despite the growth in enforced 'role-swapping' which may be occurring when husbands become unemployed.

When both partners have paid jobs, survey evidence suggests that most men's involvement with housework is low or peripheral. This was the clear conclusion of a survey of mothers (Oakley 1974b). Ginsberg (1976) found that only 15 per cent of the husbands of working wives in her sample had a 'high' level of participation in housework, although help with childcare was greater; many husbands felt that wives worked principally for their own benefit and so should not expect help with domestic chores in consequence.

Such results contrast sharply with those of Young and Willmott (1973), who concluded on the basis of a survey of married couples in the London region that the family is becoming 'symmetrical', with men and women sharing household and childcare tasks. This conclusion has been criticised (Bristol Women's Studies Group 1979) for being based on a small sample of older and more settled families, and for being premised on the continuation of a substantial rise in the average standard of living. Rapoport and Rapoport (1976) point out that it is not enough to show that tasks are divided between couples, for too often the husband sees himself as 'helping' his wife, leaving with her the responsibility for organising the household.

It may be that, in some social groups more than others, wives have to carry the burden of housework with little help from husbands. Thompson and Findlayson (1963) found that working mothers tended to come from families where there were clearly marked role differences between the sexes; as a result, these mothers received less help from husbands than non-working mothers. Gavron (1966) found that working-class husbands more than middle-class ones were increasing their contributions to household tasks. However, a study in which the difficulties of the working wife were most clearly shown was a survey of over 400 couples who were both doctors (Elston 1980): this showed (table 6.22) that male doctors received far more help from their spouses than did female doctors.

It has been argued that working wives effectively have two jobs, one paid and the other in the home, and that many accept this as 'their lot' (Shimmin, McNally and Liff 1981). It is commonly suggested that the availability of consumer durables such as washing-machines has reduced the housekeeping workload, yet American studies have shown that the invention of household appliances actually raised housework time by making possible tasks that were previously impossible. Sometimes men genuinely seem to think that

TABLE 6.22
PERCENTAGE OF EACH SEX PEFORMING CERTAIN
HOUSEHOLD TASKS WITHIN MARRIED COUPLES WHERE
BOTH PARTNERS HAVE MEDICAL CAREERS

| | Replies by female doctors Tasks undertaken by: | | | | Replies by male doctors Tasks undertaken by: | | | |
	Self	Spouse	Both	Hired help	Self	Spouse	Both	Hired help
Budgeting	27	23	50	0	39	16	45	0
Shopping	85	2	12	1	1	81	16	1
Arranging social activities	39	4	57	0	4	31	65	0
Household repairs	10	63	22	5	71	4	18	3
Cooking	81	1	12	6	1	84	14	2
House-cleaning	51	0	5	45	1	68	12	20
Looking after sick child	80	0	18	3	2	67	30	1
Major purchases	11	12	78	0	22	5	74	0

(Derived from table 5.2, Elston 1980)

a division of roles in which they look after gardening, repairs and decorating and their wives look after housework is an equal division (Hunt 1975). This is clearly not the case, and even the Young and Willmott study showed that working wives had less leisure time than their husbands.

It is revealing to examine how women actually spend their non-work time. One survey of low-paid workers (National Board for Prices and Incomes 1971) showed that, though journey-to-work distances were longer for most men, journey times were actually longer for most women because they tended not to have the use of private transport. It also seems likely that what is classed as 'leisure activities' in surveys may, for women in particular, contain an element of work or social duty as well as pleasure, though these two aspects are not easily differentiated. *Social Trends No. 5* (1974) showed that for women crafts and hobbies (principally knitting) comprised 17 per cent of leisure time as against 4 per cent for men, and the 'social activities' category (9 per cent for women, 3 per cent for men) may well have involved helping relatives and others. Men, it is true, spent some time on gardening and maintenance.

Voluntary activities form quite a substantial part of the work of the nation, which, because it is unpaid, is hidden from employment statistics. To a large degree helpers in such voluntary work are women (*Social Trends No. 5* 1974). Public-spending cuts affecting social services often involve people, mainly women, in additional voluntary work, so that the same work is done but is no longer 'visible'. In a similar manner, the care of children and elderly relatives is a task which under a different social system might well be paid work, but which in Britain is mainly done unpaid by women. According to Mackie and Pattullo (1977), there are an estimated 300,000 single women who care for elderly parents or relatives.

Probably the least-known aspect of this unpaid work is the hidden unemployment of women within family enterprises. In an attempt to exclude family-based domestic work from the employment statistics, official sources do not count either domestic servants (including au pair girls) or family workers (such as wives working for husbands in a non-supervisory capacity) as employees; they are instead counted as economically inactive. Yet Scase and Goffee (1980) suggest that small businessmen often prosper not just by their own efforts but also by those of unpaid wives. Interviews with over 120 business owners in service industries showed that women provided invaluable support to the businesses, by acting not only as housewives but also as business partners, often without remuneration. The women provided clerical, secretarial and accounting services, entertained potential customers, maintained morale of employees, and improved public relations by working for local associations or charities. Such help from wives is not confined to husbands in small businesses; an EEC (1979) survey showed that in the UK 22 per cent of wives helped in their husbands' work, 5 per cent of them giving help 'every day'.

While marriage *may* give a man an unpaid helpmate, it often gives a woman responsibilities that restrict her in the labour market. Often women gain access to the most responsible jobs, such as the directorship of firms, only if they are single (Fogarty, Allen, Allen and Walters 1971). Davidson and Cooper (1980) showed that women in managerial positions were only a third as likely as their male counterparts to be married. Turnbull and Williams (1974) neatly summed up the major constraints on married women by showing that the low proportion of married female headteachers in schools was because the school governors usually felt that family responsibilites would interfere with work, and because the women could not move to a new job because the husband would have to move too. Responsibility for children and for domestic duties can confine women to part-time work, even when they would rather work full-time (Shimmin, McNally and Liff 1981), and is a major factor in causing women to do home work rather than work outside the home (Crine 1979; Hope, Kennedy and De Winter 1976). It also results in women's having to work much nearer home than men (Mackay, Boddy, Brack, Diack and Jones 1971) and so to accept nearby jobs, however low-paid. They may be prevented from raising their pay through overtime work, and from participating in after-hours union activities (see below). Although typically women do not involve the whole family in a move to another part of the country in order to gain promotion, they are often expected to move for their husband's career, which affects their pension rights and promotion prospects.

It should not be thought that it is only married women who are confined to the less-skilled segments of the labour market. Greenhalgh (1980) shows how both industry and occupation statistics present a picture of single women following 'female career' patterns very similar to those of married women, despite their slightly higher qualifications, so that in 1975, whereas 60 per cent of married men with qualifications above A-level had a professional or managerial occupation, the proportion for single women of similar qualifications was only 16 per cent. None the less the constraints upon married women may be important because they affect the general climate of opinion about the potential of all women. Social pressures should not be forgotten, though in a survey of British people (EEC 1979) only 9 per cent of housewives said these were the main reason why they did not have a job, compared with 16 per cent who chose lack of job opportunities, and 62 per cent who chose family responsibilities, as the main factor.

A further obstacle to married women's entering employment is the system of tax and social security, which continues to perpetuate the assumption of the wife as dependent on a breadwinner husband (see also Chapter 4). One important feature of the income tax system is the wife's earned income allowance, which was introduced during the Second World War to encourage women to take up employment. It is therefore claimed that the tax system positively encourages women to work, since, if there is a choice between the tax-paying husband working overtime and the wife taking up employment, their tax bill will be lower if the wife earns the additional money and takes advantage of her tax allowance. However, this is implicitly comparing the present system with a highly distorted one in which wives have no allowances. By comparison with a system where the current total of tax concessions was reallocated so that each individual within a marriage received equal allowances, the present system where the married man receives a higher allowance than his wife makes it less imperative for the wife also to bring in an income, and this, together with the higher tax on her income, possibly acts as a disincentive to her to earn. Indeed, the original idea of the married man's tax allowance was to help him 'keep' his wife at home by compensating him for the loss of her potential earnings.

Similarly, the social security system has a number of different effects which on balance discourage married women from undertaking paid work. It is true that many unemployed women who are married to or cohabiting with a man, and who contemplate taking employment, are not dissuaded by the thought of losing social security benefits, since many women in that situation are not entitled to any such benefits in the first place. However, lack of entitlement to benefits may mean that many women do not register as unemployed – which, by cutting them off from the job market, reduces their chances of finding employment. Moreover, if her husband is unemployed and drawing social security, then above a small amount every pound the wife earns reduces his dependant's benefit by an equivalent amount. Evidence that this may discourage women from working was found in a recent survey of the unemployed (Smith 1981). The Royal Commission on the Distribution of Income and Wealth (1978a) showed that, after other influences were taken into account, the wives of unemployed husbands were 33 per cent more likely to be out of the labour force. A final effect of social security is that the statutory retirement age for women is 60, allowing retirement from employment five years earlier than men.

The tax and social security systems further discourage role-swapping arrangements where the wife is the wage-earner and the husband the house-minder. At first sight the tax system taken by itself might appear to give a positive impetus to such an arrangement, since a wife who is the sole paid worker may claim more tax allowance than a husband in the same position (she may claim the allowances that would otherwise be due to the man without losing her own allowance). However, the social security system works the other way. A man bringing up children has no right (unlike that of a woman) to be credited with National Insurance contributions; a woman cannot nominate her husband for pension rights; the couple cannot rely on her income, for if she should lose her job she cannot claim benefit for her husband as a dependant unless he is actually incapable of self-support. If her income is inadequate, a wife has no right to family income supplement and its attendant benefits. It is therefore possible that the tax and social security systems taken together may reduce the likelihood of some married women participating in paid work, adding to the other obstacles described earlier. The increase in the numbers of women who work might therefore be taken as evidence of a strong desire to work.

Oakley (1981) has criticised the sexist assumption behind the question 'Why do women work?', and yet in view of the constraints that society places on women's work, and the low earnings women can expect to get from work, people may be forgiven for asking. At least in answering the question one can dispel the notion that pay for women is not particularly important. Single women must earn to live, just as any man must. Lone mothers are responsible for both themselves and their children, and the proportion of families headed by a lone mother increased from 8 to 11 per cent over the period 1972–9 (*General Household Survey 1980* 1981). Table 6.23 suggests that paid work is crucial to such women; the proportion who work is much greater than for mothers as a whole, and income from employment is a substantial part of total income.

Within marriage, wives' earnings are often crucial (see also Chapter 4, pp. 74–8). Even before the large rise in unemployment in the 1970s, the 1971 census found that in 2 per cent of all couples the wife was the sole breadwinner. By 1977 the proportion of women who earned more than their husbands had risen to nearly 9 per cent, with a further 6 per cent earning as much as their husbands (*EOC Annual Report 1980* 1981). The significance of wives' earnings in raising family standard of living is well documented (Roberti 1974; Hamill 1978a; Royal Commission on the Distribution of Income and Wealth 1978a), and is effectively demonstrated in table 6.24. Hamill has estimated that the number of families with incomes below supplementary benefit level would have been trebled if wives had not been in paid employment. Ironically, it is often the lowest incomes that are the most crucial to the family budget; almost all the

TABLE 6.23
EMPLOYMENT AND EARNINGS OF SINGLE PARENTS, BY SEX
AND MARITAL STATUS, GREAT BRITAIN 1975

	Single woman	Widow	Separated woman	Divorced woman	Lone man
Percentage in paid work	44	56	57	50	86
Mean hours worked per week by those working	32	30	30	33	41
Income in £ per week*					
Earnings	14.3	12.0	16.6	12.7	45.4
Self-employment income	0.1	2.2	1.2	1.3	2.1
Pensions, allowances, unearned income	1.3	4.0	5.2	6.5	1.0
Original income	15.7	18.1	23.0	20.5	48.5
Net transfers (benefits less taxes)	8.3	16.5	5.7	4.8	−5.9
Total income	24.0	34.6	28.7	25.3	42.6

* Rounded to 1 decimal place
(Derived from tables 8.5 and 8.8, Royal Commission on the Distribution of Income and Wealth 1978b)

TABLE 6.24
HOUSEHOLD INCOME, BY ECONOMIC ACTIVITY OF
MARRIED WOMEN, UNITED KINGDOM 1979

	% of households with economically active woman		
Household income		*Household income*	
Under £40	7	£100 and under £120	52
£40 and under £60	12	£120 and under £160	68
£60 and under £80	29	£160 and under £200	77
£80 and under £100	43	£200 or more	75
All households	56		

(Devised from table 4.16, *EOC Annual Report 1980* 1981)

well-known surveys of homeworkers found that the money earned was required for necessities and particularly (since children were the main constraint forcing women to work from home) for children's needs (Hope, Kennedy and De Winter 1976; Advisory Conciliation and Arbitration Service 1978; Crine 1979; Hakim 1980b).

Yet is the need for money the most important determinant of a married woman's decision to work rather than rely for income on her husband? Income *is* important, as shown by the fact that a much higher percentage of housewives from lower-income households indicate that they intend to work in the future (*EOC Annual Report 1978* 1979). Many researchers have tried to find out how important money is to women workers by asking them directly why they work: for example, a survey (Marsh 1979) found that 50 per cent of the women questioned said that money was the overriding reason for working. Yet in some respects these findings are questionable. It is doubtful if men could disentangle their motivations for working, and this is surely true for women. Moreover, it is likely that, in answering, respondents may be giving the reply they believe to be most socially acceptable. Questions of a more definite nature are probably better; for example, Coote and Kellner (1980) asked workers how they would react if given a choice between working shorter hours and having a substantial pay rise, and the answers of men and women were very similar – only 33 per cent of men and 34 per cent of women preferred shorter hours.

In fact, work may generate a mixture of motivations, such as the desire to escape domestic drudgery (McNally 1979) and isolation (Hobson 1978), and a desire for job satisfaction. In this respect, one survey suggested that men and women are equally committed to work for its own sake (EEC 1979); 60 per cent of the women and 59 per cent of the men said they would continue working even if they had enough money to live comfortably.

It is possible that there are sharp differences in the attitudes towards work of the sexes in different social classes. Maizels (1970), in her study of workers under 18 years of age in London, found that girls rather less frequently than boys expressed the desire to earn money, and many fewer girls talked of promotion and advancement. It may be, however, that girls' attitudes merely reflect the realities of the situation. The EEC survey (1979) found that many fewer women than men believed they had the chance of promotion. However, a survey of 3000 women teachers in England

and Wales (National Union of Teachers 1980b) showed that 77 per cent of married women teachers saw their careers as being as important as those of their husbands. In 1979 Smith and Langrish conducted a survey of female management in the textile industry (*Guardian*, 29 November 1979) and found that women were far more motivated to succeed than men. Finally, a 1977 survey of graduates who obtained their first degrees in 1970 (see table 6.25) showed that, in choosing their latest job, women had given greater weight than men to the chance to use skill and exercise initiative, but (again perhaps reflecting the realities of the choices available) had given less weight to salary and promotion prospects. Husbands show up as a constraint on the career aspirations of wives, since more women than men were influenced by a desire to find work near that of their spouse.

From some of the surveys described above it appears that women tailor their aspirations to fit the circumstances of their likely work situations. Similarly, their reported level of job satisfaction may reflect a realism about the lack of better alternatives. The *General*

TABLE 6.25

REASONS GIVEN FOR CHOOSING LATEST JOB BY PEOPLE IN
1977 WHO HAD GRADUATED IN 1970 (PERCENTAGES)

	University		Polytechnic	
	Women	Men	Women	Men
Responsible/interesting job	19	19	20	20
Salary	10	15	12	18
Promotion/prospects	7	13	8	17
Travel/location	10	9	13	8
Opportunity to use skills/initiative	11	9	7	5
Pleasant conditions	8	7	9	7
Wider experience or change	5	6	4	8
Work near spouse/home	7	2	6	2

Notes: Only the most important factors are given in this table, and the sum of their percentages is less than 100. Those still in their first job are excluded. Not all those who had left their first job had taken a subsequent job.

(Derived from p. 624, *Employment Gazette* (June 1980))

Household Survey includes a question on job satisfaction. While the level of job dissatisfaction certainly increased among both sexes between 1971 and 1978, at the end of the period men were still more dissatisfied than women. Men's chief source of dissatisfaction was pay, whereas for women it was the kind of work they did. Considering the issue of pay by itself, a survey by Coote and Kellner (1980) found that approximately equal proportions of the sexes (women 73 per cent, men 71 per cent) thought they were fairly paid for their work. It has been suggested, though, that the 'passivity' of women in response to questions of pay is because they only compare their pay to that of other women (Hakim 1978); there is potentially much more discontent, as industrial action in the late 1960s and early 1970s in support of 'equal pay' showed.

TRADE-UNION ACTIVITY

In the field of industrial relations there is a dearth of information about the pattern of collective action of the sexes. Even such basic data as the breakdown of trade-union membership by sex are unreliable, particularly since the phasing out of separate recordings or rates of women's subscriptions to trade unions, and it seems likely that the female membership has been consistently understated (Bain and Price 1980). None the less, it is clear from data that exist (table 6.26) that men's greater share of employment, combined with the greater density of union membership among men, means that men make up over two-thirds of the trade-union movement. However, membership density has been increasing more rapidly among women than among men in recent years. This increase partly reflects the general rise in unionisation in the types of industry in which women are concentrated, particularly white-collar work and the public sector: Coote and Kellner (1980) show that the trade-union membership density of women is almost as high as that of men in the white-collar socio-economic group C1. Women are now in a clear majority of many white-collar unions (table 6.27) and in addition form sizeable minorities in some of the large general unions, including the largest, the Transport and General Workers.

Just as female workers are less unionised than male workers, so women who do join unions are less likely to hold positions of responsibility than their male colleagues. In several industries where women work in large numbers (such as textiles, potteries or

TABLE 6.26
MEMBERSHIP OF TRADE UNIONS, BY SEX, UNITED KINGDOM
1911–1979

| | *Trade-union membership (in millions)* | | *Women as % of union membership* | *% of potential membership** | |
	Women	*Men*		*Women*	*Men*
1911	0.3	2.8	10	6	23
1921	1.0	5.6	15	18	44
1951	1.8	7.7	19	25	56
1961	2.0	7.9	20	24	53
1971	2.8	8.4	25	33	58
1979	3.9	9.0	30	39	63

* i.e. membership density: the percentage of those in employment who were members of a trade union
(Devised from table 3.7, *EOC Annual Report 1980* 1981; table 12.19, *Social Trends No. 11* 1980; *British Labour Statistics 1970* 1971)

the retail trade) men retain a paternalistic control over a largely female trade-union membership. It is a question of not only the number of posts but which posts are occupied by women. A survey conducted by the National and Local Government Officers' Association (1980) found that women office holders in branches tended to occupy the more marginal posts, such as assistant secretary. To the extent that the occupations in which women are represented can be seen as extensions of the female role in the home, so can the trade-union posts held by women, such as education officer and welfare officer. None the less experience in such positions allows women a toehold in the power structure, and within NALGO women increased their share of branch officer posts from 16 to 22 per cent between 1974 and 1979. These figures concern the official trade-union structure. Information about shop stewards is more difficult to obtain, given their decentralised and informal nature. Table 6.28 shows a marginal increase in the percentage of female trade-unionists serving as shop stewards or local officials between 1976 and 1979, while there was no change in the male percentage. In respect of other union activities, the table displays small increases in female and small decreases in male participation.

TABLE 6.27
WOMEN'S SHARE OF MEMBERSHIP AND OFFICES IN
SELECTED UNIONS WITH SUBSTANTIAL FEMALE
MEMBERSHIPS IN 1980 (PERCENTAGES)

	Member-ship	Executive members	Full-time officials	TUC delegates
Association of Professional, Executive, Clerical and Computer Staff (APEX)	51	7	4	27
Association of Scientific Technical and Managerial Staffs (ASTMS)	17	8	10	10
Banking, Insurance and Finance Union (BIFU)	49	11	15	15
General and Municipal Workers' Union of (GMWU)	34	0	5	4
National Association of Local Government Officers (NALGO)	50	20	7	21
National Union of Public Employees (NUPE)	67	31	5	3
National Union of Teachers (NUT)	66	9	16	19
National Union of Transport and General Workers (NUTGW)	92	7	19	35
Transport and General Workers' Union(TGWU)	16	0	1	7
Union of Shop, Distributive and Allied Workers (USDAW)	63	19	8	21
Totals	38	11	6	16

N = 6,022,000
(Derived from Coote 1980)

The impression given is that women attend union meetings somewhat less than men but do not participate actively to the same extent in industrial action. This is a common observation of researchers, and, indeed, the extent of female participation in a factory has been used, along with other variables, to predict the amount of strike activity (*Strikes in Britain* 1978). However, throughout the last

TABLE 6.28
PERCENTAGE OF UNION MEMBERS WHO HAVE PREVIOUSLY
PARTICIPATED IN TRADE-UNION ACTIVITIES, BY SEX

| | 1976 | | 1979 | |
	Women	Men	Women	Men
Been to a union meeting	56	82	60	78
Voted in a union election	37	82	40	78
Gone on strike	22	46	24	52
Put forward a proposal at a union meeting	8	38	12	37
Stood in a picket line	6	20	5	19
Served as a local union official	3	18	6	18
Served as a shop steward	2	16	4	16
None of these	33	11	27	11

(Derived from table 8, Coote and Kellner 1980)

century there were examples of women engaging in industrial action – from the famous Matchgirls' strike of 1888, through the women's strike movement of 1911–13, to the equal-pay strike at Ford's, Dagenham, in 1968. These examples were not aberrations. In a classic study of workers in two industries, it was found that engineering workers operated collectively, while rainwear makers operated individualistically, regardless of sex (Lupton 1963). One study of the motor industry (Turner, Clack and Roberts 1967) found no relationship between the proportion of women employed in car factories and relative strike-proneness. In a more recent study of two industries in Stockport (Purcell 1979), it was found that men and women engaged in widespread action according to the tradition of the industry rather than according to sex: indeed, women in engineering had attitudes much closer to those of men in engineering than to those of women in the clothing industry.

It seems likely, then, that while women show less tendency to engage in strikes this may be associated principally with the places they work in and the work they do. Such factors may also explain why fewer women than men join trade unions. In particular, women tend to work in industries with a small-firm structure where union activity is difficult to organise (*Employment Gazette* (January 1978)). In small-scale establishments, there may be closer identification between worker and employer, and this is likely to be true in most offices – particularly between a secretary and the person she works for (Lumley 1973). Union participation and militancy also vary with type of work. Low-paid and less-skilled workers are always more difficult to unionise, and show a reduced tendency to strike (*Strikes in Britain* 1978). Part-time workers too are notoriously difficult to organise: according to one survey, only 10 per cent of part-time workers of both sexes were members of trade unions (*The Part Time Trap* 1978), though Coote and Kellner (1980) actually found a higher unionisation of female than male part-timers.

Generally, the very reasons why women work part-time (particularly domestic commitments) act as a barrier to their participation in union business, and this barrier also exists for women who work full-time. The majority of working married women have two demanding activities – their job and domestic and family responsibilities; to build in a third activity, active participation in a trade union, requires a high degree of commitment and organisation (Middleton 1977). The problem is particularly acute for mothers of young children, which explains why the gap in union membership between the sexes is greatest in the 25–34 age group (Coote and Kellner 1980).

However, it is by no means certain that such difficulties could not be overcome. When female trade-unionists in Hull were asked what would encourage them to participate in union activities, reducing home responsibilities was shown to be important, but the factors mentioned most often were holding meetings in work time and making available more information about how unions work (Stageman 1980). In the NALGO (1980) survey 85 per cent of branches were found to hold their meetings after working hours rather than at lunchtime (though even lunchtime meetings may present problems). However, the data in table 6.29 suggest that perceptions of female and male trade-union members differed most not on organisational matters – such as the timing of meetings – but on whether the union was felt to be in touch with its members and responsive to their interests and political sympathies.

It could be argued that unions fail to respond to the needs of women partly because they are run mainly by men. Even where women gain access to positions of responsibility, however, they may still be hampered. Fryer, Fairclough and Manson (1978) found that

TABLE 6.29
TRADE-UNION MEMBERS' PERCEPTIONS OF THEIR OWN
UNION, BY SEX, 1980 (PERCENTAGES)

	Women	Men
% agreeing that union:		
Would fight hard to protect my job if it were threatened	48	54
Tries hard to keep its members in touch with what the union is doing	32	46
Good at looking after the interests of people like me	40	39
Usually holds meetings at times and places that are easy for me to attend	29	34
Fights hard for equality between men and women at work	33	30
Union meetings are usually boring	18	27
Encourages people like me to get involved	19	27
Too involved in politics and not enough in advancing its members' interests	12	25
Should do more to meet the needs of workers with young children	19	15
Controlled by extremists and militants	7	12

(Derived from table 3, p. 11, *New Statesman*, 7 November 1980)

female shop stewards had poorer facilities and were able to have less time off for union duties. Within trade-union hierarchies, the representation of women has been increased through the practice of reserving some executive positions for women (for example, in 1980 there was an increase in the number of women's seats on the General Council of the TUC from two to five). However, special representation for women, particularly the formation of special committees for women, does not guarantee that the pay and employment problems of women will be dealt with by trade unions, as a recent study of ASTMS found (Harrison 1979).

Though 'deliberate non-membership' of trade unions is not extensive (Marsh 1979), there is evidence that unions were often seen as irrelevant to women's interests (Purcell 1979). In the absence of a trade union dedicated to fighting for their interests, women may have to show resistance in other ways (McNally 1979), or simply leave to find other jobs. Indeed, far from fighting for women's interests, male-dominated trade unions may even fight against them – opposing the creation of part-time jobs lest it harm the position of full-timers, and jealously guarding male/female pay differentials. The Equal Pay Act, though supported by the trade-union hierarchies, was an admission that collective bargaining would not give women equality. Neither have trade unions really attempted to tackle discriminatory attitudes and structures that perpetuate segregation in employment.

SEX DISCRIMINATION IN THE LABOUR MARKET

Despite both the increased participation of women in the labour market and in trade-union activity, women are still confined to an inferior segment of the labour market. Hakim has shown (table 6.30) that over a seventy-year period occupational segregation has declined but little. In 1971 over half of all working men were in occupations where they outnumbered women by at least nine to one, and half of all working women were in jobs where they were greatly overrepresented (at 70 per cent of the workforce) in relation to their contribution to the national labour force as a whole. Only in a few fields – education, nursing, retailing, etc. – is there actual competition for jobs between men and women, and in many of these

TABLE 6.30
OCCUPATIONAL SEGREGATION 1901–1971

	% of women working in occupations which had:				% of men working in occupations which had:			
	100% female workers	90% female workers	70% female workers	50% female workers	100% male workers	90% male workers	70% male workers	50% male workers
1901	11	52	71	82	47	74	89	95
1911	3	45	64	78	44	70	86	93
1921	0	40	56	72	29	70	83	92
1931	0	41	62	73	35	69	84	94
1951	0	31	50	68	20	61	82	92
1961	0	21	53	79	22	62	77	85
1971	0	25	51	77	14	53	77	87

(Derived from table 12, Hakim 1980a)

cases it is a matter of men infiltrating long-established women's areas.

This segregation does not arise because that is the way women prefer it. A survey of women workers (Marsh 1979) showed that only 18 per cent of professionals, 22 per cent of non-manual workers and 40 per cent of the manual grades expressed a preference to work only with women; a majority of the non-manual workforce and a third of all manual grades expressed a preference for more male colleagues. Clearly, then, the segregation of the labour force occurs either because of the way each sex is socialised and educated before entry into the labour market, or because there are discriminatory procedures operating in the labour market itself. The same survey showed that even in 1979 62 per cent of working women believed that women were discriminated against at work, and in a survey the previous year (EEC 1979) far more men than women were shown to believe that their sex gave them an advantage at work.

The extent of sexist attitudes was also displayed, particularly among men: 81 per cent of the women believed a man could do their job, but only 55 per cent of the men believed a woman could do theirs. The process of discrimination relies on the stereotyping of the sexes. In the United States Heilman and Saruwatari (1979) arranged for subjects to participate in a simulation of employee selection, and found that for managerial positions there was no discrimination against women in general, but that attractive women were assessed as less suitable and recommended for much lower salaries than unattractive ones. The National Union of Teachers found in a British survey that 60 per cent of women teachers had been asked at selection interviews about matters other than their professional life (NUT 1980b), and the union felt obliged to produce literature (NUT 1980a) to counteract the idea that the average woman teacher was married with young children and uncommitted to a career.

Men in particular are liable to have distorted ideas about women's capabilities, and this is of crucial significance since, according to a well-known survey of employers (Hunt 1975), men comprise 98 per cent of those responsible for the formulation of employment policies and 88 per cent of those who implement those policies. The survey established that the principal reasons for favouring men rather than women for particular jobs were that women were believed to have insufficient strength or stamina, and that the employer would get longer service from a man. The 1979 EOC survey was framed to allow a comparison with some of Hunt's data, thus showing how employers' perceptions changed between 1973 and 1979 (table 6.31). For most measures of performance the proportion of employers who perceived differences between men and women declined from 1973. However, on absenteeism the change was in the opposite direction; employers perceived a greater difference between the sexes on this dimension than on any other.

How far are these perceptions of employers based on reality? Surveys reveal that almost every job that one firm regards as unsuitable for women is performed by women in another company. The physical strength that women are said to lack is often a prerequisite of some jobs that women regularly do (in fact some jobs that are regarded as 'women's work', such as nursing, require considerable strength).

It is, however, more complex to decide whether there is any basis in truth for female workers being stereotyped as having high absenteeism and turnover rates. Table 6.32 shows little difference in

TABLE 6.31
EMPLOYERS' PERCEPTIONS OF THE PERFORMANCE OF WOMEN AND MEN AT WORK

	\% of all employers surveyed who believe:					
	Men better than women			Women better than men		
	1973	*1979*	*Change*	*1973*	*1979*	*Change*
Not taking days off for sickness	53	42	−11	5	6	+1
Not taking days off for other reasons	47	69	+22	10	2	−8
Staying with one firm	44	18	−26	15	23	+8
Being punctual	31	19	−12	15	12	−3
Working safely	22	5	−17	24	11	−13
Carrying out instructions	13	2	−11	18	12	−6
Working hard	12	3	−9	16	12	−4
Working conscientiously	11	4	−7	26	14	−12

(Derived from table 3, Coote and Kellner 1980)

TABLE 6.32
PERCENTAGE OF PEOPLE AGED 16 YEARS AND OVER
ABSENT FROM WORK DURING ONE WEEK, BY REASON FOR
ABSENCE, SEX AND AGE, GREAT BRITAIN 1978

	Own illness or accident		Strike/short time/lay-off		Personal and other reasons*		Total reasons*	
	W	M	W	M	W	M	W	M
Age								
16–17	5	5	0	∅	0	2	5	8
18–24	6	7	1	1	1	1	8	8
25–34	6	5	1	1	2	1	8	6
35–44	4	4	1	1	1	∅	6	6
45–54	5	5	∅	1	1	∅	6	6
55–64	5	7	∅	1	1	1	6	9
65 and over	3	2	1	1	1	∅	5	3
Total	5	5	1	1	1	1	7	7

*Excluding holidays
∅ = less than 0.5%
(Derived from table 5.10, *General Household Survey 1978* 1980)

the overall rate of absenteeism from work between the sexes. Within age groups there were marginal sex differences: of those aged 25–34, 2 per cent more women were absent; the same difference was true for those aged 65 and over. The sex difference was reversed in the age groups 16–17 and 55–64, where 3 per cent more men than women were absent.

Even if women had been shown to be absent more than men, it would be difficult to argue that this necessarily indicated less commitment to work on the part of women, since two other factors are involved. First, it is well established that low-paid and poorly trained workers, and workers in certain industries, have higher rates of absenteeism, so that differences in rates of absenteeism between the sexes probably reflect the distribution of the sexes by occupation and by industry. Second, the hours of some jobs may not have been designed to suit the needs of married women with domestic responsibilities, an idea supported by the lower rates of absenteeism among part-time and non-manual women workers, whose hours tend to be shorter or more flexible.

Women do, however, change jobs more frequently than men, as

table 6.33 shows. The higher female turnover results in part from the relative youth of the female workforce (young workers have dramatically higher turnover rates than older workers), though job mobility is actually higher for men than for women in the younger age groups (*Social Trends No. 11* 1980, table 5.12). Most if not all of the remaining difference in turnover can be explained by the fact that women are concentrated into unskilled occupations, which have high turnover rates for both sexes. Surveys often show too that women more than men leave jobs because of factors within the firm's control – for example, because they find the work unsatisfying (*General Household Survey 1978* 1980), or because of low pay or unsuitable hours (Wild and Hill 1970).

Regardless of whether or not there are sex differences in 'performance at work', a crucial element is employers' beliefs about such differences, and whether sex is used as a screening device. In the case of skilled jobs, a firm may decide to employ men, believing

TABLE 6.33
ESTIMATED PERCENTAGE OF EMPLOYEES WITH THEIR
EMPLOYER LESS THAN TWELVE MONTHS, BY OCCUPATION
GROUPS AND SEX, GREAT BRITAIN 1972

Women		*Men*	
Sales staff	32	Catering	29
Medical	26	Sales staff	23
Office and communication	23	Medical	22
Catering	22	Textiles	17
Textiles	21	Building, engineering	16
Other occupations	21	Other occupations	15
Building, engineering	20	Farming	14
Other professional and technical	19	Other professional and technical	14
		Office and communication	13
Academic	18	Transport	13
Technicians	17	Academic	13
Engineers, scientists	15	Security	11
Transport	15	Technicians	10
Security staff	15	Managers	8
Managers	9	Engineers, scientists	7
Supervisors	7	Supervisors	5

(Derived from table 17b, EEC 1974; source, table 133, *New Earnings Survey* 1972)

that their investment in training will be rewarded by continuous work over a long period. For less-skilled jobs, women are available as an 'industrial reserve army' to be called upon whenever male labour is in short supply (as in wartime or during the expansion of service industries in the 1960s) but which can be displaced from employment when no longer needed, since the institution of the family ensures that they will be provided for. Women's participation in family life has a further benefit for the firm, for their domestic commitments ensure that they are a 'secondary work-force' within a 'dual labour market', allowing firms to depress women's wage levels, and to succeed in doing this because women's lack of mobility reduces their range of alternative employment, while lack of time affects trade-union participation and action. Occupational segregation is accepted by most workers; this removes the possibility that women become dissatisfied by comparing their lot with that of men. The workforce is further segregated, since many women can work only part-time or even only at home, thus providing another basis for discrimination between women and men in terms of pay.

Economists have attempted to determine how much of the female/male wage differential is due to discrimination. Siebert and Sloane (1981) examined data from five different establishments. In only one were single women paid substantially less than single men with similar characteristics. However, Greenhalgh (1980) found in 1975 that, among people with similar educational and other back-grounds, married men earned 10 per cent more than single men, single men received 10 per cent more than single women, and single women earned 12 per cent more than married women. The extent of these differences had been reduced since 1971. The Royal Commission on the Distribution of Income and Wealth (1978a) used 1975 data to calculate the typical earnings, by sex and marital status, of people with similar backgrounds, finding that, among white people who left school at 15, after five years' work experience both single and married women would be earning over 90 per cent of the average wage of similar men; however, the earnings of women do not rise as fast as those of men, and this is true even for single women: after ten years' work experience, single women would earn less than 80 per cent of male earnings, and married women less than 75 per cent. Clearly there is a 'dual labour market', with white women and white men occupying different places within it.

ETHNIC MINORITIES IN THE LABOUR MARKET

It is often argued that the 'secondary workforce' is composed of a number of groups which when needed can be channelled into jobs of low status and pay, and that ethnic minorities as well as the majority of women are such groups. Ethnic-minority women in the labour market may have a double handicap and form a very distinct segment in terms of levels of participation and types of occupation.

In the older age ranges, males of the various ethnic groups tend to have economic activity rates that are very similar to each other, though in the younger ranges the male population of minority ethnic origin has a markedly lower economic activity rate than the rest of the population, partly because of the large number of students (Barber 1980). By contrast, the activity rates for women of minority ethnic origin are generally lower than those for women as a whole (*The Role of Immigrants in the Labour Market* 1976; Smith 1974; Barber 1980). However, although coloured women are less likely than non-coloured women to be economically active, those who do have a job are far more likely to work full-time. This is also true for women with children: coloured mothers with children under 5 work full-time far more frequently than do non-coloured mothers (Monck and Lomas 1975).

Work participation rates for white mothers with young children ranged in different towns from only 20 to 23 per cent, whereas the rates for coloured mothers varied to a much greater extent, from 13 to 33 per cent (Monck and Lomas 1975). These differences partly reflect the balance of ethnic groups within the coloured population of each town, for there is wide variation in the degree of participation of each ethnic group, as table 6.34 shows. Paid work is exceptionally common among West Indian women (74 per cent), but rare among women from Pakistan or Bangladesh (19 and 12 per cent).

In part, the differences in participation between the groups reflect their different age structures: all New Commonwealth minority ethnic groups are relatively young, with very few persons over retirement age, particularly among West Indians. Participation may also be affected by the length of time in the country, and female immigrants may have followed husbands to the UK after a considerable time lag, so that they have had less opportunity to enter an employment network. The tendency for individuals to take a job

TABLE 6.34
PERCENTAGE ECONOMIC ACTIVITY RATES, BY COUNTRY
OF BIRTH AND SEX, GREAT BRITAIN 1977

	Women	Men
United Kingdom	47	80
Irish Republic	54	86
Other EEC	55	88
Other Europe	50	79
Old Commonwealth	54	73
New Commonwealth and Pakistan:	53	83
West Indies	74	92
East Africa	58	78
India	44	83
Pakistan	19	89
Bangladesh	12	95
Rest of Commonwealth	51	70
Rest of world	43	67
Not stated or not known	52	81
All countries	47	80

(Devised from table 5.10, *Labour Force Survey 1973, 1975, 1977* 1980)

may also increase as the ethnic group becomes established. This is clearly relevant in the case of the West Indian community, and the longstanding recruitment of West Indian women by one employer (the NHS) may have contributed to their above-average participation rate.

In the main, though, variations in economic activity rates between different groups probably reflect religious and cultural factors. For example, Muslim women (a good proportion of Pakistani and Bangladeshi women) are more likely to be confined to the home and effectively excluded from paid outside work. Smith (1976) found that Asian women who could speak English were more likely to go out to work than those who could not; employers often tend to recruit only those with some knowledge of English, and this severely restricts the job chances of Asian women, since 59 per cent of them, compared with only 30 per cent of Asian men, speak English slightly or not at all.

The analysis of participation so far developed relies on traditional definitions of economic activity. It is possible that women of ethnic minorities, particularly if excluded from mainstream culture, may work from home or work intermittently for relatives, and so be classified as not in work even when they are (Monck and Lomas 1975). A second consequence of coloured women relying for jobs in their own ethnic community is that, when they do fail to find a job, they may not register at employment exchanges (Barber 1980).

It is important, therefore, to examine unemployment among minorities by looking at both registered and unregistered unemployment. The 1971 *Census of Population* showed that the rate of unemployment was substantially higher for minority-group women than for all women (9 compared with 5 per cent), and that this ethnic difference was greater than that for men (for whom the comparable figures were 7 per cent for minority men compared with 5 per cent for all men). This finding is broadly confirmed by table 6.35, particularly if one compares UK-born whites with non-whites born abroad. Despite the possible imprecisions in the figures, the table highlights the way in which the unemployment problem is acute among certain groups, particularly women from Pakistan and Bangladesh – which incidentally suggests that the low activity rate of this group may be partly due to lack of employment opportunities.

TABLE 6.35
PERCENTAGE UNEMPLOYMENT RATES,* BY SEX AND
ETHNIC ORIGIN (ENGLAND) 1977–1978

	West Indian	Indian	Pakistani/ Bangladeshi	African	Other	Non-white	White
Women							
Born UK	24	†	†	†	5.1	11.3	4.6
Born abroad	7.5	10.5	(25)	(12)	4.0	8.1	4.9
Men							
Born UK	21	†	†	†	9.5	12.3	5.3
Born abroad	9.2	7	8.6	6.9	5.1	7.3	6.1

* Including unregistered unemployed
† Less than 25 cases and therefore omitted
( ) = Based on numbers between 25 and 50
Note: Based on a 0.5% sample of private households in England, supplemented in certain areas (Derived from table 4, Barber 1980).

The employment of minority groups tends to be restricted to manual and less-skilled work, partly reflecting the concentration of those of immigrant origin into decaying central-urban areas. Both sexes of minority groups are excluded from higher-status jobs, but minority female skilled workers are very few in number indeed. Ironically, the exclusion from employment of women of Pakistani or Bangladeshi origin means that those who do have jobs tend to have work of comparatively high status. However, a very different picture emerges with those minority groups where participation is more common: in 1971 5.5 per cent of all females in Britain were employers or managers or professionals, whereas only 0.8 per cent of West Indian women had such jobs. In general, race interacts with gender further to depress occupational status. This is true even after taking into account differences in educational attainment: in a survey of 1971 school leavers in Sheffield and Bradford (Allen and Smith 1975), it was shown that half of the West Indian girls with CSE or O-level qualifications were employed in routine jobs, whereas white girls with equivalent examination successes were often in more skilled jobs.

Minority-group women are concentrated in particular occupations and particular industries, such as clothing; this factor has important consequences for conditions of work and pay. Whereas only 1 per cent of white women do night shift work, 7 per cent of those of Caribbean origin do so (Marsh 1979). Minority women tend to work in smaller establishments (Smith 1974), with all that this may imply in terms of degree of unionisation and amount of remuneration. Layard, Piachaud and Stewart (1978) suggest that belonging to the West Indian ethnic group is more clearly associated with a lowering of income levels for women than it is for men. In short, women of ethnic minorities stand even less chance than other women of gaining access to rewarding work.

LAW AND THE LABOUR MARKET

No analysis of the labour market would be complete without a consideration of the effect of the law on employment differences between the sexes. A number of laws apparently restrict the ability of employers to determine the levels of pay within their enterprises. Wage councils cover one-tenth of the country's labour force and fix statutory minimum wages in low-pay industries. The councils have potential to raise women's pay relative to that of men, since they cover one-quarter of all employed women. However, many firms pay below the agreed level, and the wages inspectorate of the Department of Employment can do little to enforce this law (Mackie and Pattullo 1977). More recently, the government has become involved in pay negotiations through the adoption of incomes policies. It has been argued that the flat-rate provisions of such policies during the 1970s favoured the lower-paid, among whom women were concentrated. However, the periods of free collective bargaining which followed such policies may have reversed at least some of the policy effects.

It might be expected, then, that the main legal weapon against the underpayment of women would be the Equal Pay Act. This states that a woman can claim payment equal to that of a man within the same firm doing the same or broadly similar work, or where the two jobs have been equally rated under a job-evaluation scheme. However, employers can subvert the intention of the Act by making extra payments which are more likely to go to men, such as those for long or unbroken service or shift work; they can also give a high weight in job-evaluation schemes to attributes such as physical strength, where men have a relative advantage, and a low weight to manual dexterity, where women have the advantage. Several studies (Office of Manpower Economics 1972; Snell 1979) have shown how employers have minimised their obligations under the Act, either by making it appear that women and men have non-comparable jobs (for example, male shop assistants have been found to be described in company books as 'management trainees') or by actually separating women and men into distinct categories of jobs, particularly by putting women on part-time work and paying them a lower hourly rate than full-timers. Women who work only with other women, mainly those in the lower-paid jobs, have no legal basis for any claim that their low pay arises because of the different treatment of their sex. It is no wonder, then, that in 1980 one-third of all applicants to industrial tribunals under the Equal Pay Act were from professional occupations.

It was partly to remedy this drawback of the 1970 Equal Pay Act that the Labour Government in 1975 supplemented it with the Sex Discrimination Act, which made illegal discrimination in employment with regard to entry, training, conditions, promotion and redundancy. Economists have argued that removing the inequality in occupational distribution (via anti-discrimination legislation) is not as important as removing inequality of payment (via equal pay legislation). This view rests on the kind of analysis presented above, where it was argued that inequality of wages is more crucial than unequal occupational and industrial distribution. However, it must be remembered that the Sex Discrimination Act may in fact be the key to reducing pay inequalities even within an occupational category, since potentially it can guarantee women access to the higher-paid grades. Moreover, if the Equal Pay Act could actually raise women's pay, then the Sex Discrimination Act would be vital to prevent employers making women redundant in the misguided belief that their productivity is less than that of men. Particularly in less-skilled occupations, employers do tend to hire and fire people according to the assumed capabilities of the group to which they belong, rather than according to individual merit. In principle, then, the Sex Discrimination Act is of great importance to working-class women.

In practice, however, it is as easy for employers to ignore the Sex Discrimination Act as it is for them to undermine the Equal Pay Act. According to the 1980 Equal Opportunities Commission Annual Report, during the previous two years 32 per cent of the complaints about discrimination in recruitment came from men, and, since 24 per cent were from organisations, only 44 per cent of complaints arose from individual women. The number of individual cases brought under the Sex Discrimination Act has fallen sharply.

Women have come to realise that the male-dominated industrial tribunals are not always in sympathy with the spirit of the Act. Moreover, a major problem for those alleging sex discrimination is that the burden of proof is on the applicant (by contrast with unfair dismissal cases where it is up to the employer to justify the dismissal). It has required much hard work and often many appeals by applicants to establish the existence of 'indirect discrimination', such as the age bars which preclude women from resuming a career after having children. However, it is almost impossible to establish the pertinence of 'informal' discrimination, such as male colleagues excluding women from their social life or fostering an atmosphere hostile to their employemnt. The EOC survey of employers (McIntosh 1980) found that one-third of men, as opposed to only one-fifth of women, had been recruited by 'informal' methods, such as private contacts or recruitment internal to the firm or enterprise;

discrimination within informal or internal labour markets is difficult to establish.

If individuals find it difficult to use the law effectively, then this makes more important the work of the Equal Opportunities Commission, which has power to make formal investigations into areas where it suspects discrimination and to issue non-discrimination notices to those who disobey the law: the Commission has, however, made little use of its enforcement powers and has been heavily criticised in the literature (for example: Hewitt 1980; Oakley 1981; Metcalf and Richardson 1980).

It seems unlikely that the law as it stands can do much to ensure that women are recruited into higher-status jobs. The Sex Discrimination Act does not require employers to produce a policy of equal opportunities, and in a survey the EOC found that only a quarter had written equal-opportunities policies, only 4 per cent had monitored progress on equality within their companies, and only 2 per cent had taken any positive action (EOC 1978a). A 1977 survey by a research team from the London School of Economics (*Equal Pay and Opportunities* 1981) did not find any employer who intended to make use of the 'positive discrimination' clauses of the Sex Discrimination Act, which allows special training for members of a sex that has traditionally been excluded from certain jobs. The Manpower Services Commission, with its responsibility for training, has only recently begun to provide training for special sections of the population; however, though it has identified as priority groups the young or long-term unemployed and racial-minority groups, it has failed to pay any special attention to the needs of women. The Sex Discrimination Act is of little use, since women tend not to apply for 'male' jobs (McIntosh 1980), and so affirmative action is needed to allay women's fears that they would be the 'lone woman' in a primarily male workforce, and ensure that women gain the qualifications and experience necessary for them to apply for higher-paid jobs.

In fact, a whole body of law precludes women from certain invaluable areas of experience. Since the armed forces are still segregated by sex, working-class men have more opportunity than working-class women to learn a trade. The protective legislation provisions of the Factories Acts limit shift work, night work and Sunday work done by women in manual occupations. The effect of this legislation is to bar women from certain high-paid jobs, such as those on car assembly lines; in certain cases, such as weaving, it has even led to women losing their jobs where factories have introduced expensive plant that needs to be worked 24 hours a day for profitability (*Guardian*, 29 April 1977); it prevents employers taking on women for certain apprenticeships because night work is required during the last two years (*EOC Annual Report 1980* 1981). The EOC Protective Legislation survey of women workers in inner urban areas reported the apparent determination of younger women not to let family commitments inhibit their intention to work shifts. None the less opinion is divided on whether the provisions of the legislation should be repealed (Coussins 1977; EOC 1979), with the Trades Union Congress and the National Campaign for Civil Liberties arguing instead for the extension to men of protection against anti-social employment conditions, at present a fairly unrealistic target. Surveys of employers also tend to suggest that legislation on shift-working is not a major obstacle to women's employment opportunities (Hunt 1975; McIntosh 1980).

These comments on the 'protective' legislation neatly point to a general conclusion that the law, framed as it is by a parliament in which the interests of men and of employers are paramount, is unlikely to be directed towards a serious attempt to erode the dual nature of the labour market. Women are channelled into secondary jobs because the values of society will then allow employers to deem those jobs worthy of lower rates of pay than would otherwise be the case, with concomitant rises in the earnings of men. Legislative concessions to the needs of women are enacted in the knowledge that such provisions will not lead to significant costs to employers – that is, will not radically disturb the status quo. Employers can be certain of this, since women are severely hampered in their attempts to undertake rewarding jobs by the domestic roles into which society socialises them. Business interests, then, find tolerable the passage of the Employment Protection Act granting women the legal right to return to work after the birth of a child, because the absence of genuine support from husbands and the failure of the state or employers to provide childcare facilities makes this right useless in practice for many women.

The lesson for women must be that it is not enough to campaign to improve women's position in law, nor is it even enough to press directly for the rights of women in the workplace. Instead, women must insist that men take an equal share in the burden of domestic duties, particularly in caring for children and other dependants. Only then will there be a genuine equality of opportunity for the two sexes in the world of work.

7

Political participation

Eileen Wormald

In discussing sex differences in political participation, it is important to remember that women have had access to the nation's political system as persons rather than personalities for only just over half a century; prior to 1918 they could make an impact directly only as monarchs or indirectly as influential political hostesses (Harrison 1978) and as the wives or mistresses of politicians. It can therefore be assumed that men have a historical base for political activity that is lacking for women, and the weight of the discussion must rest on the extent of women's penetration into a well-established male world.

The political role of women has indeed been a matter of increasing concern to students of politics since it became clear in the period following the 1939–45 war that neither the great hopes of the suffragettes nor the fears of their opponents about the impact of women on politics were being realised. There appear to have been two strands to the inquiries and discussions: why are so few women found in power positions, and what can be done about it? Committees in both the major political parties have sought to increase the number of women parliamentary candidates, the civil service as the executive branch of the government has made a detailed inquiry on the subject, and debates occur in parliament on the need to increase the number of women on public bodies as well as in the House of Commons. Yet still, while women appear to participate at the basic level of voting in equal numbers with men, beyond that there is a pyramid of participation, with fewer and fewer women to be found as one nears the top, despite the presence there from 1979 of a woman as prime minister. Explanations vary, from the presence of male-erected barriers to entry – for instance, at selection boards for local or national elected representatives, or in bodies that appoint paid employees – to differential role requirements of women (first as wife/mother, second as wage-earner and only then, additionally, as political activist), or to early socialisation into an apolitical role.

Some of the facts are indisputable; the number of elected members of parliament are published, and the small proportion of women there cannot be argued out of existence. Data on other aspects of political behaviour are more difficult to obtain, even more difficult to interpret. No figures are available on how women and men vote in elections, and none of the admirable annual Nuffield Election Surveys published relevant survey data on this until 1979. They then briefly examined the suggested 'conservatism' of women, a contentious issue in terms of both their stated voting habits and, even more, their opinions: myths, once created, die hard, and certainly where opinions are concerned data could probably be produced that on specific issues supported either side of the debate.

Again, detailed information is now annually published on the sex composition of the civil service, but for local councillors it is necessary to rely on summation of data in the annual yearbooks, or on analyses by Royal Commissions or academic inquiries. Explanations vary from quantified views of participation (as in the Maud Committee on local government) to inside assessment of the situation (Brimelow 1981, on the civil service). Explanatory difficulties are increased where the views are given of successful women on the reasons for their success (Phillips 1980, on women MPs), but the views of the unsuccessful have not been tapped.

The thrust of this chapter is to deploy such data as are available with explanatory text, but speculation about the reasons for women's political activity compared with men's is left to Chapter 9. The choice of the areas examined is either a conventional one, since that is where the data are available, or a decision based on limits of space. Thus the sections on 'The government' and 'Local government' look at elected members in politics, 'Public bodies' and 'The civil service' give information on paid and some unpaid appointments to bodies that execute political decisions, while 'Party membership' and 'Pressure groups' examine voluntary participation in political activity. Other important influences on the political process, the judiciary, industry and trade unions are to be found in Chapters 8 and 6, while some, for example the media, are left out because they would have required a lengthy theoretical explanation of diverse forms of political communication, as well as information on the sex composition of the communicators going beyond readily available sources (Hedblom 1981). Finally, 'Voting behaviour' looks at the most generally exercised form of political participation and, together with the section on 'Political opinions', discusses the supposed conservatism of women, while 'Political socialisation' examines some of the evidence about political learning.

PARLIAMENT: CANDIDATES AND MEMBERS

The vote was first given to women, if they were over 30, in 1918 (it was ten years later, in 1928, that they were given equal suffrage with men at age 21), and in the same year they were allowed to stand as parliamentary candidates after a debate in which one of their supporters, Lord Robert Cecil, advocated their cause with the double-edged words 'I think we should treat them as human beings with absolutely equal rights with men' (Brookes 1967). In the same debate Herbert Samuel accurately prophesied that 'It is rather more probable that too few will be elected rather than too many.'

Seventeen women stood for parliament in 1918 and one, Countess Markewicz, was elected, but as she was a Sinn Feiner she did not take her seat. So the first woman to sit in the House of Commons was Lady Astor, who in 1919 won for the Conservatives the Sutton division of Plymouth vacated by her husband on his succession to the peerage (Brookes 1967). Though a few women were elected in every succeeding election, there was no sharply rising curve of participation either as candidates or as elected members, and there have been only 108 women elected to parliament between 1918 and 1979.

Despite changing electoral fortunes of the two major parties, there have always been more women among the Labour MPs than the Conservatives, with the exception of 1970, when fifteen Conservative and only ten Labour women were elected (full historical tables of party distribution of women MPs are included in Conservative Women's National Advisory Council 1980). While the percentage of women MPs has fluctuated at around 4 per cent, as table 7.1 shows, the percentage of female candidates has risen gradually over sixty years to 8 per cent. This percentage varies between parties, with women comprising 4 per cent of Con-

TABLE 7.1
WOMEN CANDIDATES FOR, AND ELECTED MEMBERS OF,
BRITISH PARLIAMENTS 1918–1979

	Women candidates		Elected women members		
	Number	as % of male and female candidates	Number	as % of all female candidates	as % of male and female candidates
1918	17	1.0	1	6	0.1
1922	33	2.3	2	12	0.3
1923	34	2.4	8	21	1.3
1924	41	2.9	4	8	0.7
1929	69	4.0	14	20	2.3
1931	62	4.8	15	23	2.4
1935	67	5.0	9	13	1.5
1945	87	5.2	24	26	3.8
1950	126	6.8	21	17	3.4
1951	77	5.6	17	22	2.7
1955	92	6.5	24	26	3.8
1959	81	5.3	25	31	4.0
1964	90	5.1	29	32	4.6
1966	81	4.7	26	32	4.1
1970	99	5.4	26	26	4.1
1974*	143	6.7	23	16	3.6
1974†	161	7.2	27	17	4.3
1979	210	8.0	19	9	2.9

* February
† October
(Derived from appendix 2, Vallance 1979, and Conservative Women's National Advisory
Council 1980)

servative, 6 per cent of Liberal and 8 per cent of Labour candidates
at the ten elections 1945–74 (Le Lohe 1976).

The small number of women elected does not reflect any distaste
of the electors for women as against men candidates. Work carried
out between the two elections of 1974 showed that, where a party
put up a woman candidate at one election and a man at the other,
there was no sign that the sex of a candidate had any effect on
voting, except perhaps marginally among Liberals, who did not
appear to find a woman candidate as acceptable as a man (Steed
1975). While the general finding endorses the view of candidates
most succinctly expressed by the man who said 'I'd vote for a pig if it

wore a blue ribbon', the apparent prejudice against women among the Liberals is the more surprising, since it is among the minor parties that women have most chance of being both selected and elected proportionately to their male colleagues (Mellors 1980).

Despite the irrelevance of their sex to their electoral chances, women have to work a harder passage than men in order to obtain a parliamentary seat (table 7.2). The major parties have each attempted to ensure that there should be more female candidates (Lloyd 1963; National Labour Women's Advisory Committee 1971), but, though this has resulted in the occasional token addition of women to short lists of candidates (Rush 1969) and the doubling of the number of women candidates over the last decade, it has not substantially increased their chances of being elected. Women tend to get the 'worst' constituencies, and Dr Edith Summerskill is quoted as saying that it was not until 1955 that two women contested seats with a certainty of success (Currell 1974). In that same year it was suggested that a woman's chance of selection was only half as good as a man's (Ross 1955), and more recently it has been shown that in the February 1974 election women were less likely to be adopted for safe seats (table 7.3).

The prejudices of selection committees cannot, however, be held

TABLE 7.2
NUMBER OF FEMALE MPs WHO CONTESTED
PARLIAMENTARY SEATS PRIOR TO THEIR FIRST ELECTION
TO PARLIAMENT, 1918–1974, BY PARTY

Number of seats contested	Conserv- ative	Number of MPs Labour	Other	All parties	% of all MPs Women	Men
0	13	23	5	41	54	60
1	4	13	0	17	22	23
2	5	4	0	9	12	12
3	2	2	0	4	5	3
4	0	3	0	3	4	0.7
5	1	1	0	2	3	0.3
All women MPs	25	46	5	76		

(Derived from table 7.8, Mellors 1978)

TABLE 7.3

PERCENTAGE OF WOMEN AND MEN SELECTED FOR 'GOOD'*
AND 'POOR'† SEATS IN THE FEBRUARY 1974 GENERAL
ELECTION

| | *'Good' seats** | | | *'Poor' seats*† | | |
	Women	*Men*	*Number*	*Women*	*Men*	*Number*
Conservative	3.0	97.0	296	7.4	92.6	326
Labour	4.3	95.7	301	8.4	91.6	322
Liberal	3.8	96.2	159	9.5	90.5	358

* 'Good' seats defined as seats won, or, for the Liberals, where candidates came either first or second
† 'Poor' seats are those contested without success
(Devised from Le Lohe 1976)

fully to blame for the paucity of women MPs. Women do not present themselves for selection in the same numbers as men, and this is a major contributory factor to the disparity between male and female candidatures, with 1000 women compared to 22,500 men in the years 1918–70.

Profile of elected members

Those women who both attempt and succeed in jumping the hurdles tend to be slightly older than men (table 7.4), and their length of parliamentary service is normally shorter than that of men. In other ways too the profile of women MPs 1945–74 differs from that of men. Their occupations tend to be in the fields of 'communication' (like teaching and journalism) and not in industry, either as workers or managers. The categories of occupation in which there were at least 10 per cent of MPs during this period are shown in table 7.5. There are also differences in the educational background of women and men MPs, with the former more likely to have a secondary school/university education and the latter most likely to have a public school and/or an 'Oxbridge' background, as table 7.6 shows.

THE GOVERNMENT

The first woman to take office, five years after Lady Astor entered the House of Commons, was Margaret Bondfield, a one-time shop

TABLE 7.4
AGE OF MEMBERS OF PARLIAMENT* AT THE TIME OF THEIR FIRST ELECTION (PERCENTAGES)

	Women	Men
21–9	10	7
30–9	37	37
40–9	30	38
50–9	20	15
60–9	3	3
70+	0	0.1
Average age	43.0	41.5

* Elected during the years 1945–74
(Derived from table 7.9, Mellors 1978)

TABLE 7.5
THE OCCUPATIONS OF MEMBERS OF PARLIAMENT, 1945–1974 (PERCENTAGES*)

	Women	Men
The law	12	4
Teaching	27	10
Management	7	16
Journalism/writing	16	6
Housewife	15	0
Manual work	0	11

* Percentages do not add to 100 because only the six most common categories of occupation are shown
(Derived from table 7.12, Mellors 1978)

assistant who had left school at 13 and later became a prominent trade-union organiser and Chairman of the General Council of the Trades Union Congress. She was appointed in 1924 as the Parliamentary Under-Secretary of State at the Ministry of Labour in the first Labour Government; in the same year Susan Lawrence from a very different background, a middle-class intellectual who had taken the mathematics tripos at Cambridge, was appointed Parliamentary Private Secretary to the President of the Board of

TABLE 7.6
THE EDUCATION OF MEMBERS OF PARLIAMENT, 1945–1974
(PERCENTAGES)

	Women	Men
Any university	47	53
Elementary school only	14	16
Secondary school and university	33	19
Public school and Oxford or Cambridge	9	28
Any public school	29	48
Oxford and Cambridge	23	33

(Derived from table 7.11, Mellors 1978)

Education. In 1929 Bondfield became the first woman member of the cabinet as Minister of Labour, but it was not until 1945 that she was followed by another Labour cabinet minister, Ellen Wilkinson, and then in 1951 the first Conservative, Florence Horsburgh, was appointed Minister of Education but without a seat in the cabinet. From 1964 onwards there has always been one female minister and, on two occasions, two – first in 1968 when Barbara Castle was Secretary of State for Employment and Productivity while Judith Hart was Paymaster-General, and then in 1974 with Barbara Castle as Secretary of State for Social Services and Shirley Williams as Secretary of State for Prices and Consumer Protection. Up to 1975, however, there had still been only seven women cabinet ministers, and four of these had been Ministers of Education. Between 1974 and 1979, during the time in office of the Labour Party, nine out of nineteen women MPs were government ministers, with about one-third of them in office at the same time, the same proportion as for Labour men (table 7.7). This evidence suggests that the major barrier against women's entry into high political office appears at the point of entry to, rather than during, their political career.

It is notable that women have tended to be in offices thought to concern matters of particular interest to women (for example, education and the social services); a woman has never held the major offices of Foreign Affairs or Chancellor of the Exchequer. The designation of certain subjects as the province of women has been interpreted as an example of the setting of the political agenda

TABLE 7.7
THE NUMBERS OF WOMEN AND MEN HOLDING
PARLIAMENTARY OFFICE DURING THE YEARS 1945–1979

	Cabinet ministers		Ministers not in cabinet		Under-Secretaries		Parliamentary Secretaries	
	Women	Men	Women	Men	Women	Men	Women	Men
1945	0	8	0	34	0	10	2	21
1950	0	17	1	15	1	7	0	17
1955	0	18	0	16	0	11	1	16
1960	0	19	0	20	0	11	2	13
1968	1	23	2	31	2	15	1	19
					Women		Men	
1970	1	17	1	20	0		30	
1974	2	19	1	26	2		30	
1975	2	21	1	27	3		35	
1979	1	21	2	27	1		36	

(Devised from table 2, Currell 1974 (for 1945–68), and *Dod's Parliamentary Companion* (for 1968–79))

by men (Evans 1980). Women have, none the less, been accepted into full executive membership of the House of Commons, becoming Whips and Private Secretaries, playing a full part in, including chairing, committees, and one, a Conservative, Betty Marie Anderson (later Baroness Skrimshire), has sat in the Speaker's chair as Deputy Chairman of Ways and Means (Vallance 1979).

Although the Labour Party pioneered the entry of women into high office and Harold Wilson is reported to have been instrumental in recognising that women should be in the government as other than 'tokens' (Vallance 1979), it was left to the Conservative Party to elect in Margaret Thatcher the first woman party leader. Four years later, in 1979, she became the first woman prime minister, ironically in an election where women had the lowest percentage of seats in parliament since 1945. Though her potential electoral support was seen as lying preponderantly with women (Vallance 1979), her own election to the leadership was purported to owe everything to the activities of her male sponsors, and the essential 'patronage' role of men like Wilson and du Cann for the advancement of politically successful women has often been discussed in the literature (Currell 1974). Shirley Williams, for example, joined the Labour Party at the age of 15 but had already been befriended by Herbert Morrison (then Home Secretary), who made a point of acting as political patron to young women. She is reported as saying:

> I met him in an air raid shelter when I was 13. I got to know him quite well and he half adopted me. He used to invite me to have dinner with him at the Home Office. He said to me, it takes a lot of courage for a man to encourage a young woman to go into politics because it could be mis-understood. Most men would not want the publicity. Even more than they are now, men were reluctant to put themselves into that position. (Phillips 1980)

THE HOUSE OF LORDS

In the 'other House' women made an even later entry than into the Commons. Despite an early abortive attempt by Lady Rhondda to take her seat as a Viscountess in her own right in 1919, following the passage of the Sex Disqualification (Removal) Act, it was not until 1963 that women were admitted under the Peerage Act. Five years earlier the Life Peerages Act of 1958 had enabled both men and women to be granted non-hereditary titles. Between 1958 and 1970 twenty-five peeresses were created, and it has been argued that most have devoted a great part of their lives to political activity (Morgan 1975). By 1975 there were forty-three peeresses by succes-sion and creation, of whom some thirty-five attended regularly, compared with some 291 men out of 1062 who were eligible who attended more than one-third of the sitting days of the House (Morgan 1975). It has been noted that they play a lively part in debates, and, as in other spheres of political life, they appear to have a particular interest in matters of social concern so that, for example, they were active in pressing the Lords to amend a National Health Service Bill in order to provide free contraceptive services (Morgan 1975). On the whole, however, they do not appear a distinctive group except inasmuch as they carry fewer 'passengers' among their numbers than do the men. The composition of the House of Lords in 1981 is given in table 7.8.

THE EUROPEAN PARLIAMENT

In the first contest for the 81 United Kingdom seats in the European parliament held in 1979, 11 per cent of candidates were women, of whom 38 per cent were successful – six Conservatives, four Labour, and one Scottish Nationalist. This comparative success of women shown in table 7.9 was heralded by the views expressed in a 1978 survey of opinions by nationals of nine member states of the European Community (EEC 1979). In the United Kingdom a quota sample of 1351 respondents showed that a majority – 60 per cent of women and 45 per cent of men – thought it desirable that 'quite a lot of women should be elected to the European Parliament' as against 22 per cent of women and 36 per cent of men who thought it undesirable (the rest were 'don't knows'); only in France was there a larger majority of men (57 per cent) holding this favourable view and only in Ireland was the UK majority equalled among women.

TABLE 7.8
THE SEX COMPOSITION OF THE HOUSE OF LORDS IN 1981

	Women	Men	Women as % of total
Archbishops and bishops	0	26	0
Peers by succession	19	751	2
Hereditary peers of first creation	0	35	0
Life peers	40	276	13
All peers	59	1,088	5

(Devised from data supplied by the House of Lords' Information Office)

TABLE 7.9
THE SEX OF CANDIDATES AND THOSE ELECTED TO THE
EUROPEAN PARLIAMENT IN THE UNITED KINGDOM, 1979

	Women	Men	Women as % of total
Number of candidates	29	244	11
Number elected	11	70	14
Percentage of candidates elected	38	29	

(Devised from *Dod's Parliamentary Companion* 1980)

Moreover, the election of a high proportion of the women who did offer themselves as candidates endorsed the views expressed in the same survey about elections in general. Compared with other countries, where the main reason given why more women do not get elected to parliaments was that 'people prefer to vote for men', in the UK (and also in Denmark) the most frequent reply among both women (42 per cent) and men (37 per cent) was that too few women offer themselves as candidates.

It has been suggested (Stacey and Price 1981) that the relative success of women in this election was because the European Assembly is not seen as a prestigious or influential body, but it may equally be surmised that women were both more willing to put themselves forward as candidates and more likely to be selected where there was not a well-established tradition of male dominance.

PUBLIC BODIES

In other areas of national political life, information about sex differentials is difficult to obtain. No data are published on the composition of public boards, although all appear to contain a token woman. Maureen Colquhoun, speaking in the House of Commons on her Private Member's Bill on the Balance of Sexes, May 1965, said that according to her count there were 4500 jobs on 174 public bodies and corporations, councils and commissions and nearly all were occupied by men. Choosing some examples, she said:

I shall not be drawn into dealing with the more recherché areas of ministerial patronage. I shall merely draw the attention of the House today to some of the everyday bread-and-butter bodies that affect everybody's lives. For example, the Sugar Board has five men and no women. The Agriculture Training Board has 27 men, no women. Is it to be said that the only role of the woman in agriculture is that of the farmer's wife?

The Committee of Investigation for Great Britain has seven men, no women. I cannot think how Great Britain can be investigated without the help of women.

The Covent Garden Market Authority has six men, no women. I do not know whether that authority was responsible for the environmental damage in Covent Garden. If so, it might well have been improved with some women on the board.

The National Bus Company has seven men, no women. Of course, women do not travel on buses. Neither, apparently, do they travel on trains, because the British Railways Board has 12 men, no women.

What about the 14 male members of the Building Research Establishment Advisory Committee? Surely they need a little help from their friends. I suspect that there is one thing we can say for them. They obviously do not believe that a woman's place is in the home.

Among the 24 members of the Advisory Panel on Arms Control and Disarmament there are no women appointed, yet surely disarmament and arms control is a subject very much of interest to women. They ought to be there and they ought to be having a say. Or does the world of men still believe that 'They also serve who only stand and wait'?

I must confess that all is not entirely bleak. I was delighted with the appointments made by my right hon. Friend the Secretary of State for Prices and Consumer Protection, whose Department has just set up the National Consumer Council with 13 women and five men. That is something for the Guinness Book of Records. I suspect that it is the only Government-appointed body with a majority of women. (Hansard 1965, pp. 933–4)

The bill, which sought to increase the number of women on such public bodies, was not passed into law. Efforts to involve women in industrial tribunals led to an increase of 75 women on the tribunals in two years, so that by 1974, of the 1200 members, 125 (11 per cent) were women (Milburn 1976). In general, however, there is no record of how many women are members of the 360 public bodies, some like the Rent Assessment Panels having fifteen branches, which are listed in the *Directory of Paid Public Appointments* (1978).

LOCAL GOVERNMENT

The influence of comments such as those from Ruth Dalton explaining why she intended to leave parliament where she had been 'keeping warm' a constituency for her husband, Hugh Dalton – that she was returning to local politics because 'There we do things, here it seems to be all talk' (Vallance 1979) – has led to the frequent suggestion that women prefer local political activity to national politics. This has been argued both on pragmatic grounds, that it is easier for them to combine their supposedly primary role of wife and mother with the work of local government, as well as on the grounds that its concern with domestic and community matters is of immediate importance to them in that role. Chamberlain (1975) suggests that women on a parish council view their work as an extension of their interest and activity in village affairs, being about something concrete that they know and understand; but it seems unlikely that this view could as readily be held by women on the powerful Greater London Council, where they have constituted a relatively high proportion of the membership (20 per cent in 1975), and where it was noted that fears have been expressed about their impact (Sullerot 1977).

In comparing the relatively greater participation of women in local than in national politics, it is important to remember that they gained entry to local government well before any of them were first granted the parliamentary suffrage: the 1831 Hobhouse Act gave the local vote to all ratepayers, male or female, while the 1870 Education Act permitted the election of school boards by rate-payers of either sex, and women were not barred from standing as candidates (Smellie 1968). As a result, many years before 1918, women were active in local authorities (Middleton 1977). Their current contribution has been examined by two Royal Commissions: the Committee on the Management of Local Government (Maud Committee 1966–9) and the Committee of Inquiry into the System of Remuneration of Members of Local Authorities (Robinson Committee 1977).

Candidates and councillors

The Robinson Report was based on a sample of 6980 councillors out of a total of 25,741, and a 73 per cent response rate was achieved. This compares with a sample of 3721 for Maud and a response rate of 88 per cent. Robinson used the Maud data as baseline, so that comparisons could be made over the intervening decade. The report noted an increase of female councillors from 12 to 17 per cent of the total but commented on the continued underrepresentation of a group that comprised over 52 per cent of the total population.

Two years later Bristow (1978a) showed that 18 per cent of council members in English shire counties, 13 per cent in metropolitan counties and 11 per cent in Welsh counties were women; and more recently (Bristow 1980) he demonstrated that over all the local authorities there was a slight increase in the proportion of women councillors between 1974 (15 per cent), when there was local government reorganisation, and 1977 (17 per cent).

Although there is a much higher percentage of female candidates in local than in parliamentary elections, in other ways a similar picture of their electoral chances can be seen: women do not put themselves forward for selection at the same rate as men, and when they do they have slightly less chance of obtaining a winnable seat, but there is little evidence of bias by the electorate against women (Bristow 1978a). In contrast to parliamentary elections, the Conservative Party nominates many more female candidates for local elections than does the Labour Party (Bristow 1978a; Le Lohe 1976), as shown in table 7.10. As a result, it is in the Conservative-controlled districts, such as the counties of the South of England, that women fare the best. Bristow concludes that women's representation (except for London) is most closely associated with both affluence and Conservatism (table 7.11).

TABLE 7.10
COUNTY COUNCIL ELECTION CANDIDATES* IN ENGLAND,
1973 AND 1977, BY SEX (PERCENTAGES)

| | Candidates | | | | % of candidates elected | |
| | Conservative | | Labour | | | |
	Women	Men	Women	Men	Women	Men
1973	18	82	15	85	41	45
1977	21	79	15	85	37	39

* In a sample of eight county council elections
(Derived from Bristow 1978b)

TABLE 7.11
SEX OF ELECTED MEMBERS ON DISTRICT COUNCILS, BY
PARTY IN CONTROL OR IN FIRST POSITION, 1974 AND 1977
(PERCENTAGES)

| | 1974 | | 1977 | |
	Women	Men	Women	Men
Conservative	17	83	18	82
Labour	14	86	16	84
Independent	16	84	17	83
Others	17	83	15	85

(Derived from Bristow 1980)

Profile of local councillors

The age distribution of the two sexes in local councils in 1976 was similar, and in other features of the councillor profile – education, income, occupation, dwelling tenure – the sexes were also not differentiated except in so far as 7 per cent of women classified themselves occupationally as housewives in 1976, as they had in 1964 (Robinson Committee 1977).

The marital status of men and women is distinguished in the Robinson Report and shows that four times as many women (17 per cent) as men (4 per cent) are widowed, divorced or separated, and in this respect the sex differential accurately reflects the proportions in the total population. Although there is no British evidence on the point, it is possible that the Dutch findings on local councillors (Van Arnhem and Leijenaar 1981) – that for women much more than for men it is important, for continued political activity, that the family, both spouse and children, should accept their political activities – holds true in Britain, and that it is therefore easier for those without marital ties to be active in political life.

Local government activity

In examining the local government activity of councillors, the Robinson survey discovered that, while women spent slightly less time than men on council and committee meetings, they spent rather more time on dealing with electors' problems (table 7.12).

Women councillors also differ from men in the areas of council work they appear to find most attractive. In examining the offices held by women in English and Welsh counties, Bristow (1978c) showed that they most commonly chaired committees on the social services, education and amenities, and least often chaired policy, planning and transportation committees. An unpublished study by Bruce (Bristow 1978c) of a sample of 646 district councillors in Greater Manchester found a similar sex differential in *membership* of committees, women being found preponderantly on education and social services committees, and male membership being spread more evenly across all committees. It is not known whether this is the result of women's choice or whether these are the committees they are most likely to be offered because they deal with matters believed to be their primary concern (Evans 1980).

TABLE 7.12
PERCENTAGE OF TOTAL TIME SPENT ON COUNCIL DUTIES
GIVEN TO VARIOUS TYPES OF DUTY, BY SEX OF COUNCILLOR

	Women	*Men*
Council and committee meetings		
Attendance at	26	30
Preparation for	21	23
Travelling to and from	10	10
Other duties		
Party meetings	7	7
Dealing with electors' problems	19	16
Meeting organisations on behalf of council	11	10
Other	5	5
Total	100	100

(Derived from table 23, Robinson Committee 1977)

Local government offices

Just as fewer women candidates are elected than are nominated, so fewer of them become committee chairmen and fewer still attain the post of chairman, vice-chairman and leader of the council (Bristow 1978c). This was not so in 1964, when the Maud Report said of all types of local authority: 'Women are nearly as well represented (11 per cent) amongst the chairman [of authorities] as are men (12 per cent) . . . and . . . are just as likely as men to be chairmen of committees.' Bristow (1978c) shows that in 1977–8 only 7 per cent of women councillors held chairs as against 10 per cent of men, and these, as noted above, are predominantly in committees devoted to personal services (a pattern similar to the one of ministerial offices held by women in the national government).

There had, however, been an improvement in the number of chairs held by women in county councils between 1976 (9.8 per cent) and 1978 (11.2 per cent), and this may have been due to the swing to the Conservatives, since in local government this appears to be the party most favourable to the advancement of women (table 7.13).

TABLE 7.13
COMMITTEE CHAIRMEN OF ENGLISH AND WELSH COUNTY
COUNCILS IN 1976–1978, BY SEX (PERCENTAGES)

	Women	*Men*
Party in power		
Conservative	12	88
Labour	6	94
Independent	8	92
All councils	11	89

(Derived from Bristow 1978c)

Local government and parliamentary candidatures

Local government experience has often been considered an avenue to parliament for both men and women (Brown 1980). In 1974 some 40 per cent of the Labour members of parliament and 30 per cent of the Conservatives had been local authority councillors (Mellors 1978). Using data on all the 1758 MPs who have successfully contested one or more of the ten elections between 1945 and October 1974, Mellors produced a table showing their previous local government experience. A striking difference appears between women and men Conservatives, where almost 50 per cent of the women had served on a local authority compared with 25 per cent of the men. He concurs with an earlier view (Currell 1974) that, together with party activism and voluntary work, municipal experience ranks as 'probably the most significant pre-election experience' of MPs; and for Conservative women, in particular, whose chances of success in local government appear greater than for Labour women, it may be an invaluable way of establishing credibility in the political arena.

PARTY MEMBERSHIP

Information on the sex composition of the general membership and of the local and regional executives of the national political parties is not readily available. The Maud Committee on Local Government Organisation in 1967, investigating what they described as 'the community conscious elector', found in their sample of 989 men and

1195 women that 7 per cent of men and 8 per cent of women said they were paid-up members of political parties. In 1971 the National Labour Women's Advisory Committee report on women and the Labour Party said that 'although no analysis exists it appears that in the majority of constituencies, on the General Committee and the Executive Commitee, there are more men than women', and went on:

> The imbalance in the power position of men and women can be clearly discerned in Labour youth organisations. The 1971 Young Socialists Conference had only 25 per cent girls as delegates and there are no girls at all out of a total membership of 11 on the National Committee of Young Socialists. On the National Organisation of Labour Students, there are three girls out of a membership of 22.

Rush has estimated that over half the members of local Conservative associations are women, yet, in the selection committees he observed, only three out of nine members were women. He concludes that 'Whatever their numerical strength, women do not dominate selection, nor would it seem that their influence is commensurate with their numbers' (Rush 1969). The existence of separate women's sections in the parties, while sometimes a cause of controversy, has at least ensured women's presence in the national party executives and, as shown in table 7.14, was fundamental to their appearance in the chair of the national party (Vallance 1979). The NEC of the Labour Party has a 'closed' section for women, so that there are always at least five on that body; while the Central Council of the Conservative Party may be composed of nearly 50 per cent women, although the requirement is only that between one-third and a half should be women (Brown 1980).

TABLE 7.14
FEMALE CHAIRMEN OF NATIONAL POLITICAL PARTIES
BETWEEN 1926 AND 1979

	Conservative	Labour	Liberal
Number	16	13	6
% of all chairmen	30	26	11

(Devised from Conservative Women's National Advisory Council 1980)

PRESSURE GROUPS

Another major avenue of political involvement for women, particularly in the Labour Party, is through trade-union membership; the data are dealt with in Chapter 6. They also have the opportunity through such membership to participate in pressure group activity. It has been estimated (Shipley 1979) that there are some 2000 pressure groups and representative associations, but the sex composition of their membership is not published. Shipley includes information obtained by questionnaire on 600 groups; in the twelve that were listed as Women's Organisations, where it might be expected that the majority of subscribers would be female, there were 22,100 members. These figures excluded the 417,000 members of the Women's Institutes and the 210,000 members of the Townswomen's Guild, which, while they are non-political, may be an avenue into local political activity (Chamberlain 1975). It has recently been suggested (Evans 1980) that phenomena such as the Women's Aid Movement and the National Abortion Campaign demonstrate that women's political interest and activity are high when focused on matters of intense political concern but which are often thought to be outside or above the customary political agenda of party politics. Such activity may lead into a variety of byways, as with the Clean-Up TV Campaign (later the National Viewers and Listeners Association), which originated because its founder, Mary Whitehouse, felt that her personal representations to the BBC had impact neither on the programmes nor on the renewal of their charter. She decided, she wrote, 'Well, there's nothing left is there but for the women of the country to rise up and say that we have not borne our children nor built our homes to have them undermined like this' (Whitehouse 1967). That participation may follow protest has in her own case been amply demonstrated and in different but equally contentious areas may provide an example for other women who feel that the present agenda of 'politics' is devised by men and tends to ignore matters of most concern to women (Goot and Reid 1975).

VOTING BEHAVIOUR

Women were granted equal suffrage with men in 1928; for the previous ten years, from 1918, while all men could vote at the age of

21, women had to wait until they were aged 30, in order that they might not outnumber men at the polls in the aftermath of the death toll of the Great War.

Voting is the most basic and freely accessible level of political activity, and over three-quarters of the population in Britain exercise their suffrage at general elections: 78.8 per cent in October 1974 and 78.9 per cent in May 1979. No information on voters other than total turnout and votes cast for each party are published, and other information has to be obtained through opinion polls or academic surveys. There is little written about sex differential in turnout – which may be because it does not exist: an early analysis showed that, where non-voters and voters for other than the main parties were lumped together, they constituted 16 per cent women and 17 per cent men (Blondel 1966). Of greater interest and concern has been the party preferences of men and women: the idea that women are more Conservative than men appears in many texts (Pulzer 1967). Summarising the position, Rose (1974) concluded that 'because the two parties are so closely matched it is technically correct to suggest that an exclusively male franchise would give Labour a victory at every British general election and an exclusively female franchise would give the Conservatives recurring victories'. Using Gallup Poll data for 1970 based on a nationwide quota-sample survey, Rose showed that a Conservative bias could be located among working-class women (table 7.15). He explained this as partly a function of the longer life of women and the tendency of older people to vote Conservative, and noted that there is a particular preponderance of women of pensionable age among the working class. Other opinion polls have reinforced this explanation (Evans 1980), and it should also be noted that, commenting on earlier Gallup Polls in 1945–66 which showed a Conservative bias among women, Durant, the Gallup Poll director, said 'the [sex] differences are so small proportionately that sex has little accuracy as a predictor of the vote of an individual' (Rose 1969). A National Opinion Poll in 1978 found women favouring the Conservatives in each age group, but in 1979, although the Conservatives had a lead among women at the beginning of the campaign, by voting day they collected exactly the same percentage of women's and men's votes (table 7.16), and it was the men whose voting had swung proportionately more towards the Conservative Party since 1974 rather than the women, where the swing was towards the Liberals (Kellner 1980).

TABLE 7.15
VOTING INTENTIONS 1970, BY SOCIAL CLASS AND SEX
(PERCENTAGES)

	Conservative	Labour	Other	% of sample
*Upper middle class**				
Women	71	21	8	6
Men	70	23	7	9
Lower middle class†				
Women	54	34	11	13
Men	53	40	7	9
Working class§				
Women	41	48	11	34
Men	35	56	10	30

* Higher managerial/professional/administrative jobs
† Other non-manual jobs
§ All manual jobs
N = approx. 1000
(Derived from table 23, Rose 1974, based on Gallup Poll in 1970)

TABLE 7.16
VOTING IN THE GENERAL ELECTION OF 1979, BY SEX
(PERCENTAGES)

	Women	Men
Conservative	45	45
Labour	36	40
Liberal	17	12
Swing to Conservatives since 1974	4	7
Swing back to Labour during campaign	5	−1
All voters	49	51

(Derived from Butler and Kavanagh 1980; source, MORI poll)

POLITICAL OPINIONS

A related argument is that women hold more conservative views than men. There is some difficulty in defining such views as well as in locating either consistent or coherent opinions of individuals or groups (Evans 1980). In examining the issues of the 1970 election campaign, Francis and Peele (1978) used data based on the Butler and Stokes (1969) survey of a stratified sample of the adult population of the UK (excluding Northern Ireland), of whom 52 per cent were women. It appeared that while there was divergence along sex lines on most issues – for example, tax reduction against increased social service expenditure, and attitudes to immigration – there was a convergence of views among the younger age groups in which the sexes have shared a more common life experience than their elders (Francis and Peele 1978). Thus, in choosing between increases in social services or tax cuts, more women preferred the latter, and this 'conservative' tendency increased with age. On attitudes towards 'immigrants', on the other hand, there is a shift towards a more 'liberal' policy among the two youngest age cohorts of women to a level not reached by the men, but taking all age groups together there is little difference in attitudes of men and women (table 7.17).

TABLE 7.17
WOMEN'S AND MEN'S ATTITUDES TOWARDS TAX
REDUCTIONS, SOCIAL SERVICES AND NEW
COMMONWEALTH IMMIGRANTS (PERCENTAGES)

	Women	Men
Would prefer		
Tax cuts	68	63
Increases in social services	24	31
'Don't know'	9	6
Would		
Assist sending immigrants home	20.0	19.6
Allow to stay but stop further immigration	49.5	48.0
Allow in immigrant families and skilled workers	21.4	21.4
Other or 'Don't know'	10.1	10.7

N = 1845
(Derived from tables 5 and 8, Francis and Peele 1978)

On other matters – for example, withdrawal from Northern Ireland, continued abolition of capital punishment – no clear pattern of sex differential emerges.

Ten years later an opinion poll carried out by MORI in February 1981 produced similar inconclusive evidence on sex differences in conservative views. A national quota sample of 1911 respondents showed only marginal differences; for example, 2 per cent more women than men believed that more industries should be nationalised, and 5 per cent more men than women believed public schools should be abolished. There is some evidence that women are more conservative than men in their views on parliamentary institutions: the MORI survey of July 1980 showed that 45 per cent of men but only 35 per cent of women favoured abolition of the House of Lords.

In analysing a number of earlier NOP polls, Evans (1980) has equally shown that there is no clear pattern of more 'conservative' opinions being held by women than by men, and it is possible that data from other polls would produce evidence to be used on either side of the debate. It may be concluded, therefore, that there is no firm evidence for the belief that women are generally more right wing than men.

THE CIVIL SERVICE

The civil service is the executive branch of the political system and is a career entered into by appointment or competitive examination. As the modern industrial state has become increasingly complex, so have the civil servants become increasingly involved in the management of that state. The extent of their political power is now frequently under discussion, but women are absent from the public debate, since, although they constituted 39 per cent of all civil servants in 1979, they are mainly concentrated in the clerical group or in the junior grades of the executive and administrative grades (table 7.18).

In 1970 a departmental committee was set up under Kemp-Jones to consider the employment of women in the civil service and to examine ways in which the opportunities for their employment might be improved. It discovered that, although there had been an increase between 1950 and 1970 (table 7.19) in the percentage of women in all classes except the Science and Technical II, the num-

TABLE 7.18
SEXUAL COMPOSITION OF THE VARIOUS GRADES* IN THE
CIVIL SERVICE, 1979 (PERCENTAGES)

	Women	Men	Total Number†
Open structure levels‡			
Permanent Secretary	0	100	41
Deputy Secretary	2	98	158
Under-Secretary	4	96	615
Executive directing grades			
Middle band	4	96	52
Lower band	0	100	18
Administration group			
Assistant Secretary	5	95	1,155
Senior Principal	3	97	710
Principal	8	92	4,456
Senior executive officer	8	92	8,060
Higher executive officer (A)	28	72	387
Higher executive officer	16	84	22,382
Administration trainee	30	70	488
Executive officer	37	63	47,395
Clerical officer	65	35	89,436
Clerical assistant	79	21	75,329

* Staff's substantive grade at 1 January
† Part-time staff counted as half-units
‡ Includes period appointments
(Derived from table 4, *Civil Service Statistics* 1980)

bers were still small. Only in the clerical group had there been a striking increase, to the point where there were then about equal numbers of men and women in that branch of the service. When women do succeed in entering the civil service, it appears that they have less chance of promotion, as the report of the Fulton Committee (1968) showed by comparing the 1967 positions of women and men established before 1940; only 37 per cent of women compared to 70 per cent of men were in the upper grades. Brimelow (1981) suggests that any discrimination does not stem from promotion boards but from assessments of suitability for promotion, and that such prejudices may be most telling at the level of promotion to higher executive officer (table 7.20).

In their discussion of the reasons for the sex discrepancies in

TABLE 7.19
PERMANENT STAFF IN THE MAJOR CATEGORIES OF THE
CIVIL SERVICE, BY SEX, 1950–1970 (PERCENTAGES)

	1950*		1970†	
	Women	Men	Women	Men
Administrative	7	93	9	91
Executive	20	80	21	79
Clerical	35	65	50	50
Professional Science and Technical I	3	97	6	94
Science and Technical II	8	93	5	95

* As at 1 April, including Post Office
† As at 1 January, not including Post Office
(Derived from table 1, Civil Service 1971)

TABLE 7.20
WOMEN AND MEN* PROMOTED IN THE CIVIL SERVICE FROM
EXECUTIVE OR LOCAL OFFICER GRADE 1 TO HIGHER
EXECUTIVE OFFICER, 1976–1979

	Number promoted*		All promoted	Women as % of Executive officers	Local officers grade 1
	Women	Men			
1976	415	1,448	22	32	42
1977	367	1,577	19	34	45
1978	554	1,838	23	35	47
1979	497	1,457	25	37	48

* Part timers counted as half units
† Figures as at 1 January, and subject to updating
(Derived from tables 5 and 9, *Civil Service Statistics* 1980)

employment, the Kemp-Jones Committee (Civil Service 1971) found little discrimination against women but commented on the expectation that there would be unbroken service for all entrants until retirement – an expectation that militated against otherwise good conditions of service for women – and they recommended measures to help women to combine family responsibilities with a career. In monitoring the progress made in implementing the recommendations of that report, the department noted in 1975 that one-third of all entrants as administrative trainees (previously

Assistant Principal grade), who are usually graduates, were now women, a proportion approximately equal to the number of women graduating, while women entrants to the executive officer and equivalent grades averaged 43 per cent in the five years 1970–4 (*Civil Service Statistics* 1975). A slight improvement in promotion prospects for women, particularly among those with between five and nine years' service, was also noted, but voluntary wastage among women (12 per cent) is still more than twice that of men (5 per cent) across all age groups. As a result of the increase in the number of women entrants in the decade since the Kemp-Jones Report was published, there has been a considerable increase in the proportion of women in the administrative, executive and clerical grades (compare table 7.18 with table 7.19), but their chances of promotion are still less than for men (Brimelow 1981). There are currently no female Permanent Secretaries (the top grade of the structure), although there have in the past been three, Evelyn Sharp in the Ministry of Housing and Local Government (1955–6), Mary Smieton at the Ministry of Education (1959–63) and Mildred Riddelsdall in the Department of Health and Social Security (1971–3).

In her recent discussion of the position of women in the civil service, Brimelow (1981) has again concluded that, while there *may* be bias in committees that select for promotion, the most obvious explanation for their exclusion from top positions lies in women leaving or interrupting their careers to have children; a solution is sought in part-time work, childcare facilities or rights of reinstatement after child-rearing.

POLITICAL SOCIALISATION

The comparative lack of political participation by women has been generally acknowledged, and the argument, or myth, that women are less politically knowledgeable, interested and active than men has been described as the 'orthodoxy of women's lesser achievement' (Evans 1980). The idea of apolitical women has a long history: the nineteenth-century prime minister, Gladstone, thought that granting women the suffrage would 'trespass upon their delicacy, their purity, their refinement, the elevation of their whole nature', and as recently as 1955 Duverger wrote:

While women have legally ceased to be minors they still have the mentality of minors in many fields and, particularly in politics, they usually accept paternalism on the part of men. The man, husband, fiancé, lover or myth, is the mediator between them and the political world. (Duverger 1955)

This has often been explained by early differential political socialisation of boys and girls. Stradling (1978), in a nationwide survey of adolescents based on questionnaires administered to 4033 pupils in a stratified sample of 100 schools selected from grammar, secondary modern and comprehensive, of which 72 agreed to participate, located lower levels of political knowledge among girls than boys (table 7.21).

At an earlier date, however, Dowse and Hughes (1971) had not found significant sex differences in general political socialisation. They drew on a sample of 627 schoolchildren aged 11–17 years in the Exeter area; while finding that, controlling for education, girls tended to be less well informed politically than boys, 26 per cent of boys and 27 per cent of girls in secondary modern schools expressed interest in politics, while 44 per cent of boys and 43 per cent of girls in grammar schools classed themselves as politically interested. All other findings about sex differences in politicisation were ambiguous, and they concluded that 'boys and girls, in the Exeter state school sector, at least, are not obviously and grossly differentially socialised in terms of political attitudes'. And a recent inquiry using intensive interviews rather than questionnaires has disputed the existence of early political sex differences among working-class

TABLE 7.21
PERCENTAGE OF GIRLS AND BOYS WITH HIGH SCORES* ON
ASPECTS OF POLITICAL KNOWLEDGE

	Girls	*Boys*
Political office holders	29	51
Local politics	15	21
Political institutions	8	15
Issue awareness	18	28
International affairs	8	19

* Those obtaining high marks on a set of questions about politics
N = 1972 girls, 2061 boys
(Derived from table 21a, Stradling 1978)

adolescents in Britain (Wormald 1981). This would support the suggestion that questionnaires used in political knowledge surveys have a sex bias (Goot and Reid 1975), and that this accounts in part for any perceived sex differentials.

Further, it must be noted that the very concept of political socialisation as the manner in which humans 'learn their political behaviour early and well and persist in it' (Hyman 1959) has been under attack since its heyday in the 1960s (Marsh 1971). Even if girls did appear more politically passive than boys, there is no evidence to suggest a direct link between early political learning and later political behaviour. Adult experiences may have been a more potent influence in creating apolitical women. Greater female politicisation as a result of the increasing employment of women outside the home has been noted in America (Andersen 1975), and it seems probable that in Britain as in America sex differences in political activity are decreasing except at the level of holding political office (Verba, Nie and Kim 1978).

OVERVIEW

The general picture appears to be of increased political activity of women where access is freely open to them, but in any field where selection and competition is involved women still lag behind men.

Though this may be due to women's acceptance of a subordinate political role, what Lane (1961) has called 'the properly dependent role of her sex', it seems more likely that they are held back by the situational or institutional constraints, the demands of the dual role of mother and employee, together with the knowledge that politics is a man's game played according to rules made by and for men. The wife of Stanley Baldwin, the inter-war prime minister, summarised the position when she said of the House of Commons that it was 'essentially a man's institution evolved through centuries by men to deal with men's affairs in a man's way'. Yet women have broken into that male preserve, and it seems likely that, if women are made aware of the possibilities of entry into political life, are sustained in that effort to enter, and see increasing signs of success for the pioneers, they might obtain truly equal political participation in the nation's political system and no longer find that they have equal rights but, apparently, unequal opportunities to participate in public and political life at both national and local levels.

8

Involvement in crime

Erica Stratta

An examination of the official statistics over the past fifty years underlines the fact that women, in contrast to men, form a very small proportion of the criminal population. The effect of this was that for many years research was mainly carried out into crimes committed by men, as they constituted the majority of those involved in criminal acts, and generalisations, if any, about female crime were derived from this research. Women's crime was seen to be a kind of appendage to that of men.

Crime, however, is a social problem, unlike the other areas examined in this book. A continuing increase in crime, and of offences committed by women in particular, has not surprisingly spurred on the search for explanations and solutions to the problem. One result of this has been the increasing recognition in the 1960s of the sex variable as a contributory factor to criminal behaviour. Early research into this focused at the level of the individual, and sought to isolate supposedly innate female characteristics, such as passivity, specific bodily processes and low intelligence, as reasons both for the involvement of women in crime and the kinds of crime carried out by them (Pollak 1961; Cowie, Slater and Cowie 1968). This was often considered in conjunction with an underlying assumption that for women, unlike men, criminal behaviour was contrary to normal gender roles, and therefore pathological.

It is only very recently that this emphasis on 'innate' characteristics has been challenged, resulting in a shift from intrinsic and biological explanations of women's crime to an emphasis on the effect of the social structure of the society, and of the social processes. As a consequence, criminologists have focused on a different set of reasons for women's crime in contrast to that of men, such as the nature of women's employment opportunities, their lack of power, the sex stereotyping of the agencies of social control, and the fact that laws are defined by men.]The result of this radical change in emphasis has been to challenge the validity of the official statistics and definitions of illegal behaviour. These are now no longer considered as given, but have come to be considered as highly problematic, as much a reflection of the male-dominated processes of social control, and therefore of power relationships between the sexes, as they are an indication of crime in general, and female crime in particular, within our society (Rosenblum 1975; Smart 1976).

This chapter traces the shifting debate and also considers other important factors relevant to a discussion of sex differences in crime. It begins with an examination of the criminal statistics (these, however, are recognised as being problematic), moves to a consideration of 'the dark figure' and its implications for the official data, analyses the statistical evidence related to the processes of social control as exemplified by sentencing policy and penal institutions, and finally examines sex differences in relation to the experience of victimisation.

Thus the argument tries to suggest that the reasons for female involvement in crime are more complex than the evidence presented either by the statistics or by any one theoretical perspective.

SEX AND CRIME: THE OFFICIAL STATISTICS

It has already been pointed out above that crime is very much a male-dominated activity. A scan through the official statistics and the volumes of research into deviance as a whole, and juvenile delinquency in particular, confirms this. Table 8.1 gives details, over a fifty-year period, of the sex ratio of adult offenders. While

TABLE 8.1
PERCENTAGE OF PERSONS FOUND GUILTY OF INDICTABLE
OFFENCES, BY SEX

	1930	*1950*	*1960*	*1970*	*1975*	*1979*
Women	11	14	12	13	15	14
Men	89	86	88	87	85	86

(Devised from table 4, Smart 1979)

the proportion of women in comparison to men has risen slightly during this period, male offenders continue to account for approximately 85 per cent of all persons found guilty of indictable offences in England and Wales. Recent research in America has shown that the figure is over 90 per cent male, if the sample is limited to offenders who have experienced four or more previous arrests (Datesman and Scarpetti 1980).

Traditionally it has been argued that the low level of female involvement is one reason why they, unlike male offenders, have attracted very little attention until recently, either from researchers or from the public in general (Heidensohn 1968; Walker 1973). A further reason for this lack of attention may well be due to the fact that the kinds of crime with which women have been traditionally associated, such as prostitution, are often victimless. There is also a considerable emphasis on the part of the police and courts in linking female juveniles to what are commonly termed juvenile-status offences, such as truancy, moral danger and illicit sexual activity (which are illegal only because the offender is under age) – which means that female delinquency has tended to be seen as a relatively minor problem. (This is in contrast to the treatment of male offenders, whose behaviour is more frequently categorized as criminal offence (Ingleby 1960; Richardson 1969; Smart 1976).) This attitude has been reinforced by the fact that these types of behaviour are no longer considered once women have reached the age of 18.

The last decade, however, has seen increasing recognition of the relevance of the sex variable in any general theories of deviance (Simon 1975; Harris 1977). This is, in part, a reflection of the recent interest in women's studies and female emancipation; it is also related to the dramatic rise in the female crime rate (table 8.2) and to the subsequent speculation that, as women move into what has been traditionally a male-dominated activity, this represents a break from gender role behaviour. In the category of violent offences against the person (excluding sexual offences), for example, female crime rose by 192 per cent between 1969 and 1978 in comparison to 86 per cent in the case of male offenders. Further, the dramatic presentation in the media of the activities of women as members of radical revolutionary groups, and as gun-carrying hijackers and bank robbers, has heightened the public awareness of female deviance, and has mirrored the evidence that female crime is on the increase. Percentage increases, however, have to be

TABLE 8.2
PERCENTAGE INCREASES IN SELECTED CRIMINAL
OFFENCES BY WOMEN AND MEN BETWEEN 1969 AND 1978

	Women	Men
Violence against the person and sexual offences	188	65
Offences against property with violence*	44	4
Offences against property without violence†	57	19
Motoring offences	53	15

* Includes burglary and robbery
† Includes theft, handling stolen goods, fraud and forgery
(Devised from table 5.1, *Criminal Statistics for England and Wales 1979* 1981)

measured against the actual figures on which they are based. The number of female criminals in any single category is so small that the addition of a few hundred can represent a considerable increase when translated into percentage terms. By comparison, the number of male offenders has to increase by a much greater amount in order to make the same impact (table 8.3).

Table 8.3 indicates that the proportion of crimes of violence committed by women has more than doubled as a proportion of the total crime committed by them between 1969 and 1978. This is also true of criminal damage in the case of both women and men. On the other hand, there has been a slight decline for both sexes in the category of theft and handling stolen goods. The biggest differences between male and female involvement are in the two categories of burglary, and theft and handling stolen goods. It is important to note that comparisons with any figures on type of offence compiled after 1978 are difficult, owing to the introduction in 1979 of a new offence and tabulation procedure. Any comparisons with earlier figures need, therefore, to be adjusted to take account of this new procedure, otherwise the figures could be construed as revealing, after 1979, larger increases in certain types of offences than those which had in fact occurred.

The extent to which the figures for a single decade can be said to represent a new trend, however, is called into question when a more historical perspective is taken (Smart 1979). Table 8.4 indicates that the size of the increase in female offences since the mid-sixties is not

TABLE 8.3
OFFENDERS FOUND GUILTY OF INDICTABLE OFFENCES AT
ALL COURTS, ENGLAND AND WALES 1969 AND 1978

	1969 Women	Men	1978 Women	Men
Number of offenders				
Violence against the person	1,120	19,735	3,267	36,729
Sexual offences	31	6,466	51	6,489
Burglary	1,797	65,101	2,599	66,788
Robbery	138	2,388	196	3,161
Theft, handling stolen goods	33,290	153,528	51,976*	181,796*
Fraud and forgery	2,514	12,052	4,393	15,741
Criminal damage	834	18,474	3,091	41,929
Other (excluding motoring offences)	654	3,847	463*	5,393*
Total	40,378	281,591	66,036	358,026
Percentage of offenders				
Violence against the person	2.7	7.0	4.9	10.3
Sexual offences	0.1	2.3	0.1	1.8
Burglary	4.5	23.1	3.9	18.7
Robbery	0.3	0.8	0.3	0.9
Theft, handling stolen goods	82.5	54.5	78.7	50.8
Fraud and forgery	6.2	4.3	6.7	4.4
Criminal damage	2.1	6.6	4.7	11.7
Other (excluding motoring offences)	1.6	1.4	0.7	1.5

* The size of this figure is in part affected by the fact that, from 1978 onwards, offenders found guilty of 'abstracting electricity' were no longer categorised under 'Other offences' but under 'Theft and handling stolen goods'.
(Derived from table 5.1, *Criminal Statistics for England and Wales 1979* 1981)

unique, and that from time to time there have been considerable increases in these offences since the mid-1930s. This would seem to suggest that rises in the female crime rate cannot be attributed solely to the revival of the women's movement in Britain from the sixties onwards, and that the search for mono-causal explanations for female crime is as inappropriate as in the case of male crime. An attempt will therefore be made to indicate some of the other variables that need to be taken into account in any consideration of the interrelationship between male and female crime rates as recorded in the official statistics.

TABLE 8.4
PERCENTAGE INCREASES AND DECREASES IN PERSONS
FOUND GUILTY OF INDICTABLE OFFENCES, OVER FOUR
DECADES

	1935–46		1946–55		1955–65		1965–75	
	Women	Men	Women	Men	Women	Men	Women	Men
Violence against the person	+94	+70	−30	+108	+111	+102	+225	+100
Offences against property with violence	+365	+199	+97	+74	+129	+176	+149	+55
Offences against property without violence	+68	+32	−5	−0.7	+127	+84	+66	+46
All indictable offences	+68	+46	−1.5	+14	+121	+103	+95	+83

(Derived from table 3, Smart 1979)

The limitations of the official statistics as sources of evidence on the extent and form of criminal behaviour in a society are, however, well recognised (Kitsuse and Cicourel 1963; Wiles 1970). The figures given so far relate to offences known to the police which have subsequently been cleared up. They do not, therefore, include crimes that have not been reported or recorded by the police, or crimes that have not been traced to particular offenders. These crimes are classified by criminologists as 'the dark figure', since they are not recorded in the official statistics. The relationship between the official statistics and 'the dark figure' is unknown, and it is therefore open to speculation whether an increase in the official statistics merely represents a shift from 'the dark figure' into the recorded statistics or is, in fact, an actual increase. Thus any examination of sex differences with regard to the committing of crime, or speculation about changes in that relationship, must clearly take into account the evidence related to 'the dark figure', as revealed by self-report studies. This is discussed in the following section.

THE EFFECT OF 'THE DARK FIGURE'

The existence and extent of unreported, unrecorded crime ('the dark figure') has been recognised for some time as being relevant to any consideration of sex differences in crime rates. For example,

Pollak (1961) argues that the actual extent of female criminality is comparable to male but that this fact is masked in the official statistics because of women's position in the home and family, resulting in their leading a more privatised existence in comparison to men.

Pollak's theorising has been followed by several attempts to measure 'the dark figure' in relation to sex differences in criminal behaviour, particularly in the case of juveniles (Jensen and Eve 1976; Campbell 1977; Wise 1967). The technique used is known as self-report, a method of questioning whereby respondents are asked to indicate which of a variety of activities, legal and illegal, they have been involved in. It thus seeks to eliminate bias and filtering, which occurs when police and welfare reports are the sole source of evidence concerning illegal behaviour. In this form of research, however, the effects of lying have to be taken into account, but the results suggest that only a small proportion of the responses are lies (approximately 11 per cent: Campbell 1977), and that there is no sex difference in the extent of lying (Mawby 1980). This is obviously relevant to any consideration of the extent of, and reasons for, sex differences in criminal behaviour which emerge from self-report studies.

The results of these anonymous, self-report studies have, however, confirmed that, while there is a difference between male and female involvement in crime, it is not as great as when the official statistics are the sole source of evidence. The latter indicate a ratio in the case of juvenile delinquents of between four and six boys committing an offence for every one girl, and for more serious crimes a ratio of 7:1 (Cowie, Slater and Cowie 1968), whereas the results of the self-report studies show the ratio to be more even. Campbell (1977), for example, after averaging all the offences in her study, found that the boy to girl self-admission ratio was 1.12:1; and Wise (1967) concluded that boys and girls participated almost equally in sexual offences (50.1 per cent boys, 49.9 per cent girls) and alcohol offences (50.8 per cent boys, 49.2 per cent girls), and that, whereas there was not equal participation in other offences, differences were less than those reported in the official statistics. A recent study in Sheffield (Mawby 1980), using the self-report method, found that on a checklist of nineteen items there was a consistent difference between the sexes in the level of involvement, with a higher proportion of boys than girls committing the offence in fourteen out of the fifteen items listed (table 8.5). An interesting point to emerge from the data below is that within several of the broad categories there are sex differences. In the case of 'vandalism' the only offence in which there was not a significant difference between the sexes was 'graffiti', which could be characterised as relatively non-violent and victimless.

In considering the evidence from self-report studies in relation to sex differences, it is obviously important to bear in mind the choice of incidents that respondents are asked to consider. In the Sheffield study (Mawby 1980) the sample was not asked to record their

TABLE 8.5
PERCENTAGE OF EACH SEX SAYING THEY HAD COMMITTED
VARIOUS OFFENCES

	Girls	Boys
Corporate theft		
From building site	8	41
Shoplifting	39	54
From school	44	42
From kiosks, machines, etc.	4	10
Burglary		
Housebreaking	1	6
Burglary of shop, school, factory, etc.	1	12
Breaking into empty building	8	37
Attempted breaking offence	5	19
Vandalism		
Breaking window, property, etc.	18	53
Graffiti	46	49
Firework vandalism	5	33
Arson	5	14
Violence		
Hit or kicked causing bruising or bleeding	50	64
Robbery by threat	12	25
Violence using a weapon	8	19

N = 266 girls, 340 boys
(Derived from table VI, Mawby 1980)

participation in sexual offences or those involving alcohol. These are both categories in which female offenders have been shown to have a high proportion in relation to males (Wise 1967), and this must affect any comparison between women and men for offences over all.

THE PROCESS OF SOCIAL CONTROL

The discrepancy between the official figures and self-report studies has led some researchers to suggest that there are double standards of morality operating in the courts, depending on the sex of the offender. This, it is argued, is the result of gender-role expectations on the part of the police, social workers and the judiciary, who have a tendency to see female deviance as being in the main related to sexual behaviour and male deviance to be concerned with a wider range of indictable offences (Smart 1976). This argument would seem to be confirmed by figures such as those related to the juvenile-care proceedings for the United Kingdom in 1973 (Smart 1976, table 1.3(a)). These show that, in the age group 10–17, 87 per cent of girls, as compared to 12.4 per cent of boys, were put into care for reasons of exposure to moral danger; and 20 per cent more girls than boys were put into care for being beyond parental control. It is also interesting to note that both these categories are status offences and are therefore limited to juveniles. In the case of indictable offences, however, the position is reversed, with 63 per cent of boys being put into care because of an indictable offence, as compared to 37 per cent of girls.

Further support for the argument that double standards of morality operate in the courts is also to be found in the research into juvenile delinquents in institutions. This has shown that concern about the sexual behaviour of female offenders results in a higher proportion than males being referred to the care of social workers, and being committed to institutional care, even though, by comparison with males, their records of delinquency are less extensive. A study by Terry (1970) revealed that girls committed only 18 per cent of all the offences in the police records but were responsible for nearly 50 per cent of the charges related to sexual offences and being beyond parental control. Richardson (1969), in a study of girls in approved schools, pointed out that only 24 per cent of her female sample were admitted for criminal offences, the majority being admitted for reasons of moral danger or because they were in need of care and protection. In the case of boys, however, 95 per cent were sent to an approved school because they had committed an indictable offence (Ingleby 1960). Further, over one-third of Richardson's female sample were institutionalised after a single court appearance, whereas in the case of boys long-term institutionalisation of a first offender was found to be a rare occurrence (Stratta 1970). Further evidence of differential processing in a recent report (NACRO 1977) showed that female juvenile first offenders were five times more likely to be sentenced to an institution than male juvenile first offenders.

On the basis of this evidence, therefore, it is suggested that the discrepancy between the official and self-report figures, in male and female criminal involvement, can be accounted for to some degree by the perception and processing of the deviant on the part of the agents of social control. The evidence suggests a dual standard in relation to the treatment of male and female juvenile delinquents, which is reflected in the fact that girls are sentenced largely on the basis of their potential for delinquency, and boys as a result of being found guilty of an indictable offence.

The numbers of women and men in those agencies responsible for the processing of offenders would therefore seem relevant to the overall discussion. As can be seen from table 8.6, these are male dominated – which, as will be subsequently argued, has certain implications for the processing of offenders, not least in the stereotyping of offenders on the basis of sex. It will be argued that

TABLE 8.6
SEX COMPOSITION OF AGENCIES RESPONSIBLE FOR
PROCESSING CRIMINALS

| | Number | | Percentage | |
	Women	Men	Women	Men
Police	11,843	115,987	9	91
Probation officers	1,744	3,289	35	65
Magistrates	9,543	15,141	39	61
High Court and circuit judges	6	467	1	99

(Devised from table 4.1, *Annual Abstract of Statistics* 1981; table 10, EOC 1978b; and correspondence with the Magistrates' Association and the Lord Chancellor's private office)

the proportion of women and men in the agencies of social control is relevant to any consideration of the relationship between female and male crime rates, and the relationship between the sex of the offender and the particular categories that are applied to certain forms of criminal behaviour.

It is interesting, for example, to speculate on what might be the effect in the future of the fact that the number of women police officers has increased by 145 per cent over the past nine years, compared to a 13 per cent increase in the number of male officers (*Annual Abstract of Statistics* 1981). In relation to prostitution, for example, women police officers have been observed to be much more scrupulous than men in following the letter of the law; this could result in an increase in arrests for this offence (Cunnington 1980).

FEMALE AND MALE INVOLVEMENT IN CRIME

Figures for offenders found guilty of a particular category of offence (table 8.7) indicate that for both sexes the highest number of offences are concerned with motoring. This is also the category in which, over the past ten years, there has been the second largest increase in convictions for both sexes together. Examination in more detail of the global figure for motoring offences shows that the sex ratio is not evenly distributed. Twice as many men (15 per cent) as women (7 per cent) are convicted of dangerous driving offences, and among men there are 11 per cent more convictions for driving while disqualified. The other categories in table 8.7 embrace a wide range of offences, and it is only after a close examination of the kinds of offence that fall within each of these categories that further sex differences begin to emerge. These differences are also seen when one examines the ways in which similar crimes are carried out by each sex. Pollak (1961) argues that 'Women commit all types of crime, but their procedure is different to that used by men in their criminal pursuits.'

One reason why differences arise is the existence of crimes which by reason of their legal definition are sex-specific. Examples of these, within the overall category of sexual offences, are the crimes of rape (which can be committed only by men) and prostitution (which can be committed only by women). The English law clearly recognises that both men and women can be prostitutes, for it is an

TABLE 8.7
FEMALE AND MALE OFFENDERS FOUND GUILTY, ENGLAND
AND WALES 1969 AND 1979

| | *1969* | | *1979* | |
	Women	*Men*	*Women*	*Men*
Number of offenders				
Offences against the person (violence and sexual offences)	1,151	26,201	3,940	51,925
Offences against property with violence (burglary, robbery)	1,935	67,489	2,399	59,919
Offences against property without violence (theft, handling stolen goods, fraud and forgery)	35,804	165,580	52,555	188,929
Other (including criminal damage)	38,674	323,041	56,584	380,298
Motoring offences	60,947	885,906	93,171	1,008,432
Total	138,511	1,468,217	208,649	1,689,503
Percentage of offenders				
Offences against the person	0.8	1.8	1.9	3.1
Offences against property with violence	1.4	4.6	1.4	3.5
Offences against property without violence	26	11	25	11
Other	28	23	27	23
Motoring offences	44	60	45	60

(Derived from table 5.1, *Criminal Statistics for England and Wales 1979* 1981)

offence for either sex to live off the earnings of a male or female prostitute. However, the single category 'offence by prostitute', in the official statistics, contains figures only in the column headed 'female', which in 1979 were shown as 3014, compared to a nil figure in the male column. Charges of male prostitution, however, are placed in a different legal category, described as 'soliciting by', or 'indecency between males'. This use of a different category for the same offence, depending on the sex of the offender, would seem an obvious example of the differential processing of women and men by the police and other agents of social control.

It is also widely recognised that some crimes can be described as sex-related (Pollak 1961; Smart 1976; Caplan 1980). In the case of these crimes the level of involvement of a particular sex is higher than their involvement in other offences. A comparison between female and male involvement in a group of sex-related offences is given in table 8.8. Further evidence of the sex-specific nature of certain offences is given in table 8.9, where the statistics for shoplifting offences over the past decade show that, unlike the majority of

TABLE 8.8
SOME EXAMPLES OF SEX-RELATED CRIME 1969–1979

	Female offenders as % of all those found guilty	Male offenders as % of all those found guilty	Number of persons found guilty
Offence by prostitute and related offences*	79	21	3,924
Shoplifting	45	56	72,525
All larceny	22	78	220,569
Car theft	3	97	38,371
All burglary	4	96	59,130

* Includes 'aiding offence by prostitute', 'brothel keeping' and 'soliciting by a male'
(Devised from table 1.2(a), Smart 1976; and *Criminal Statistics for England and Wales 1979* 1981)

TABLE 8.9
RATE PER 100,000 OF THE POPULATION OF WOMEN AND MEN
IN ENGLAND AND WALES FOUND GUILTY OF SHOPLIFTING,
1969–1979

	1969	1970	1971	1972	1973	1974	1975	1976	1977	1978	1979
Women	83	87	92	93	90	111	125	138	147	140	128
Men	72	80	89	94	94	124	142	155	176	167	168

(Derived from table 1.1, Smart 1976; and *Criminal Statistics for England and Wales 1979* 1981)

criminal offences, the number of women found guilty has at times exceeded that of men. Sex differences also emerge in relation to the kind of items stolen and their value; women tend to shoplift items of lower value (Gibbens and Prince 1962). This suggests that female involvement may well be higher than that recorded in the official figures, since petty shoplifting is an offence where retailers have traditionally not brought charges against offenders because of the time-consuming prosecution procedures.

Further types of crime where women have a higher involvement than in other offences (table 8.10) are offences against children, theft by an employee, theft from an automatic machine or meter, handling stolen goods, blackmail, forgery, and violence against members of one's own family (Wolfgang 1958; Pollak 1961; Smart 1976). Crimes where men predominate are breaking and entering, homicide, and violent offences against persons unknown.

TABLE 8.10
SEX COMPOSITION OF OFFENDERS, BY TYPE OF OFFENCE, 1979

| | Number of offenders | | Percentage of offenders | |
	Women	Men	Women	Men
Murder	10	126	7	93
Attempted murder	1	26	4	96
Other wounding*	3,484	41,541	8	92
Theft by employee	1,990	9,174	21	79
Theft from a machine	747	2,817	21	79
Handling stolen goods	2,971	18,846	14	86
Forging and uttering	1,160	2,554	31	69
Child stealing	4	11	27	73
Cruelty to a child	86	57	60	40
Drunkenness, simple	3,916	48,358	8	92
Drunkenness with aggravation	4,266	49,082	8	92
Social security offences	4,307	10,202	30	70
Other motoring offences[†]	90,857	920,733	9	91

* Refers to wounding other than that endangering life
[†] Refers to offences excluding driving or being in charge of a vehicle while unfit, reckless or dangerous driving, and driving while disqualified
(Derived from categories from table 1.4, Smart 1976, and data from *Criminal Statistics for England and Wales 1979* 1981)

These differences would seem to be related to traditional gender roles, 'female' crime being concerned with those kinds of behaviour that do not require a great deal of strength and reflect feminine concerns and women's more privatised existence; 'male' crime, on the other hand, requires more force and specialised skill, and reflects a greater access to the public arena, as exemplified in male dominance in crimes such as car theft and burglary.

In the case of juveniles, sex differences relating to the charges brought have already been referred to (p. 212). Further differences in the type of offence can also be seen in the results of a recent large-scale Canadian research (Caplan 1980). Here the proportion of boys (12 per cent) charged with some form of violent offence against property was much higher than the proportion of girls (3 per cent); this was also the case when the value of the property stolen was in excess of $200. The pattern was, however, reversed in the case of truancy, where the proportion of girls involved (20 per cent) was twice as high as the proportion of boys (10 per cent).

SEX AND CRIME: THEORETICAL EXPLANATIONS

Theoretical explanations for the differences between women and men in criminal behaviour, which have attempted to look behind the surface manifestations, have concentrated, first, on variables that can be said to operate with differential effects on women and men and, second, on the reaction to, and processing of, women and men whose deviance is similar. These theoretical attempts would seem to fall into four broad headings: biological and physiological; socialisation; sub-cultural; social interaction (Davies 1980).

Biological and physiological

Researchers concerned with biological and physiological explanations argue that the sex differences in criminal behaviour can be traced to basic biological differences between women and men, and the consequent adaptive learning (Pollak 1961). Other researchers have sought to establish the particular variables that distinguish the deviant from the non-deviant, and in particular the characteristics that are sex-related. Thus Cowie, Slater and Cowie (1968) point to such variables as the below-average intelligence of their sample of delinquent girls and their widespread educational retardation; the higher incidence of broken homes than in a comparable group of delinquent boys; and the fact that a large proportion of their sample (52 per cent) were diagnosed as psychiatrically abnormal. This latter fact, they suggest, indicates that the behaviour of delinquent girls was likely to be affected by psychiatric abnormality, in contrast to social factors in the case of boys. This point is emphasised by Konopka (1966), who concludes that female delinquents are more abnormal than male delinquents in that, for females, delinquent behaviour is the result of a confused or masculine sex-role identity; it is a perversion of their natural role.

Socialisation

Researchers concerned with socialisation explanations argue that differences in criminal behaviour can be traced to the differential experience of women and men, which in turn reflects gender-role typifications and expectations. Thus the family is seen as having a major influence, for example in its sex-related emphasis on aggressive or non-aggressive behaviour, the effects of which can be borne out in sex differences in criminal behaviour. This is offered as an explanation of why men predominate in crimes involving violence, physical strength and skill, whereas women are more involved in crimes requiring less physical strength, and are also to be found in secondary supportive roles in traditional male crime, such as robbery (Wolfgang 1958; Hoffman-Bustamente 1973). Further sex differences in criminal behaviour, it is argued, are the result of a greater emphasis on conformity in female socialisation, and the fact that parents exercise more control over their daughters than their sons (Newson and Newson 1976). Thus boys are not discouraged from delinquency-related, risk-taking behaviour in the same way as girls, since this is seen as much more appropriate to their sex and status (Hagan, Simpson and Gillis 1979).

Sub-cultural

Sub-cultural causes were a major research concern, particularly throughout the fifties and sixties, in the search for an explanation of male juvenile delinquency; researchers emphasised the effects of a closely knit, single-sex, delinquent gang upon the behaviour of individual members (Downes 1966; Gill 1977). Some theorists hypothesised that gang membership was a consequence of the frustrations of male working-class adolescents at their lack of occupational mobility; the delinquent gang was postulated as an alternative means of achieving status (Cohen 1955; Cloward and Ohlin 1960). Empirical studies have not totally supported this hypothesis, and have put forward alternative explanations for the existence of the male delinquent gang. Downes (1966) stressed the influences of adolescent culture, while Gill (1977) emphasised the complex inter-relationship of particular structural determinants, such as housing policy, low income and the effects of an inner-city social environment. In the case of girls, there is as yet no evidence to suggest that the single-sex gang is relevant to an explanation of female delinquency. Adolescent girls would appear to be more concerned with attracting boys, and are therefore found as members of male-dominated groups in which they nevertheless take an active part (Shacklady-Smith 1978). It is suggested, therefore, that sex differences in gang membership reflect different focal concerns; for women, status is achieved through association with men which in turn is a reflection of the inequalities between the sexes existing within society as a whole.

Social interaction

In this approach explanations are related to the social interaction between the deviant and non-deviant and are concerned with differences in the application of rules and the processing of deviants. Such studies have found considerable sex differences (whether informally as related to social interaction, or formally through the legal system), as this chapter has already indicated. This has been demonstrated in the discussion of sex differences revealed when comparing the official statistics with self-report studies – in the examination by sex of the proceedings brought under the Children and Young Persons Act (1969) (Smart 1976; and see pp. 212–13 above), and in the research of Terry (1970), related to sexual offences and parental control, and Richardson (1969), who examined the criteria for sentencing female juveniles to institutions. Additional evidence on the processing of adult offenders is provided by recent research in the United States into court proceedings in New York State. It concluded that women were less likely than men to spend time in prison, either awaiting sentence or after a conviction; and if convicted they were less likely than men to receive the more severe sentences (Nagel 1981). In addition to the official agencies of social control, this chapter has also made reference to the different socialisation processes of women and men within the family (Newson and Newson 1976; Hagan, Simpson and Gillis 1979).

It is argued by some criminologists, however, that to concentrate as these studies have done on interaction at the micro-level, with its consequent emphasis on sexism and stereotyping, as reasons for female/male differences, is to ignore the underlying assumptions and structure of the society as a whole. Thus Greenwood (1981) maintains that the reasons for the differences between women and men in criminal behaviour are located in the power of the state, which through its economic, political and legal institutions determines relationships between the sexes, as well as their division of labour.

In conclusion, it would seem that on the basis of the research to date the most fruitful line of inquiry, in relation to explanations of criminal differences between women and men, is that which stresses, at the macro-level, the regulatory control on the relations between the sexes wielded by the institutions of a society, in conjunction with the process of socialisation and interaction at the micro-level.

SENTENCING POLICY

As is evident from the types of sentences shown in table 8.11, the police and the courts have a wide range of sentences from which they can select in dealing with individual offenders. These range from a caution (a non-custodial sentence) at one end of the spectrum to a Borstal or prison sentence (a custodial sentence) at the other end.

In arriving at a decision about the sentencing of a particular offender, the courts take into account easily quantified criteria, such as the type of crime committed, the existence and length of previous criminal records, and the experience (if any) of particular types of sentence. However, the additional use of medical and social workers' reports also indicates that less easily quantified criteria, such as the offender's family background and commitments, the availability of certain forms of treatment, and the sex of the offender, are also taken into account in determining sentence. Thus, in

TABLE 8.11
PERCENTAGES* OF TYPES OF (a) NON-CUSTODIAL AND (b)
CUSTODIAL SENTENCES GIVEN TO ALL TYPES OF OFFENDER,
BY SEX, 1979

(a)	Caution	Absolute/ conditional discharge	Probation	Super- vision order	Fine	Community service order	Attendance centre	All
Women	39	14	9	2.6	36	1	0.1	93
Men	17	8	4	3.0	42	3	2	79

(b)	Detention	Care order	Borstal	Prison Suspended	Immediate	Otherwise dealt with	All
Women	†	0.7	0.3	4	2	0.7	8
Men	3	0.9	2	6	9	1	22

* Percentages over 1 rounded except those for supervision order
† There are no detention centres for women
N = 90,312 women, 418,623 men
(Devised from tables 5.4 and 6.2, *Criminal Statistics for England and Wales 1979* 1981)

the case of women as compared to men, such factors as their often exclusive responsibility for running the home and caring for dependent children, the belief that the effects of removal from the home environment into an institution are more painful for women than for men (NACRO 1980), the fact that an offender is pregnant, the public image of female establishments as providing more therapeutic facilities than male establishments – these can all affect sentencing decisions.

The court decisions related to non-custodial sentences, summarised in section (a) of table 8.11, reflect the influences of both the offender's criminal history and social factors. But the fact that a higher proportion of women (93 per cent) than men (79 per cent) are either cautioned or receive non-custodial sentences could also be interpreted as reflecting traditional beliefs about the nature of female crime in comparison to male crime, as well as a concern for the traditional female role in relation to the family and child-bearing, and the effect on that role of a period of time in an institution.

Women, then, would appear to be treated more leniently than men, with twice as many being cautioned, and a higher proportion receiving a discharge or a probation order. The one exception would seem to be a community service order (Criminal Justice Act 1973), a recently introduced, enlightened, non-custodial sentence; according to the Conference of Chief Probation Officers, a woman's chances of receiving a community service order are four times less than those of a man (NACRO 1980).

Sex differences solely in relation to the experience of cautioning (table 8.12) again reflect leniency towards women, but this is particularly noticeable in the case of juveniles up to the age of 17. The same pattern of leniency to women is also reflected in custodial sentences, which are applied to a much smaller proportion of female offenders (8 per cent) in comparison to males (22 per cent) (see section (b) of table 8.11). The exception is the use of remand for prisoners awaiting either trial or sentence. In this case magistrates are more likely to remand women in custody than men (Dell 1971), a factor that obviously contributes to the gross overcrowding in female remand centres (see table 8.15). Having received a custodial sentence, the length of that sentence would appear to be shorter for the majority of women in comparison to men; 25 per cent of women served three months or less in 1979 compared to 20 per cent of men (Heidensohn 1981). Details of the length of sentence for a particular offence are given in table 8.13. The *Report of the Work of the Prison Department* (1979) noted that the fact that only 7 per cent of women received a sentence of over eighteen months, compared to 14 per cent of men, probably reflects their less extensive criminal records. It also probably reflects that a higher proportion of women were

TABLE 8.12

OFFENDERS CAUTIONED AS A PERCENTAGE OF OFFENDERS FOUND GUILTY OR CAUTIONED FOR INDICTABLE OFFENCES, BY AGE AND SEX

| | *Age* | | | |
	10–14	*14–17*	*17–21*	*21+*
Female	85	59	5	10
Male	66	34	3	3

(Derived from table 5.6, *Criminal Statistics for England and Wales 1979* 1981)

charged with the less serious offence of shoplifting under the particular offence category in this table.

THE CUSTODIAL SENTENCE

Between 1969 and 1979 the number of women in penal institutions rose by 103 per cent in comparison with a 23 per cent increase for men (table 8.14), but despite this the ratio of male to female offenders in penal institutions is still about 30:1 (see table 8.16). Latest figures for the daily average population indicate (not surprisingly), however, that for both sexes there is a serious problem of overcrowding. In female establishments the total population is 14 per cent in excess of the accommodation available, and in male

TABLE 8.13
RECEPTION OF ADULTS UNDER SENTENCE FOR THEFT,
HANDLING, FRAUD AND FORGERY,* BY SEX AND SENTENCE
LENGTH, 1979 (PERCENTAGES)

	Women	Men
3 months or less	33	23
4–6 months	30	26
7–18 months	30	37
Over 18 months	7	14

* Excluding fine-defaulters
N = 1067 women, 12,621 men
(Derived from table 5(c), *Report of the Work of the Prison Department* 1979)

TABLE 8.14
NUMBER OF RECEPTIONS INTO PRISON UNDER SENTENCE OF
IMPRISONMENT

	Women	Men	All
1969	1,037	29,669	30,706
1975	1,351	30,664	32,015
1979	2,109	36,423	38,532

(Derived from table 4.8, *Annual Abstract of Statistics* 1981)

establishments the figure is 9 per cent (*Report of the Work of the Prison Department: Statistical Tables* 1979, table 1(a)). The more detailed figures given in table 8.15 indicate, however, that the overcrowding is not evenly distributed across all institutions. In the case of men, it occurs only in local prisons and remand centres, whereas for women the number of offenders is considerably in excess of the accommodation in all institutions, except open prisons and Borstals.

Figures showing the distribution of type of offence among women and men given a custodial sentence (table 8.16) reveal a similar sex distribution to that revealed by earlier tables (see table 8.10). In the

TABLE 8.15
PERCENTAGE EXCESS OF POPULATION OVER ACCOMMODATION IN PENAL ESTABLISHMENTS, BY SEX

	Local prisons	Training prisons Open	Closed	Remand centres	Borstals Open	Closed	Detention centres Senior	Junior
Women	48*	1	29	54	5	28	†	†
Men	45	0	0	22	0	0	0	0

* Includes figures for Holloway Prison, which also serves as a local prison
† There are no detention centres for women
(Devised from appendix 3, *Report of the Work of the Prison Department* 1979)

TABLE 8.16
TYPE OF OFFENCE COMMITTED BY OFFENDERS IN INSTITUTIONS, BY SEX (PERCENTAGES)

	Women	Men
Violence against the person	17	18
Sexual offences	0.7	5
Burglary	10	30
Robbery	4	7
Theft, handling, fraud and forgery	47	28
Other offences	16	10
Not known	5	3

N = 1147 women, 34,581 men
(Devised from table 1.5, *Report of the Work of the Prison Department: Statistical Tables* 1979)

case of women, almost half of them have been sent to an institution because of some form of non-violent offence against property (a sex-related crime category), whereas, in the case of burglary, the proportion of men sent to an institution is three times that of women. This again supports the evidence that burglary is related to the male sex, as shown in an earlier section (see table 8.8).

Table 8.17, giving details of the sentencing of women and men to different types of institution, also reveals some interesting differences in the treatment of the sexes. Thus, of the female population, the highest proportion, 61 per cent, is concentrated in training prisons, in comparison to 42 per cent of the male population. However, in the case of local prisons, which are characterised by severe overcrowding, lack of training facilities and a high turnover in the population, the proportion of male prisoners detained in these establishments is more than twice that of female prisoners (Sparks 1971). This, however, is counterbalanced by the high proportion of women, as compared to men, who are detained in remand centres, which are essentially short-stay institutions intended for offenders awaiting trial, sentence, or transfer to another institution.

Differences in female/male institutional experience are also likely to be affected by the size of the respective populations, a male/female ratio of about 30:1. Thus there are fourteen institutions for female offenders compared to 123 for men, and the former are widely dispersed around the country; in the case of specialist female institutions, the position is even further exacerbated, there being only one open Borstal to deal with the needs of all women offenders

TABLE 8.17
SENTENCED POPULATION, BY TYPE OF INSTITUTION
(PERCENTAGES)

| | Remand centres | Local prisons | Training prisons | | Borstals | | Detention centres | | Number |
			Open	Closed	Open	Closed	Senior	Junior	
Women	12	14	34	27	4	10	*	*	1,147
Men	1	36	9	33	4	10	4	2	34,581

* There are no detention centres for women
(Devised from table 1.5, *Report of the Work of the Prison Department: Statistical Tables* 1979)

under 21 who require long-term treatment in open conditions. The *Report of the Work of the Prison Department* (1979) noted that 'many women have to serve their sentences at long distances from their home areas making visiting difficult or impossible'. In addition, Home Office provisions to aid the rehabilitation of prisoners, such as temporary release to obtain a job, or interviews with a probation officer from their own area, often cannot take place in female institutions because of the travelling distances involved. Heidensohn (1981) concludes that, as a consequence of the population size, the visiting needs of female prisoners cannot be related to the geographical distribution of institutions, and specialist provisions, such as education or trade training, are not found to the same extent as in male institutions. It is argued that the cumulative effect of these limitations on female institutions is to create an environment within them which emphasises traditional female gender-role stereotypes, rather than encouraging independence and preparation for the world of work (Price 1977).

The view that crime, in the case of women, is considered to be more abnormal, and associated with personality disorder, has already been referred to (p. 219) and may be reflected in the higher proportion of women than men who are allocated to training prisons. Evidence for this point of view could, however, be provided by the level of violence experienced in women's establishments, where the incidence of assaults is over three times that in men's (*Report of the Work of the Prison Department* 1979); in a closed female Borstal a high incidence of self-mutilation has been noted (NACRO 1980). In 1979, 135 women prisoners in all institutions were diagnosed as suffering from some form of mental disorder, as compared to 605 men prisoners; this comprised 12 per cent of the female population in custody in comparison to 2 per cent of males (*Report of the Work of the Prison Department: Statistical Tables* 1979, table 10.8).

Here again, it would seem important to note that this sex difference in the incidence of mental disorder is problematic, as was revealed in the evidence to the Parliamentary Sub-Committee examining women in prison (Heidensohn 1981). The fact that more women prisoners are diagnosed as mentally ill may, in part, reflect traditional attitudes towards female offenders and may give rise to a subsequent heightened expectation of abnormality which does not operate to the same extent with male offenders.

Table 8.18, giving details of the previous custodial experience of prisoners (though note that the 'unknown' category for women is 49 per cent), indicates that a much higher proportion of men than women have had experience of a previous custodial sentence. This could be said to reflect the more lenient sentencing policy towards women, which has already been noted, as well as the fact that women, as a whole, have shorter criminal records than men: 51 per cent of men in prison have a record of 6 or more previous convictions, compared to 27 per cent of women in custody awaiting sentence (*Report of the Work of the Prison Department* 1979).

Thus it would seem that, in relation to sentencing decisions, a higher proportion of women are treated more leniently than men. Those women who receive custodial sentences are more likely, however, to experience overcrowding as a consequence of the increase in their numbers in recent years, and less likely to experience diversity in terms of the overall institutional provision.

TABLE 8.18
RECEPTIONS INTO PRISON, BY NUMBER OF PREVIOUS
CUSTODIAL SENTENCES (PERCENTAGES)

	Unknown	*0*	*1*	*2*	*3*	*4–5*	*6 or more*
Women	49	28	11	5	3	3	2
Men	16	21	14	12	9	11	16

N = 2,109 women, 36,423 men
(Derived from table 4.8, *Annual Abstract of Statistics* 1981)

VICTIMS OF CRIMES

Research into victimisation, carried out in three inner London boroughs (Sparks, Genn and Dodd 1977), concluded that, when all the offences were combined, a slightly higher proportion of men (49 per cent) reported one or more incidents of victimisation in the preceding year than women (43 per cent). The researchers emphasise, however, that this difference in overall victimisation rates attained significance only in the case of crimes of violence (assaults, robbery and thefts from the person). As indicated in table 8.19, the proportion of men reporting one or more incidents of violence was

TABLE 8.19
PERCENTAGE OF WOMEN AND MEN REPORTING HAVING
BEEN THE VICTIM OF VIOLENCE*

	Women	Men
Once	7	13
Twice or more	2	4
None	90	83

* In the year prior to interview
N = 303 women, 242 men
(Derived from table IV.4, Sparks, Genn and Dodd 1977)

almost twice as high as that for women. For burglary and for thefts other than from the person, only a slightly higher proportion of women than men reported incidents. This tendency for men to have greater experience of victimisation is borne out by research at national level in the United States. Here the National Opinion Research Centre has shown that for all crime committed only one-third of the victims are women.

Reasons for the difference in experience between men and women as victims of crime could well be attributed to the same kind of factors which have already been discussed in relation to the differences in criminal behaviour, such as the privatised nature of women's lives by comparison to men's, and the fact that their work and home experience do not often result in their handling amounts of money of the size that would make them attractive victims for an attack.

However, if one begins to examine particular types of offence in more detail, then the ratio of women to men as victims looks somewhat different. One obvious example of this is the crime of rape, of which the only victims can be women, and which is not legally recognised as an offence when it takes place within marriage. The most recent statistics show that, during 1979, 375 men were sentenced for the crime of rape, compared to a figure of 653 for the number of men proceeded against, and 1170 for the number of offences recorded by the police (*Criminal Statistics for England and Wales 1979* 1981). The difference between offences of rape which are reported to the police (but not officially recorded), which are officially recorded by them, and which are officially proceeded against, reflects the powers of discretion exercised by the police, which are then reflected in the official statistics such as those reported above. This suggests that the conviction rate for rape is low in comparison to the number of offences known to the police, and in comparison with other types of offence (Smart 1976). Further, these figures, taken in conjunction with the evidence provided by self-report studies which show that the actual incidence of rape is four times that recorded in the official statistics (Bowker 1978), indicate that the number of women who are victims of rape attacks is much larger than can be deduced from the criminal statistics. This clearly has implications in any consideration of the ratio of women to men as victims of crime.

A similar situation could be said to apply in the case of crimes committed within marriage. Although marital homicides have been shown to be equally distributed between the sexes, an overwhelming majority of assaults are committed by husbands against wives (Bowker 1978). Interestingly, however, marital assault does not appear as a separate legal category, being subsumed under the general term 'assault'. Perhaps related to this point is the fact that until relatively recently attacks by husbands on their wives have not aroused a great deal of public concern or been an aspect of behaviour where outside intervention, either by the police or through the courts, has been regarded as relevant or appropriate. The effects of these attitudes on the likelihood of victims of marital assault reporting these offences, and on the reaction of the police on receiving such reports, must have implications for the number of incidents that appear in the official statistics, and on any estimate of the number of victims involved.

However, in the case of homicide in general a different pattern is to be found. Table 8.20 gives details of the age and sex of all homicide victims between 1969 and 1978. A comparison of the totals points to the fact that, while men have always been in the overall majority, the differences between the sexes as victims of homicide has widened from 3 in 1969–73, to 36 in 1974–8, and to 39 in the single year 1979. An examination of each particular age group, from 1969 to 1973 and from 1974 to 1978, reveals that the differences between women and men are, in fact, quite small, but that in all seven age groups (apart from exceptions in three of them) men have always been in the majority, and it is in the three age

TABLE 8.20
NUMBER OF OFFENCES* RECORDED AS HOMICIDE, BY AGE
AND SEX OF VICTIM, 1969– 1973 AND 1974–1978

| | 1969–73* | | 1974–8* | |
	Females	Males	Females	Males
Age				
Under 1 year	17	23	16	17
1–4 years	16	18	11	18
5–15 years	14	11	15	16
16–29 years	48	51	58	66
30–49 years	48	44	60	75
50–69 years	23	33	34	49
70 years and over	20	9	24	12
Total	186	189	217	253

* Average per year
(Devised from table 10.6, *Criminal Statistics for England and Wales 1979* 1981)

groups between 16 and 70 that the main increases have occurred in recent years. A contributory factor to this difference is likely to be the greater exposure of men to the public arena, together with the overall increase in homicides of 196 (52 per cent) in a ten-year period.

Researchers who have examined sex differences in reaction to the experience of victimisation have also noted significant differences. Thus Maguire (1980), in his research into the impact of burglary upon victims, found that the most frequent male response was one of anger, while a higher proportion of women reacted with shock, fear or upset (table 8.21). These sex differences are confirmed by research carried out in Toronto on the long-term effects of the experience of burglary. This found that a much higher proportion of women (42 per cent) in comparison to men (2 per cent) experienced fear of being alone; and that 36 per cent of women were afraid of going into their homes in comparison to 8 per cent of men (Waller and Okihiro 1978).

It appears, then, that for crime over all, and in particular offences such as homicide, men are in the majority in any comparison of the sex of victims. It has been suggested, however, that the overall figure related to sex differences needs to be modified to take

TABLE 8.21
FIRST REACTION ON DISCOVERING BURGLARY, BY SEX
(PERCENTAGES)

	Women	Men
Anger/annoyance	19	41
Shock	29	9
Upset/tears/confusion	20	13
Surprise/disbelief	6	11
Fear	13	4
No strong reaction	13	21

N = 159 women, 163 men
(Derived from table 1, Maguire 1980)

account of 'the dark figure', particularly in relation to crimes such as rape and marital assault, in which women are overwhelmingly the majority of victims.

OVERVIEW

In examining the relationship between sex and crime, this chapter has confined itself to the evidence presented by the official statistics, supplemented by data from recent research where relevant. It has not, therefore, examined in any great depth the considerable amount of theoretical speculation that has emerged in relation to crime generally and sex differences in particular, nor the research derived from this. In addition, it has made no reference to any legislative changes – for example, the Domestic Violence and Matrimonial Proceedings Act (1976) – which have implications for the official figure in relation to female/male involvement in crime and experience as victims.

The examination of the official statistics has shown that, while in the last decade crime has increased over all, this increase has been proportionally greater for female than for male offenders. The belief that this recent increase represents a significant shift by women into what had been a traditionally male-dominated activity has been challenged, however, by an analysis of the figures from the official statistics, taken over four decades. Further analysis has also shown that certain crimes are sex-specific, as in offences such as rape and prostitution, and sex-related, with female crime tending to cluster only in certain categories, such as non-violent offences against property.

The fact that criminal statistics cannot be regarded as unproblematic was confirmed by the evidence of self-report studies into juvenile-delinquent populations. These showed that the overall ratio of female to male criminal involvement is less than that officially recorded, although differences are still significant in traditional 'male' crime, such as that involving violence against property. Examination of charges brought against juveniles provided evidence of sex stereotyping; thus girls were, in the main, charged with behaviour such as sexual deviance or truancy, in contrast to boys, who were found, in the main, to have committed indictable offences. It was argued that this sexism was, in part, the result of the male domination of the agencies of social control, such as the courts and the police.

Theoretical explanations of the relationship between sex and crime revealed a number of different emphases, including biological explanations, socialisation experience and social interaction. The latter included both micro-level analysis – for example, of the judicial processes – and macro-level analysis related to the role of the state in determining relationships between the sexes. The argument that stressed the interrelationship between institutions of a society, their influence on the socialisation processes and hence sex differences in crime was felt to be the most powerful, thus locating the characteristics associated with crime and gender within an overall social framework.

Sentencing policy showed that in general women tended to be treated more sympathetically than men, with a higher proportion receiving a caution or non-custodial sentence. This was not shown to be the case in relation to institutional experience, however, where women prisoners were found to have less opportunity for rehabilitation and specialist provision.

In relation to victimisation, a higher proportion of men were found to be victims of violent offences, but it was argued that women's experience of victimisation in the case of rape and marital violence was very much under-recorded, and that this therefore distorted the official figures. Considerable sex differences existed in relation to the experience of victimisation.

Unlike other areas examined in this book, it would seem that in the case of crime women are not always at a disadvantage in relation to men. The fact, however, that the political and legal institutions are dominated by men does mean that women enjoy that advantage only as a consequence of male discretion.

9

Sex differences in Britain

Eileen Wormald and Ivan Reid

In choosing the areas in which to examine sex differences, there was no conscious or deliberate intention to choose those that would best illustrate similarities or identities or pinpoint discrimination, inequality, subordination or constraints. Moreover, in restricting the data largely to the last decade, it was intended to abstain from an examination of historical development in either the increase or diminution of sex differences.

Such intentions, however, did not prevent two clearly observable trends emerging as the chapters were assembled. First, where historical data were used to illuminate the current position, what was demonstrated was that, despite deliberate attempts in many areas to equalise opportunities for the sexes, women remained a subordinate group. Second, although there is a common assumption or myth that there has been a massive change in women's position in the twentieth century, the data here suggest otherwise. The creation of the myth is in itself of interest in studying sex differences: women's increasing self-consciousness – the determined effort of an active and vociferous group to participate fully in all aspects of social life – appears to have led to the idea that the battle for sex equality – that is, the 'longest war' (Tavris and Offir 1977) – has been won. Certainly we have moved a long way historically from the view of sex differences and relationships contained in the following extract from the fourth edition of the *Encyclopaedia Britannica* (1800–10):

> The man, more robust, is fitted for severe labour, and for field exercise; the woman, more delicate, is fitted for sedentary occupations, and particularly for nursing children. The man, bold and vigorous, is qualified for being a protector; the woman, delicate, and timid, requires protection. Hence it is that a man never admires a woman for possessing bodily strength or personal courage; and women always despise men who are

totally destitute of these qualities. The man, as a protector, is directed by nature to govern; the woman, conscious of inferiority, is disposed to obey. Their intellectual powers correspond to the destination of nature. Men have penetration and solid judgement to fit them for governing, women have sufficient understanding to make a decent figure under a good government; a greater portion would excite dangerous rivalry between the sexes, which nature has avoided by giving them different talents. Women have more imagination and sensibility than men which make all their enjoyments more exquisite; at the same time that they are better qualified to communicate enjoyment. Add another capital difference of disposition: the gentle and insinuating manners of the female sex tend to soften the roughness of the other sex; and wherever women are indulged with any freedom, they polish sooner than men.

These are not the only particulars that distinguish the sexes. With respect to the ultimate end of love, it is the privilege of the male, as superior and protector, to make a choice; the female preferred has no privilege but barely to consent or refuse. . . . Among all nations it is the practice for men to court, and for women to be courted; and were the most beautiful woman on earth to invert this practice, she would forfeit the esteem, however by her external grace she might excite the desire, of the man whom she addressed. The great moral virtues which may be comprehended under the general term integrity are all absolutely necessary to make either men or women estimable; but to procure esteem to the female character, the modesty peculiar to their sex is a very essential circumstance. Nature hath provided them with it as a defence against the artful solicitations of the other sex before marriage, and also as a support of conjugal fidelity.

At the same time, as will be clear to all its readers, this book bears witness to the extent of sex differences and inequalities and how very far our society has yet to go really to affect and change them.

LEGISLATION FOR SEX EQUALITY

The passing in Britain of legislation to end the disadvantages of women seemed to suggest that the general public was prepared to accept equality and that Acts of Parliament would ensure it. The Equal Pay Act was passed in 1970, and amended and supplemented by the Sex Discrimination Act (1975) and the Employment Protection Act (1975). Broadly speaking, the 1970 Act gives a woman the right to equal treatment with a man when she is employed in like work to that of a man or employed in a job which, even if different from that of a man, has been given the same value as a man's job under a job-evaluation scheme. While it clearly established the principle of equal pay for equal work for women and men and therefore might be said to have helped to create a climate that militated against discrimination on the grounds of sex, it could not ensure complete equality. Thus it did not enable comparison to be made between sex-segregated employment – so that, for example, women secretaries cannot claim comparability with unqualified but highly paid male clerical staff. Other, complementary, legislation such as the minimum-wage machinery is not well enforced, with the result that the intention to improve the position of women is not implemented. The Sex Discrimination Act was a remarkably comprehensive Act which set out penalties and compensation for infringement of its directives. It made unlawful discrimination on the grounds of sex in employment, certain organisations (such as trade unions), education and professional training, public appointments, provision of goods, facilities and services, property disposal, and certain related matters such as discriminatory advertisements. Concurrently there was established the Equal Opportunities Commission, which was empowered to work for the elimination of discrimination, to promote equality of opportunity generally between women and men, and to keep under review the Acts of 1970 and 1975. The Commission was empowered to support individual complainants in the industrial tribunals and the courts and themselves initiate action.

That this legislation has not been fully effective may be judged by reports from the Commission of the European Communities. The EEC has been in the vanguard of proclaiming the need for equality between the sexes and has issued three directives: on Equal Pay (1975), Equal Opportunities (1976) and Equal Treatment in Social Security (1978). While applauding Britain's early legislation, described above, it has recently shown concern that the Equal Pay Act may allow a restrictive interpretation of 'equal pay for equal work or work of equal value' because a firm has to operate a job-evaluation scheme before an employee can claim equal pay, and only a minority of firms have produced such schemes.

Other ambiguities in the British laws have been brought to the European Court of Justice, and in ratifying the court's decisions the British Court of Appeal has confirmed that the EEC legislation has priority over British law where there are ambiguities. So women now have the umbrella protection of legislation not only in Britain but also in the EEC, together with the Equal Opportunities Commission, in claiming their equal rights. However, there has clearly been either inadequate publicity of these rights or unwillingness and inability to understand them, since in a recent survey it was shown that 42 per cent of the British sample either did not know about or thought there were no laws regarding equality of treatment at work, and 66 per cent did not know about, or were not concerned with, what the European Community might be doing in this respect (*Women of Europe: Supplement 5* 1980).

A conclusion might therefore be drawn that women are not always aware of their disadvantage or, if they are, are disinclined to do anything about it, because the idea of women's subordinate position is so ingrained in the social structure. Equally pervasive is the notion that equal opportunities exist regardless of sex; thus the chief officer of a public body offers the following explanation for the lack of women among appointments: 'I must state that invitations to join any of our committees are issued on the basis of the suitability of people to do the job and they did not take much account of other factors such as sex' (Kerr 1979).

SEXISM AND STATISTICS

If we look at any of the preceding chapters we can see that women as a group are frequently disadvantaged as a result of their gender. It appears, as is forcefully argued in Chapter 2, that a woman's position in society is constrained partly by her place in the family and very largely by her position in the labour market. Not all of this picture can be shown in a book based on readily available data about women and men. The prevalence of sexism (see below) in official statistics obscures some of the realities of sex differences in the social structure. This was shown in a seminar funded by the EOC in 1980 called 'Women in Government Statistics'. It was called too late to have impact on one major source of data, the 1981 census form, but it is possible that it may influence the subsequent analysis (Nissel 1980).

In discussing sexism in official statistics, which constitute the major sources of data for this book, the Oakleys (1979) define sexism as a type of discrimination between people based on their social classification as female or male where sex is not, as for instance it is with childbirth and lactation, a relevant characteristic.

They suggest that sexism in statistics is found in the *areas* chosen for statistical analysis, the *concepts* used to organise and present the statistics, the way the *collection* of data is organised, the *processing* of the statistics and the *presentation* of the data.

In applying these criteria to the data in this book we can see that the authors have noted gaps in the information available in certain *areas* – for example, the number of hours spent on housework (Chapter 6), as well as notable instances such as electoral statistics (Chapter 7) where in processing data these are not broken down by sex. They have further drawn attention to the *concepts* or assumptions about the basic familial role of women which underly, for instance, the studies of income distribution and the difference in the data when 'household' is used as a base rather than family (Chapter 4). Similarly, Nissel (1980) has demonstrated how concepts such as 'head of household' or 'housewife' are relics of nineteenth-century assumptions that no longer relate to reality and has drawn attention to the dangers of trying to deduce household characteristics from the characteristics of one individual of either sex. Equal dangers are inherent in the *collection* of data on, for example, employment, where limited definitions hide important contributions to the economy (Chapters 4 and 6). It also confuses the concept of social class, which is customarily defined according to the occupational status of the head of the household, usually taken as being a man; this instance of sexism has aroused considerable discussion at least among sociologists. While the relationship of sex and social class is one of the areas not covered in this book, it has been confronted in Reid (1981). Finally it must be noted in this context that many data that are collected are not *processed* – for example, information about wives' earnings and dependants' allowances available in the Inland Revenue which could help to provide invaluable information on family finances (Nissel 1980).

Since this is not a book of original data but a review of other people's work, it has not been possible to change the sexism inherent in many statistics. However, where data are available, processed and published, it is usual for men to be taken as the base against which women are compared, so in our presentation we reversed this process by making women the focus of our interest, and to this end women appear first in each table. By highlighting gaps in the data about sex differences, we have also drawn attention to information that we feel is needed in order to inform discussion about sex differences and about discrimination against either women or men.

OPPORTUNITY AND ACHIEVEMENT: SEX AND GENDER DIFFERENCES

As we have noted, the picture that emerges in these chapters is of women consigned to a gender-specific role which is not in any sense natural or ordained but is culturally produced. In Chapter 2, after distinguishing sex and gender, the author examines theories of how this gender role is constructed in our society and locates the ideology of gender in the sexual division of labour and the familial role of women. The way in which these two intertwine to deprive women of equality in social security provisions is most readily exemplified in Chapter 4. The state has enhanced the idea of the dependent role of women in the family, despite evidence, explored in Chapters 2, 3 and 6, that for a long period of their life many women do not live in a family setting with a man to 'depend on' and that increasingly women play an important part in the economy as well as often being the sole breadwinners for dependent relatives. It would appear that the state is using a 'myth' of women's primary role as wife and mother both as an instrument of social control and as a support for an ideal notion of uninterrupted family life – as well, perhaps, as a means of saving money.

Where women do not appear to be transgressing their familial role, the state now encourages them to share equal opportunities with men; in education (as Chapter 5 shows) the potential is there, but it seems that women are not fully grasping the opportunities open to them. If we assume an equal distribution of intelligence between the sexes, then women are disadvantaged in education if we mean by this that they achieve less in terms of qualifications and career. In some ways – for example, linguistic skills – men are disadvantaged in comparison with women, but this does not, on the whole, hold them back from career achievement. The tendency to lay the blame for women's inequalities on a male-dominated society neglects the cultural assumptions of the social role of the sexes and the extent to which these are as readily embraced by women as by men.

As is shown in Chapter 5, in the educational race girls start equal with boys but at some point drop out of the competition, and by the time they are ready to leave school one in four of girls who are qualified to do so fail to participate in higher education, compared with only one in nine of boys. It is suggested that women establish themselves as rapidly as possible in an occupational role through early post-school training and that many of the occupations they embrace are gender-specific. We do not know, since the evidence appears conflicting, whether there is differential ability (for example, in mathematics) between boys and girls, but there is some evidence that there are expectations that influence both choice of curriculum subjects and achievement within them, and that these are reinforced in coeducational schools. The self-image of girls is one where they are seen, and therefore often see themselves, primarily as home-makers and not as future wage-earners, and this clearly influences their educational progress. The importance of the 'hidden curriculum' within the school, reinforced by family expectations and media influence, in limiting the educational achievement of women is touched on in Chapter 5, and the analysis points clearly to the social construction of sex differential in educational achievement. For many women the result may be entirely satisfying; they may be pleased to have a strong reason for not striving and competing, for accepting gender-specific occupations. However, it cannot be ignored that the evidence of women's desire to take up education again in later life suggests that a number regret the limitations of their early educational aspirations and achievements. Moreover, if we assume an equation between level of education and occupation, we see that women's subordinate position in the workforce (Chapter 6) is due in part to their being channelled, as a result of inadequate educational qualifications reinforced by interrupted career patterns, into unskilled occupations and jobs in service industries. As a result they have poor earnings relative to men and appear to be used as a buffer for the workforce needs of an economy subject to boom and recession. Yet, as Chapter 6 shows, for some households the woman's wage is either the sole or an essential part of the household economy. Moreover, women's desire to work in paid employment for job satisfaction and companionship as well as in order to earn money suggests that girls should be counselled from an early age about the career implications of their educational activities as well as, or in relationship to, the familial role into which they are socialised. For the majority of women their occupation will, over long periods, be as central to their lives as is their child-bearing and home-making role. In this respect it seems essential that, if women wish to advance their cause in education and careers based on educational certification, they must be more prepared to assume responsibility for themselves, assessing their individual skills and interest irrespective of expectations arising from their gender; to do this their whole perception of the female role may need to change and their understanding of the realities rather than the myths of female activity must be revised.

This appears equally true in the field of politics. There is little evidence that children are socialised into a sex-specific political role (Wormald 1982), perhaps because politics is not salient in the lives of most young people, and though attempts have been made to show that girls do not learn political skills as readily as boys (Rapoport 1981) the description of these skills may assume a given male-oriented political world. At the level of access to the political hierarchy, girls may be put off or put down by the historical barriers to their entry. If we compare the number of candidates, both successful and unsuccessful, with elected members of the House of Commons, we can see that more women wish to enter politics than are allowed to, and, while this is probably equally true of men, it cannot be assumed that an explanation in the women's case lies in the notion that they are apolitical. Women are, as was seen in Chapter 7, as politically interested as men, but they may not translate their ideas into active involvement to the extent that men do because they meet early rejections in a polity in which men are, historically, well entrenched. Alternatively, having noted that the structures of our society are such that barriers are erected against their political recruitment, they may make a rational response and turn away from political activism towards areas where they may hope for easier rewards, in the way that they may reject careers traditionally regarded as 'men's jobs' (Wormald 1982).

One of the results, however, in politics, as perhaps in other careers such as medicine (Chapter 3), is that women do not constitute a large enough group to make an impact as women, and, though in both the Commons and the Lords on matters of immediate concern to their sex the women tend to stand firmly together, on the whole they appear to adopt the ideology of the male world they have successfully entered (Phillips 1980). Whether, if more women were present in the political hierarchies, they would be able to adopt a different stand is open to speculation, but they would certainly, if they wished, then be in a position to press for the end to anomalous distinctions in matters such as social policy discussed in Chapter 4.

In the areas of education and politics, therefore, it would seem that women, though currently disadvantaged, need not be imprisoned by their gender any more than they are by their basic biology or supposed psychology. In the latter areas, however, as shown in Chapter 3, women have both advantages and disadvantages compared with men. From before birth until death women have a greater chance of survival than do men; moreover, they are less likely to be malformed and also less likely to suffer accidents – so that both infancy and childhood are safer for girls than for boys. Yet despite their greater survival rate and their longevity women feel they have more health problems than do men. Moreover, their view of their health is reflected in women's greater use of medical services and by a much higher rate of hospital admissions. Although survival and health differences may seem innate, some of them are culturally contrived. The higher accident rate for boys is in part due to the fact that they are encouraged to be more adventurous than girls (cf. Chapter 5), are probably allowed out on bicycles more frequently and in more hazardous conditions and, at a later age, are more likely to ride motor cycles, while the male preponderance among road-traffic injuries and the female bias in home injuries is clearly a gender and not a sex differentiation. Other differences are biological; childbirth fatalities are clearly sex-specific. Illness resulting from contraceptive usage, on the other hand, is a result of medical research's focusing on chemicals and internal devices that limit the fertility of the woman not the man, who cannot, therefore, suffer from 'side effects'. In turn, this research focus may be the result of the imbalance in sex composition of the medical profession (Chapter 3 and see Roberts 1981). Women have the advantage of greater longevity than men, and this may be due to the less stressful life their subordinate and dependent role allows them, although their higher incidence of mental illness seems to negate this notion. It also seems possible, however, that women are more likely to have problems diagnosed as mental; this idea is reinforced by the discussion of supposed causes of female crime (Chapter 8). It is easy to speculate why this is so, but why women are twice as likely to be operated on than men is much more difficult to explain. As in other areas, the familial role of women can be perceived in the lower rate of male referrals to hospital and their lower average length of stay, with the assumption that men are more likely to be cared for in the home than are women, although this 'caring' work by women is not computed as a contribution to the national income (see Chapter 6).

Is it despite or because of their approach to their own health – more willingness to consult a doctor, more likelihood that they will have operations – that women have a higher life expectancy than men? As in other areas (e.g. the supposed conservatism of women – Chapter 7) some of the differences in the vital statistics may be due to the different age structure, others to occupational differences, of women and men, and the balance may change as women penetrate more into occupational categories previously designated for 'men only', and as the demographic structure changes, with men for the first time predominating in age groups up to the middle forties (Chapter 3). Additionally, increases in alcohol consumption and smoking among women may also reduce their longevity, and role reversal could ensure fewer hospital admissions for women, as men increasingly share in the caring roles in the family. This is clearly an area where, despite biological differences, the possibility of equalisation of life chances between the sexes seems possible and, to some extent, predictable.

The most problematic area may well be that of occupational opportunity, which is fundamental to the whole social structure. The inequalities in career opportunities, in promotion prospects and in pay between the sexes seems basic to the relative positions of women and men in the social structure. It is also the area of most mystification in gender roles: the contradictory myths that women work outside the home only for 'pin money' and that they would not work if they did not have to exist side by side as part of a cultural ethos that seems bent on depressing the value of any female activity other than that of wife and mother. The process can be seen at work in the recurrence of inequalities of pay after a brief period of increasing equalisation as a consequence of the Equal Pay Act (1970), as Chapter 6 shows. The difficulties inherent in an Act that seeks to end discrimination in an occupational system which is itself discriminatory can clearly be seen; where some occupations appear to be designated 'female' and others 'male', wage comparability is difficult to obtain, and it is economically beneficial to employers to maintain that discrimination, since it enables them to keep the level of certain wages depressed. It is, as Chapter 2 has shown, difficult to ascertain what accounts for the social and sexual division of labour, which seems grounded in industrial society, since it appears in various degrees under all forms of production systems. It may be suggested that the economy is based on a social structure that maintains a 'cheap' labour force both by encouraging an ideology of devotion to family life and the responsibility for maintaining family members and by ensuring that large areas of maintenance of the family (housework and childcare) are produced free of economic cost. This can be interpreted either in functional terms, by suggesting that the needs of the system of production determine the sexual division of labour, or in conflict terms, by supposing that a patriarchal society maintains its control by accustoming women not to compete in the labour market on equal terms with men but instead provide unpaid comfort and support for the male worker. What is clear, whichever position one adopts, is that work is perceived as that which is paid. Where there is no payment, there are sometimes assumptions that need is not there and at other times that need should be supported differently. Thus some social security benefits exclude the married woman – for example invalid care allowance – because she is assumed to be not in paid work, while insurance benefits generally are based on interruption of earnings, so that those not in the paid economy are reliant on less attractive, means-tested benefits.

The increasing employment of women outside the home may induce a change in these patterns, though currently the picture is obscured by unemployment; and the failure of many women to register as unemployed (Chapter 6) suggests an acceptance of the idea that gainful employment is a supplementary and not a primary female role. The familial role of women seems thus to be bolstered at every point; even where women break from the mould, the tendency is for them to be 'placed' in a context related to family interests – as both in the occupational structure, where they are predominantly employed in the 'caring and catering' services, and in the political arena, where they tend to specialise in education, the social services, consumer protection.

In one area this family context appears to benefit women: the familial role is emphasised in the analysis in Chapter 8 of sex differences in crime. Women appear to gain advantage from the view generated by male-dominated agencies of social control that their crimes are of a different order (not just a different type) from that of men's and that they should be allowed for as long as possible to continue their caring role in the family. The reduction in the number of women in prison from 43,382 in 1886 to 7408 in 1976 (Greenwood 1981) leads to the speculation that the home-centred, privatised ideal of women is a product of twentieth-century adaptation to an established economic system; Pinchbeck's (1930) work on women in the industrial revolution, which shows their part in establishing the industrial economy of Britain, demonstrates that any idea of keeping these women out of prison in order to succour the family at home would have represented a travesty of the real world. Increasingly, as women again penetrate the paid economy, it may be anticipated that the recent 'increase' in recorded female crime may continue, though the impact of unemployment could skew the picture. For the moment, however, their perceived gender role benefits women, who appear to be less apprehended for crime and to be more likely than men to be cautioned rather than charged; once, however, it is established that a woman has deviated from her traditional familial, non-criminal role, and has been relabelled as deviant to the point where she must be imprisoned, this is often explained as a result of mental aberration and is endured within a setting that appears to encourage and reinforce her subordinate role.

Because crime is seen as a 'problem', it has been investigated at length, and theories about its incidence among both men and women are to be found in a way that cannot be so readily uncovered, for example, in examining sex differentials in political participation or in the use of medical services. Attempts have to be made to 'solve' problems, whereas unequal access to resources may simply be accepted as biologically ordained or as a necessary function of the way in which society is ordered according to 'given' sex roles. If women should be in the home, it is clearly important to discover the extent to which they are, instead, out committing crimes and to search for explanations for this aberration; whereas women's non-participation in politics can be looked on as a 'natural' acceptance of their primary role as wife and mother, with any excursion into politics directed into interests seen as an extension of that role. Sexism may be a less tenable description of women's experience in crime than elsewhere, since both female and male offenders are stereotyped as deviants from the norm and each sex suffers, or benefits, from the labelling process. Nor can the criminal statistics be accused of 'hiding' women, since any sex differentiation occurs before people appear in those statistics, and, once there, sex is one of the basic variables used. However, questions still remain unanswered; it appears that the designation of what is a crime is related to gender-typing, so that, for example, violence in the family assumes the dominant position of men, but we do not know the extent to which such typing actually determines the sex roles. Are women supported in assuming a subordinate role by the expectations of those like the police and judiciary who interpret the law according to the way in which women and men accept their given roles? In this area too the concept of socialisation may need careful examination; although it has been suggested in Chapter 7 that a deterministic idea of socialisation is inappropriate in the learning of political behaviour, it seems more appropriate in the case of criminal behaviour, since socialisation is one of the ways in which gender-role expectations are mediated, resulting in more conformist, less aggressive and, therefore, less 'deviant' behaviour among women than among men. That this behaviour, if thoroughly internalised, may militate against participation in certain other areas and may reinforce the values underlying the sexual division of labour is a possibility but at best is non-proven.

We are aware that in pursuing further any argument related to sex differences we would have to look outside the confines of this book. The consequences of legislation (Coote and Gill 1977) in areas other than those mentioned in this and other chapters is almost certainly important in gender-typing, and the subject of women in the media would require much more than the cursory mention it receives here (see King and Stott 1977). Even within the chapters, some important aspects have had to be neglected because of the concentration on the visibility of women as they appear in the statistics; when, for example, sex differences in education are examined in Chapter 5, the impact of the 'hidden curriculum' can only be touched on, since it appears so very rarely in the data. It is clear, however, that schools are a major agent of socialisation and social control (Reid 1978); not only the organisation of the school itself and of the curriculum within the school, selection procedures and success through conformity but also teacher roles and teacher expectations have all been examined as means by which the continuity of the social structure, including gender roles, is ensured. It could be argued that, given the weight of this process, the wonder is not that so little but that so much has changed.

CONTINUITY AND CHANGE

That is the picture which emerges: the past fifty years *have* seen changes in the relative position of women and men in Britain. Yet, despite the raising of female consciousness, despite legislation to end the disadvantages of women, despite the effort of feminists for the past hundred years, sex differences in Britain today are on the whole weighted in favour of men. It is, however, problematic to claim that this is a result of *deliberate* oppression by men; many women do not take advantage of all the opportunities open to them, and it is interesting to speculate why. It may be because their position is a result of their physiology: they do give birth to children and they can suckle them, and these facts may have resonances that no amount of deliberate attempts at change can alter. Gender role may indeed be so irrevocably ordained that we should not be surprised that the biblical measurement (Leviticus 27:3–4) of a woman's worth as three-fifths of a man's should be reflected in current wage distribution (see Chapter 6, p. 124).

Yet, even if this is true, girls clearly have to learn what it means to be a woman, and the whole culture from birth congratulations cards onwards is bent on ensuring that they learn their 'properly depen-dent role' (Lane 1961). Socialisation theories have, however, moved from one of strict determinism or the 'over-socialised con-ception of man' (Wrong 1961) to a view of an individual as adapting to the various social situations she or he meets, so that there can be immense variability of 'normal' opinions, knowledge and behaviour (White 1977). Early socialisation studies inquired into socialising agents and tested their relative importance in the learning of expected behaviour; later ones looked at the process from the viewpoint not of the socialiser but of the learner playing an active role in learning and adaptation, rather than passively absorbing transmitted ideas, and thereby strongly challenged the passive, subject role of 'man in society'.

The latter view of the socialisation process, however, chiefly serves, in the short term, to explain attitudes and behaviour aber-rant from a general trend. Women politicians or women judges, by this standard, have either been differentially socialised – as with the Euro-MP Barbara Castle, a former cabinet minister, the daughter of parents who taught her a clearly political role (Phillips 1980) – or have rejected their socialisation into a subordinate role as a result of their own interpretations of their place in the world, as Phillips suggests is true of the first woman prime minister, Margaret Thatcher, or, indeed, been subject to a combination of the two. Another view of the process (in some ways as deterministic as early socialisation studies) is that human beings accustom themselves to a social sex role, embracing it willingly, indeed fervently, as superior to any alternative (Willis 1978). According to this explanation, girls, for example, would deliberately choose not to pursue education as far as they are capable because they believe that their most desirable activity is not to build a career but to devote themselves primarily to being wives and mothers. This may explain early sex-role performance, but the findings, for example, that many more women than do so would actually like to work outside the home (Chapter 6) and their later entry into further education (Chapter 5) suggest that they have been supported by cultural norms into making a choice which later they may regret. In the long run, therefore, more women as well as men may embrace different gender roles when these are increasingly portrayed as legitimate alternatives within the current social structure. What might be hoped for, then, is that the sexes could live and express themselves unencumbered by cultural prescriptions, social constraints and a legal and social system based on sexist principles or assumptions. In such a situation the range of choice and the diversity of behaviour and roles would be very greatly heightened. Women and men might be enabled to negotiate their relationships as people, rather than as members of their sex. For many readers such a view may well appear as utopian, if not undesirable. However, two factors ought to be borne in mind. First, there are indications of such negotiation between couples at present in our society, and, while there may have been elements of this since time began, it would seem that they are becoming more common and prominant – though, at the same time, quite how such a negotiation might be achieved at societal level, given the relationship of the sexes to the basic structure of society (see Chapter 2 and *passim* in this book), remains far from clear. Second, it needs to be recognised how far we, as a society, have moved in this direction, not only in recent years but spectacularly in history.

It cannot, moreover, long escape the attention of girls and women that in certain areas the designated female role as familial and dependent on men works to everyone's disadvantage: the poverty imposed on women by social security rules (Chapter 4) can scarcely be something that they would knowingly embrace by internalising their given role. So it may be that the question that most immediately needs to be addressed is not whether girls are taught and/or eagerly embrace a female role but what is the process by which gender roles are ideologically constructed (Chapter 2).

OVERVIEW

Equally there is a need to examine the extent to which, in any of the areas examined in this book, the position of women could be altered, to confront the question of social determinism of the position of women, and to discover what are, in a given social structure, the parameters of possible change. We would assert that the limit has certainly not been reached; social justice requires that the state should recognise that the family, however desirable, is increasingly a structure of considerable variety (as Chapters 3 and 4 show), and that to base crisis support on the concept of women as dependants of the male breadwinner is to ignore the reality of life for millions of women. Further, women should be encouraged, and where necessary aided, to enter careers where they can fulfil their potential and contribute whatever talents they have to the common weal, though the current occupational structure and unemployment may be a constraint on any major change. It is, however, necessary to face the fact that the economic base of the current social structure may be on the brink of a dramatic change. If many of the sex differences in Britain are a function of the sexual division of labour in industrial society, then the impact of new technology may have a profound effect. If micro-processors allow increasing leisure and can be largely worked from within the home by either women or men or both, then the need, if such it is, for women to elaborate their child-bearing role into other areas of domesticity while men 'go out' to work may no longer be operative. Job-sharing may become a commonplace for wife and husband rather than a headline-hitting rarity. It seems possible, however, that for the moment some of these changes may reinforce the disadvantage of women (Downing 1980), and at all times vigilance is necessary, combined with action through pressure groups and trade unions, and political activism to decrease sex differences where these work to the disadvantage of either sex. In particular, since the ultimate social control operates through state legislation, it seems imperative that women should claim an equal share with men in political decision-making, administration and adjudication. They then might achieve not identity between the sexes – since the very nature of sex would defy such an objective – but genuine equality. If we substitute 'people' for 'men' in the following quotation, it provides a sound and bold challenge to our present concern.

> So to criticise inequality and to desire equality is not, as is sometimes suggested, to cherish the romantic illusion that men are equal in character and intelligence. It is to hold that, while their natural endowments differ profoundly, it is the mark of a civilised society to aim at eliminating such inequalities as have their source not in individual differences, but in its own organisation: and that individual energies, which are a source of social energy, are more likely to ripen and find expression if social inequalities are, as far as practicable, diminished. (Tawney 1931)

Few, however, whether women or men, are natural pioneers fighting against the odds, breaking through the barriers. Most people do not translate their perception into action, their ideas into weapons. Some, however, will blaze the trail, and there seems nothing incapable of change, or avoidance, in gender-typing that should prevent the less bold and dedicated from following. Any other view looks like the proclaiming of defeatist ideas, of which both women and men would do well to be wary. What appears to be crucial, then, is that people should be freed from those inequalities, or lack of choice, imposed upon them by the structure of the society or the culture in which they live.

Notes on the contributors

Andrew Cooper graduated from the University of Southampton and received his doctorate from the University of Bristol. He currently lectures in the Social Science Division at Worcester College of Higher Education.

Tony Kidd studied at the universities of Manchester, Exeter and Birmingham, and has taught in colleges of further education, education and higher education. He is currently Head of the Social Science Division at Worcester College of Higher Education.

Ivan Reid trained as a teacher at St John's College, York, and taught in secondary schools. Subsequently, he read a first degree in sociology at the University of Leicester and part-time higher degrees at the universities of Liverpool and Bradford. He taught main-course sociology in Edge Hill College of Education before joining the teaching staff of Bradford University where he is currently senior lecturer in educational sociology and Chairman of the Undergraduate School of Applied Educational Studies. He is probably best known as an author through his two books *Social Class Differences in Britain*, second edition (Grant McIntyre, 1981) and *Sociological Perspectives on School and Education* (Open Books, 1978).

Erica Stratta graduated from Bedford College, University of London, and studied for her doctorate at the London School of Economics. As well as being a mother, she has taught in both secondary schools and further education. Currently she is senior lecturer in the Social Science Division at Worcester College of Higher Education. She is author of *The Education of Borstal Boys* (Routledge & Kegan Paul, 1970).

Michael Webb graduated from Oxford University, taught in a sixth-form college in Southampton and researched at Leeds University. He currently lectures in economics and industrial sociology at Worcester College of Higher Education.

Margaret Wilkin trained and practised as a primary teacher before going to Exeter and Bristol universities to study sociology and education. She is currently senior lecturer in the Educational Studies Division at Worcester College of Higher Education.

Eileen Wormald graduated from the London School of Economics and has since had a varied career as research officer, abstractor, social worker, teacher and mother. When this book was planned and written she was Head of Social Science at Worcester College of Higher Education where she is now Dean of the Faculty of Arts and Sciences. She is joint editor (with Robin Alexander) of *Professional Studies for Teaching* (SRHE, 1979) and (with Ivan Reid) of *Sociology and Teacher Education* (ATCDE, 1974), and author of a number of journal papers.

Bibliography and author index

Figures in italics at the end of entries are page and/or table numbers in this book.

The following abbreviations are used: CSO for Central Statistical Office; DES for Department of Education and Science; DHSS for Department of Health and Social Security; DoE for Department of Employment; EEC for European Economic Community; EOC for Equal Opportunities Commission; HMSO for Her Majesty's Stationery Office; NACRO for National Association for the Care and Resettlement of Offenders; NFER for National Foundation for Education Research; OECD for Organisation for Economic Co-operation and Development; OPCS for Office of Population Censuses and Surveys; PEP for Political and Economic Planning.

ABELL, R. A. (1976) *An Investigation into Some Aspects of Visual Handicap*. DHSS, Statistical and Research Report Series No. 14. London: HMSO *45*

ABRAMS, P. (1978) *Work, Urbanism and Inequality*. London: Weidenfeld and Nicolson *271*

ACKER, S. (1980) 'Women, the other Academics'. *British Journal of Sociology of Education* 1(1), 81–91 *108*

ACKER, S. (1981), 'No-Woman's Land: British Sociology of Education 1960-1979'. *Sociological Review*, 29 (1), 77–104 *16*

ADELSTEIN, A. M., *et al.* (1976) *Child Health: Collection of Studies*. OPCS Studies on Medical and Population Subjects No. 31. London: HMSO *254*

ADELSTEIN, A. M., and WHITE, G. C. (1976) 'Causes of Children's Deaths: Analyses by Social Class'. In Adelstein *et al.* (1976) *34*

ADVISORY CONCILIATION AND ARBITRATION SERVICE (1978) *The Toy Manufacturing Wages Council Report No. 13*. London: ACAS *137, 152*

ALLEN, S. and SMITH, C. (1975) 'Minority Group Experience of the Transition from Education to Work'. In Brannen (1975) *169*

AMSDEN, A. (1980) *The Economics of Women and Work*. Harmondsworth: Penguin *268*

ANDERSEN, K., (1975) 'Working Women and Political Participation'. *American Journal of Political Science*, 19 (3), 439–53 *203*

Annual Abstract of Statistics (1979 and 1981) CSO. London: HMSO *214; 4.10, 6.1, 8.6, 8.14, 8.18*

APU Mathematical Development Primary Survey (1980) Report No. 1. DES. London: HMSO *88*

Aspects of Secondary Education in England (1979) DES. London: HMSO. *97*

BAIN, G. S., and PRICE, R. (1980) *Profiles of Union Growth*. Oxford: Basil Blackwell *154*

BAIRD, I. M., SILVERSTONE, J. T., GRIMSHAW, J. J., and ASHWELL, M. (1974) 'Prevalence of Obesity in a London Borough'. *Practitioner*, 212, 706–14 *3.8*

BARBER, A. (1980) 'Ethnic Origin and the Labour Force'. In *Employment Gazette* (August), 841–8 *166, 168; 6.35*

BARKER LUNN, J. C. (1970) *Streaming in the Primary School*. Slough: NFER

BARKER LUNN, J. C. (1972) 'The Influence of Sex, Achievement and Social Class on Junior School Children's Attitudes'. *British Journal of Educational Psychology*, 42 (1), 70–4 *85, 101*

BARKER, D. L., and ALLEN, S. (1976a) *Dependence and Exploitation in Work and Marriage*. London: Longman *14, 256, 262*

BARKER, D. L., and ALLEN, S. (1976b) *Sexual Divisions and Society*. London: Tavistock *14, 263*

BARRETT, M. (1980) *Women's Oppression Today: Problems in Marxist Feminist Analysis*. London: Verso *19, 21, 22, 24, 25, 26*

BAXANDALL, R., EWEN, E., and GORDON, L. (1976) 'The Working Class Has Two Sexes'. *Monthly Review* (July–August), 1–9 *127*

BEDEMAN, T., and HARVEY, J. (1981) 'Young People on YOP'. In *Employment Gazette* (August), 362–4 *6.16*

BEECHEY, V. (1977) 'Female Wage Labour in Capitalist Production'. *Capital and Class*, 3, 12–26 *20, 21*

BEECHEY, V. (1978) 'Women and Production: A Critical Analysis of Some Sociological Theories of Women's Work'. In Kuhn and Wolpe (1978) *18*

BELOTTI, E. G. (1975) *Little Girls*. London: Writers and Readers Publishing Co-operative *10, 95*

BENET, M. (1972) *Secretary*. London: Sidgwick & Jackson *115*

BERAL, V. (1979) 'Reproductive Mortality. *British Medical Journal*, 2, 362–4 *42*

BERG, S., and DALTON, T. (1977) 'UK Labour Force Activity Rates: Unemployment and Real Wages'. *Applied Economics*, 9 (3), 265–70 *143*

BEVERIDGE, W. (1942) *Report of a Committee on Social Insurance and Allied Services*. Cmnd 6404. London: HMSO *63, 64, 83*

Birth Statistics 1978 (1980) OPCS, Series FMI, No. 5. London: HMSO *33*

BLACKSTONE, T. (1975) 'Women Academics in Britain'. In Piper (1975) *106, 108*

BLONDEL, J. (1966) *Voters, Parties and Leaders*. Harmondsworth: Penguin *195*

Bolton Committee of Enquiry into Small Firms (1971) London: HMSO *136*

BOSANQUET, N., and TOWNSEND, P. (1980) *Labour and Equality: A Fabian Study of Labour in Power 1974–1979*. London: Heinemann *262*

BOSTON, S. (1980) *Women Workers and the Trade Union Movement*. London: Davis-Poynter

BOWKER, L. H. (1978) *Women, Crime and the Criminal Justice System*. Lexington, Mass.: Lexington Books   230

BRADLEY, J., and SILVERLEAF, J. (1979) 'Women Teachers in Further Education'. *Educational Research*, 22(1), 15–21   107

BRANNEN, P. (1975) *Entering the World of Work*. London: HMSO   254

BRIMELOW, E. (1981) *Women in the Civil Service*. London: Haldane Society   176, 199, 201

BRISTOL WOMEN'S STUDIES GROUP (1979) *Half the Sky: An Introduction to Women's Studies*. London: Virago   145

BRISTOW, S. L. (1978a) 'Women Councillors'. *County Councils Gazette* (May), 38–40   188, 189

BRISTOW, S. L. (1978b) 'Women Councillors'. *County Councils Gazette* (November), 229–30   7.10

BRISTOW, S. L. (1978c) 'Women Councillors'. *County Councils Gazette* (December), 272–4   190, 191; 7.13

BRISTOW, S. L. (1980) 'Women Councillors: An Explanation of the Under-Representation of Women in Local Government'. *Local Government Studies* (May–June), 73–90   188; 7.11

British Labour Statistics 1970 (1971) DoE. London: HMSO   6.8, 6.26

BROOKES, P. (1967) *Women at Westminster*. London: Peter Davies   177

BROWN, G. W., and HARRIS, T. (1979) *Social Origins of Depression*. London: Tavistock   41

BROWN, H. P. (1977) *The Inequality of Pay*. Oxford: Oxford University Press

BROWN, M. (1974) *Sweated Labour: A Study of Homework*. London: Low Pay Unit

BROWN, R. (1980) *Going Places: Women in the Conservative Party*. London: Conservative Political Centre   192, 193

BROWN, R. (1976) 'Women as Employees'. In Barker and Allen (1976a)

BROWNMILLER, S. (1975) *Against Our Will*. New York: Simon & Schuster   22

BRUEGEL, I. (1978) 'Bourgeois Economics and Women's Oppression'. In *MF*, 1, 103–11

BURMAN, S. (1979) *Fit Work for Women*. London: Croom Helm   267

BUTLER, D., and KAVANAGH, D. (1975) *The British General Election of 1974*. London: Macmillan   270

BUTLER, D., and KAVANAGH, D. (1980) *The British General Election of 1979*. London: Macmillan   7.16

BUTLER, D., and STOKES, D. (1969) *Political Change in Britain*. London: Macmillan   197

BUTLER, N. R., and BONHAM, D. G. (1963) *Perinatal Mortality, First Report*. London: Livingstone   34

BYRNE, E. M. (1975) 'Inequality in Education – Discriminal Resource – Allocation in Schools'. *Educational Review*, 27 (3), 179–91   102

BYRNE, E. M. (1978) *Women in Education*. London: Tavistock

CAMPBELL, A. (1977) 'What Makes a Girl Turn to Crime'. *New Society*, 27 January, 172–3   210

CAPLAN, P. J. (1980) 'Sex Differences in a Delinquent Clinic Population'. *British Journal of Criminology*, 20 (4), 311–26 *216, 218*

CHAMBERLAIN, M. (1975) *Fenwomen: a Portrait of Women in an English Village*. London: Virago *187, 194*

CHASSERIAUX, E., and REILLY, E. (1978) *Women Working in London*. Research Memorandum. London: Greater London Council

CHESTER, R., and PEEL, J. (1977) *Equalities and Inequalities in Family Life*. London: Academic Press *263*

CHIPLIN, B., CURRAN, M., and PARSLEY, C. (1980) 'Relative Female Earnings in Great Britain and the Impact of Legislation'. In Sloane (1980) *126, 131, 135*

CHIPLIN, B., and SLOANE, P. (1974) 'Sexual Discrimination in the Labour Market'. *British Journal of Industrial Relations*, 12 (3), 371–402 *123, 130*

CHIPLIN, B., and SLOANE, P. (1976a) *Sex Discrimination in the Labour Market*. London: Macmillan *130, 136*

CHIPLIN, B., and SLOANE, P. (1976b) 'Male/Female Earnings Differences: A Further Analysis'. *British Journal of Industrial Relations*, 77–81

CHODOROW, N. (1978) *The Reproduction of Mothering: Psychoanalysis and the Sociology of Gender*. Berkeley, Cal.: University of California Press *22*

CIVIL SERVICE (1971) *The Employment of Women in the Civil Service*. Kemp-Jones Report. CSD Management Studies 3. London: HMSO *200; 7.19*

Civil Service Statistics (1975 and 1980) London: HMSO *201; 7.18, 7.20*

CLARK, J. P., and HAUREK, E. (1966) 'Age and Sex Roles of Adolescents and their Involvement in Misconduct: A Reappraisal'. *Sociology and Social Research*, 50, 496–508

CLOWARD, R. A., and OHLIN, L. E. (1960) *Delinquency and Opportunity: A Theory of Delinquent Gangs*. New York: The Free Press *220*

COHEN, A. K. (1955) *Delinquent Boys: The Culture of the Gang*. New York: The Free Press *220*

COMER, L. (1972) *Wedlocked Women*. London: Feminist Books *10*

Comprehensive Education (1981) Issue 42

CONSERVATIVE WOMEN'S NATIONAL ADVISORY COUNCIL (1980) *Women in Politics*. London: Conservative Party *177; 7.1, 7.14*

COOTE, A. (1979) *Equal at Work: Women in Men's Jobs*. London: Collins

COOTE, A. (1980) 'Powerlessness and How to Fight it'. *New Statesman*, 7 November *6.27*

COOTE, A., and GILL, T. (1977) *Women's Rights: A Practical Guide*. Harmondsworth: Penguin *247*

COOTE, A., and KELLNER, P. (1980) *Hear This Brother: Women Workers and Union Power*. London: New Statesman *152, 154, 158; 6.28, 6.31*

COUNTER-INFORMATION SERVICES (1981) *Women in the 80s*. London: CIS *141*

COUSSINS, J. (1977) *The Equality Report*. National Campaign for Civil Liberties (Rights for Women Unit). London: NCCL *173*

COWIE, J., SLATER, E., and COWIE, V. (1968) *Delinquency in Girls*. London: Heinemann   *204, 210, 218*

Criminal Statistics for England and Wales 1979 (1981) Cmd 8098. London: HMSO   *229; 8.2, 8.3, 8.7, 8.8, 8.9, 8.10, 8.11, 8.12, 8.20*

CRINE, S. (1979) *The Hidden Army*. London: Low Pay Unit   *136, 148, 152*

CUNNINGTON, S. (1980) 'Some Aspects of Prostitution in the West End of London'. In West (1980)   *214*

CURRELL, M. (1974) *Political Woman*. London: Croom Helm   *179, 184, 192; 7.7*

Curricular Differences for Boys and Girls (1975) DES. London: HMSO   *96, 98, 100; 5.6*

DALE, R. R. (1974) *Mixed or Single Sex Schools*, vol. 3. London: Routledge & Kegan Paul   *98*

DATESMAN, S. K., and SCARPETTI, F. R. (1980) *Women, Crime and Justice*. Oxford: Oxford University Press   *206*

DAVIDOFF, L. (1973) *The Best Circles*. London: Croom Helm   *2*

DAVIDSON, M., and COOPER, C. (1980) 'The Women Under Pressure'. *The Guardian*, 9 October   *138, 147*

DAVIES, L. (1980) 'Deviance and Sex Roles in Schools'. Unpublished PhD thesis. University of Birmingham   *218*

DAVIES, R. (1975) *Women and Work*. London: Hutchinson

DEACON, A. (1976) *In Search of the Scrounger: The Administration of Unemployment Insurance in Britain 1920–31*. London: Bell   *65*

DEEM, R. (1978) *Women and Schooling*. London: Routledge & Kegan Paul   *95, 103*

DELAMONT, S. (1980a) *Sex Roles and the School*. London: Methuen   *94, 95, 102, 104*

DELAMONT, S. (1980b) *The Sociology of Women: An Introduction*. London: Allen & Unwin   *114*

DELL, S. (1971) *Silent in Court*. Occasional Papers on Social Administration No. 42. London: Bell   *223*

Dod's Parliamentary Companion. Hailsham: Dod's.   *7.7, 7.9*

DOUGLAS, J. W. B. (1964) *The Home and the School*. London: MacGibbon & Kee   *86, 87*

DOWNES, D. (1966) *The Delinquent Solution: A Study in Subcultural Theory*. London: Routledge & Kegan Paul   *219, 220*

DOWNING, H. (1980) 'Word Processors and the Oppression of Women'. In Forester (1980)   *250*

DOWSE, R. E., and HUGHES, J. A. (1971) 'Girls, Boys and Politics'. *British Journal of Sociology*, 22 (1), 53–67   *202*

DUVERGER, M. (1955) *The Political Role of Women*. Paris: UNESCO   *202*

EDWARDS, E. G., and ROBERTS, I. J. (1980) 'British Higher Education: Long-Term Trends in Student Enrolment'. *Higher Education Review*, 12, 7–43   *6, 92*

EEC (1974) *Women and Employment in the United Kingdom, Ireland and Denmark*. Brussels: EEC   *6.33*

EEC (1979) *European Men and Women in 1978: A Comparative Study of*

Socio-Political Attitudes in the European Community. Luxemburg: EEC *147, 148, 152, 161, 185*

EEC (1980) *European Women in Paid Employment*. Brussels: EEC

ELIAS, P. (1980) 'Labour Supply and Opportunities for Women'. In Lindley (1980) *6.19*

ELSTON, M. A. (1980) 'Medicine: Half our Future Doctors?'. In Silverstone and Ward (1980) *145; 6.22*

Employment Gazette. Department of Employment. London: HMSO *125, 142, 144, 157; 6.3, 6.9, 6.14, 6.18, 6.19, 6.20, 6.25*

EOC (1977) *Women and Low Incomes*. Manchester: EOC

EOC (1978a) *Equality Between the Sexes in Industry: How Far Have We Come?* Manchester: EOC *172*

EOC (1978b) *Women in the Legal Services*. Manchester: EOC

EOC (1979) *Research Bulletin, No. 1.1*. Manchester: EOC *162, 173*

EOC (1980a) *The Experience of Caring for Elderly and Handicapped Dependants*. Manchester: EOC *62; 4.1*

EOC (1980b) *Women and Government Statistics*. EOC Research Bulletin No. 4. Manchester: EOC *238, 264, 266*

EOC (1981) *Women and Underachievement at Work*. EOC Research Bulletin No. 5. Manchester: EOC

EOC Annual Report 1978 (1979) Manchester: EOC *128, 152*

EOC Annual Report 1979 (1980) Manchester: EOC *133; 6.17*

EOC Annual Report 1980 (1981) Manchester: EOC *150, 171, 173; 6.13, 6.24, 6.26*

Equal Pay and Opportunities (1981) Manpower Paper No. 20. DoE. London: HMSO *172*

EVANS, J. (1980) 'Women and Politics: A Reappraisal'. *Political Studies*, 28 (2), 210–21 *183, 190, 194, 195, 197, 198, 201*

Family Expenditure Survey (1979) London: HMSO *4.13*

FINER, M. (1974) *Report of the Committee on 1-Parent Families*. London: HMSO *80*

FOGARTY, M., ALLEN, A. J., ALLEN, I., and WALTERS, P. (1971) *Women in Top Jobs: Four Studies in Achievement*. London: Allen & Unwin *147*

FOGARTY, M., ALLEN, I., and WALTERS, P. (1981) *Women in Top Jobs 1968–79*. London: Heinemann

FOGARTY, M. P., RAPOPORT, R., and RAPOPORT, R. N. (1971) *Sex, Career and Family*. London: Allen & Unwin *18, 19*

FONDA, N., and MOSS, P. (1976) *Mothers in Employment*. Uxbridge: Brunel University *260*

FORESTER, T. (1980) *The Micro-Electronics Revolution*. Oxford: Blackwell *258*

FRANCIS, J. G., and PEELE, G. (1978) 'Reflections on Generational Analysis: Is there a Shared Political Perspective Between Men and Women?'. *Political Studies*, 26 (3), 363–74 *197; 7.17*

FRANKFORT, E. (1972) *Vaginal Politics*. London: Times Books *22*

FREIDL, E. (1975) *Women and Men: An Anthropologist's View*. Eastbourne: Holt, Rinehart & Winston *2*

FRYER, R. H., FAIRCLOUGH, A. H., and MANSON, T. B. (1978) 'Facilities for

Female Shop Stewards: The Employment Protection Act and Collective Agreements'. *British Journal of Industrial Relations*, 16, 160–74   *158*

FULTON COMMITTEE (1968) *The Civil Service*. London: HMSO   *199*

GARABEDIAN, P. G., and GIBBONS, D. C. (1970) *Becoming Delinquent*. Chicago, Ill.: Aldine Press   *271*

GARDINER, J. (1975) 'Women's Domestic Labour'. *New Left Review*, 89, 47–58   *21*

GARDINER, J. (1977) 'Women in the Labour Process and Class Structure'. In Hunt (1977)   *27*

GAVRON, H. (1966) *The Captive Wife*. Harmondsworth: Penguin   *145*

General Household Survey 1972 (1975) OPCS Social Survey Division. London: HMSO   *38*

General Household Survey 1976 (1978) OPCS Social Survey Division. London: HMSO   *45, 56, 144; 3.9*

General Household Survey 1977 (1979) OPCS Social Survey Division. London: HMSO   *34, 41, 42, 45; 3.3*

General Household Survey 1978 (1980) OPCS Social Survey Division. London: HMSO   *144, 164; 6.4, 6.15, 6.32*

General Household Survey 1980 (1981) OPCS Social Survey Division. London: HMSO   *118, 120, 150*

GEORGE, V., and WILDING, P. (1972) *Motherless Families*. London: Routledge & Kegan Paul

GIBBENS, T. C. N., and PRINCE, J. (1962) *Shoplifting*. London: ISTD   *217*

GIDDENS, A. (1975) *The Class Structure of the Advanced Societies*. London: Harper & Row   *17*

GILL, C. (1977) *Luke Street: Housing Policy Conflict and the Creation of the Delinquent Area*. London: Macmillan   *219, 220*

GINSBERG, S. (1976) 'Women, Work and Conflict'. In Fonda and Moss (1976)   *145*

GOFFMAN, E. (1979) *Gender Advertisement*. London: Macmillan   *104*

GOLDTHORPE, J. (1980) *Social Mobility and Class Structure in Modern Britain*. Oxford: Clarendon   *16*

GOOT, M., and REID, E. (1975) *Women and Voting Studies: Mindless Matrons or Sexist Scientism*. London: Sage   *194, 203*

GORER, G. (1971) *Sex and Marriage in England Today: A Study of the Views and Experiences of the Under 45s*. London: Nelson (London: Panther, 1973)   *72*

GRAY, A. (1974) 'The Working Class Family as an Economic Unit'. Unpublished PhD thesis. University of Edinburgh   *69, 72*

GRAY, P. G., TODD, J. E., SLACK, G. L., and BULMAN, J. S. (1970) *Adult Dental Health in England and Wales in 1968*. OPCS Social Survey Division for DHSS. London: HMSO   *45*

GREENHALGH, C. (1977) 'A Labour Supply Function for Married Women'. *Economica*, 44, 249–65   *143*

GREENHALGH, C. (1980) 'Male/Female Wage Differentials in Great Britain: Is Marriage an Equal Opportunity?'. *Economic Journal*, 90, 751–75   *138, 148, 165; 6.6*

GREENWOOD, V. (1981) 'The Myth of Female Crime'. In Morris (1981)   *221, 246*

GREER, G. (1971) *The Female Eunuch*. Maidenhead: McGraw-Hill   *22*

GRIMES, J. A. (1978) 'The Probability of Admission to a Mental Illness Hospital or Unit'. In *In-Patient Statistics from the Mental Health Enquiry for England 1975* (1978)   *44*

HADOW COMMITTEE (1927) *The Education of the Adolescent*. London: HMSO   *103*

HAGAN, J., SIMPSON, J. H., and GILLIS, A. R. (1979) 'The Sexual Stratification of Social Control: A Gender-Based Perspective on Crime and Delinquency'. *British Journal of Sociology*, 30 (1), 25–38   *219, 221*

HAKIM, C. (1978) 'Sexual Divisions Within the Labour Force: Occupational Segmentation'. *Employment Gazette* (November), 1264–8   *132, 154*

HAKIM, C. (1980a) *Occupational Segregation*. Research Paper No. 9. DoE. London: HMSO   *132; 6.11*

HAKIM, C. (1980b) 'Homeworking: Some New Evidence'. *Employment Gazette* (October), 1105–10   *136, 152, 159; 6.30*

Half The Story (1979) Bristol: Women's Study Group   *10*

HALSEY, A. H. (1972) *Trends in British Society Since 1900*. London: Macmillan   *7, 8, 9*

HAMILL, L. (1978a) *Wives as Sole and Joint Breadwinners*. Government Economic Service Working Paper No. 13. DHSS. London: HMSO   *75, 78; 4.6, 4.7*

HAMILL, L. (1978b) *An Exploration of the Increase in Female 1-parent Families Receiving Supplementary Benefit*. Government Economic Service Working Paper No. 14. DHSS. London: HMSO   *80; 4.12*

HARDING, J. (1979) 'Sex Differences in Examination Performance at 16+'. *Physics Education*, 14 (5), 280–4   *98*

HARRIS, A. (1977) 'Sex and Theories of Deviance: Towards a Functional Theory of Type Scripts'. *American Sociological Review*, 42 (1), 13–16   *206*

HARRIS, C. (1979) 'The Sociology of the Family'. *Sociological Review Monograph*, 28   *10*

HARRIS, J. (1977) *William Beveridge: A Biography*. Oxford: Clarendon Press   *63*

HARRISON, B. (1978) *Separate Spheres*. London: Croom Helm   *175*

HARRISON, G. A., and BOYCE, A. J. (1972) *The Structure of Human Populations*. Oxford: Clarendon Press   *270*

HARRISON, M. (1979) 'Participation of Women in Trade Union Activities'. *Industrial Relations Journal* (Summer), 41–55   *159*

HARTLEY, D. (1980) 'Sex Differences in the Infant School: Definitions and Theories'. *British Journal of Sociology of Education*, 1, 93–105   *85*

Health and Personal Social Services Statistics for England 1978 (1980) DHSS. London: HMSO   *3.5, 3.6, 3.10*

HEATH, A. (1981) *Social Mobility*. London: Fontana

HEDBLOM, M.(1981) *Women and Mass Media*. European Consortium for Political Research/IPSA Workshop. Lancaster: University of Lancaster   *177*

HEIDENSOHN, F. (1968) 'The Deviance of Women: A Critique and an Enquiry'. *British Journal of Sociology*, 19 (2), 160–73   *206*

HEIDENSOHN, F. (1981)) 'Women and the Penal System'. In Morris (1981)   *223, 227*

HEILMAN, M., and SARUWATARI, L. (1979) 'When Beauty is Beastly: Effects of Appearance and Sex on Evaluations of Job Applicants for Managerial and Non-Managerial Jobs'. *Organisational Behaviour and Human Performance*, 23 (3), 360–72   *161*

HEWITT, P. (1980) 'Sex Equality'. In Bosanquet and Townsend (1980)   *172*

HOBSON, D. (1978) 'Housewives: Isolation as Oppression'. In Women's Study Group: Centre for Contemporary Cultural Studies (1978)   *152*

HOFFMAN-BUSTAMENTE, D. (1973) 'The Nature of Female Criminality'. *Issues in Criminology*, 8 (2), 117–36   *219*

HOLTER, H. (1970) *Sex Roles and Social Structure*. Oslo: Universitets Forlaget   *10*

HOPE, E., KENNEDY, M., and DE WINTER, A. (1976) 'Homeworkers in North London'. In Barker and Allen (1976a)   *148, 152*

Hospital In-Patient Enquiry (1980) DHSS, OPCS and Welsh Office, Series MB4, No. 7. London: HMSO   *42; 3.7*

HOUSE OF LORDS (1968) *House of Lords Reform*. Cmd 3799. London: HMSO   *75, 78*

HUNT, A. (1968) *A Survey of Women's Employment*. London: HMSO

HUNT, A. (1975) *Management Attitudes and Practices Towards Women at Work*. OPCS Social Survey Division. London: HMSO   *128, 146, 161, 173*

HUNT, A. (1977) *Class and Class Structure*. London: Lawrence & Wishart   *260*

HYMAN, H. H. (1959) *Political Socialization*. New York: Free Press   *203*

INGLEBY, J. D. (1960) *Report of the Committee on Children and Young Persons* (Ingleby Report). London: HMSO   *206, 213*

INGLEBY, J. D., and COOPER, E. (1974) 'How Teachers Perceive First Year School Children'. *Sociology*, 8 (3), 463–73   *85*

In-Patient Statistics from the Mental Health Enquiry for England 1977 (1980) DHSS Statistical and Research Report, Series No. 23. London: HMSO   *3.6*

IRVINE, J., MILES, I., and EVANS, J. (1979) *Demystifying Social Statistics*. London: Pluto Press   *266*

ISAACSON, Z., and FREEMAN, H. (1980) 'Girls and Mathematics: A Response'. *Mathematics Teaching*, 90, 24–6   *99*

JAMES, W. P. T. (1979) *Research on Obesity*. DHSS Medical Research Council. London: HMSO   *3.8*

JENSEN, G., and EVE, R. (1976) 'Sex Differences in Delinquency: An Examination of Popular Sociological Explanations'. *Criminology: An Interdisciplinary Journal*, 13, 427–48   *210*

JOSHI, H. (1978) *Secondary Workers in the Cycle: Married Women and Older Workers in Employment Fluctuations, GB 1965–74*. DHSS. London: HMSO   *142*

KAMERMAN, S. B., and KAHN, A. J. (1978) *Family Policy: Government and Families in Fourteen Countries*. New York: Columbia University Press *59, 264*

KELLNER, P. (1980) 'Not a Defeat a Disaster'. *New Statesman*, 18 May, 704–6 *195*

KELSALL, R. K., POOLE, A., and KUHN, A. (1972) *Graduates*. London: Methuen *92*

KERR, E. (1979) Letter from the Chief Officer of the Council for National Academic Awards, London, to one of the Editors *238*

KEYS, W., and ORMEROD, M. B. (1977) 'Some Sex Related Differences in the Correlates of Subject Preference in the Middle Years of Secondary Education'. *Educational Studies*, 3 (2), 111–16 *101*

KING, J., and STOTT, M. (1977) *Is This Your Life? Images of Women in the Media*. London: Virago *247*

KITSUSE, J. I., and CICOUREL, A. V. (1963) 'A Note on the Use of Official Statistics'. *Social Problems*, 11 (2), 131–9 *209*

KLEIN, V. (1965) *Britain's Married Women Workers*. London: Routledge & Kegan Paul *18, 19*

KONOPKA, G. (1966) *The Adolescent Girl in Conflict*. Englewood Cliffs, NJ: Prentice-Hall *219*

KUHN, A., and WOLPE, A. (1978) *Feminism and Materialism*. London: Routledge & Kegan Paul *19, 255, 271*

Labour Force Statistics 1968–1979 (1981) Paris: OECD

Labour Force Survey 1973, 1975, 1977 (1980) EEC Commission/OPCS. London: HMSO *6.1, 6.21, 6.34*

LABOUR PARTY (1974) *Obstacles to Women in Public Life*. London: Labour Party

LABOUR RESEARCH DEPARTMENT (1978) 'Women at Work'. *Labour Research* (December) *133*

LA FONTAINE, J. S. (1978) *Sex and Age as Principles of Social Differentiation*. London: Academic Press *2*

LAND, H. (1969) *Large Families in London*. London: Bell *69, 70, 73; 4.3*

LAND, H. (1971) 'Women, Work and Social Security'. *Journal of Social and Economic Administration*, 5 (3), 183–91

LAND, H. (1975) 'The Myth of the Male Breadwinner'. *New Society*, 29 February, 71–3

LAND, H. (1976) 'Women: Supporters or Supported?' In Barker and Allen (1976b) *22*

LAND, H. (1977) 'Inequalities in Large Families'. In Chester and Peel (1977)

LAND, H. (1978) 'Who Cares for the Family?'. *Journal of Social Policy*, 7 (3), 259–85

LAND, H., and PARKER, R. (1978) 'United Kingdom'. In Kamerman and Kahn (1978) *59*

LANE, R. (1961) *Political Life*. New York: Free Press *203, 248*

LAYARD, R., PIACHAUD, D., and STEWART, M. (1978) *The Causes of Poverty*. (Background Paper to Royal Commission on the Distribution of Income and Wealth 1978b). London: HMSO *169*

LEETE, R. (1977) 'Changing Marital Composition'. OPCS, *Population Trends*, No. 10. London: HMSO *55, 56*

LEETE, R. (1979a) *Changing Patterns of Family Formation and Dissolution in England and Wales 1964–76*. OPCS Studies on Medical and Population Studies. London: HMSO *54, 56*

LEETE, R. (1979b) *Divorce and Remarriage: A Record Limitage Study*. OPCS, *Population Trends*, No. 16. London: HMSO *56*

LE LOHE, M. J. (1976) 'Sex Discrimination and Under-Representation of Women in Politics'. *New Community* (Summer), 118–19 *178, 189; 7.3*

LEONARD, D. (1980) *Sex and Generation: A Study of Courtship and Weddings*. London: Tavistock *69*

Life Tables (1979) The Registrar General's Decennial Supplement for England and Wales, Series DS, No. 2. London: HMSO *49; 3.11, 3.14*

LINDLEY, R. M. (1980) *Economic Change and Employment Policy*. London: Macmillan *259*

LLOYD, S. (1963) *Report to the Chairman of the Party Organisation and the Executive Committee of the National Union of Conservative and Unionist Associations*. London: Conservative Party *179*

LOBBAN, G. (1975) 'Sex Roles in Reading Schemes'. *Educational Review*, 27 (3), 202–9 *96*

LUMLEY, R. (1973) *White Collar Unionism in Britain*. London: Methuen *158, 173*

LUPTON, T. (1963) *On the Shop Floor*. Oxford: Pergamon *157*

MACFARLANE, A. (1979) 'Child Deaths from Accidents: Place of Accident'. *Population Trends*, 15, 10–15 *34*

MACFARLANE, A. (1980) 'Official Statistics and Women's Health and Illness'. In EOC (1980b) *30*

McINTOSH, A. (1980) 'Women at Work: A Survey of Employers'. *Employment Gazette* (November), 1142–9 *126, 127, 171, 172, 173*

McINTOSH, N. E. (1979) 'Women in Distance Education: The Open University Experience'. *Educational Broadcasting International*, 12 (4), 178–83 *110, 112; 5.13*

MACKAY, D. I., BODDY, D., BRACK, J., DIACK, J. A., and JONES, N. (1971) *Labour Markets Under Different Employment Conditions*. London: Allen & Unwin *148*

MACKIE, L., and PATTULLO, P. (1977) *Women at Work*. London: Tavistock *147, 170*

MCNABB, R. (1977) 'The Labour Force Participation of Married Women'. *The Manchester School*, 43 (3), 221–35 *143*

MCNALLY, F. (1979) *Women for Hire: A Study of the Female Office Worker*. London: Macmillan *133, 138, 152, 159*

MACRAE, D. G. (1972) 'Classlessness'. *New Society*, 26 October, 208–10 *16*

MAGUIRE, M. (1980) 'The Impact of Burglary Upon Victims'. *British Journal of Criminology*, 20 (3), 261–75 *231; 8.21*

MAIR, L. (1971) *Marriage*. London: Scolar Press. (Harmondsworth: Penguin) *10*

MAIZELS, J. (1970) *Adolescent Needs and the Transition from School to Work*. London: Athlone Press *152*

MANLEY, P., and SAWBRIDGE, D. (1980) 'Women at Work'. *Lloyds Bank Review*, 135 (January 1980), 29–40

Marriage and Divorce Statistics 1978 (1980) OPCS Series FM2, No. 5. London: HMSO *54, 56; 3.15, 3.16*

MARSDEN, D. (1969) *Mothers Alone*. London: Allen Lane *73*

MARSH, A. (1979) *Women and Shiftwork: The Protective Legislation Survey Carried Out for the EOC*. OPCS. London: HMSO *133, 152, 159, 161, 169*

MARSH, D. (1971) 'Political Socialisation: The Implicit Assumptions Questioned'. *British Journal of Political Science*, 1, 45–65 *203*

MAUD COMMITTEE (1966–9) *Royal Commission on Local Government*. London: HMSO *176, 188, 191, 192*

MAWBY, R. (1980) 'Sex and Crime: The Results of a Self-Report Study'. *British Journal of Sociology*, 31 (4), 525–43 *210, 211; 8.5*

MAXWELL, J. (1977) *Reading Progress from 8–15*. Slough: NFER *87*

MEAD, M. (1950) *Male and Female*. London: Gollancz *13, 14*

MELLORS, C. (1978) *The British MP*. London: Saxon House *179, 192; 7.2, 7.4, 7.5, 7.6*

METCALF, D., and RICHARDSON, R. (1980) 'Labour'. In Prest and Coppock (1980) *172*

MIDDLETON, L. (1977) *Women in the Labour Movement*. London: Croom Helm *158, 188*

MILBURN, J. F. (1976) *Women as Citizens: A Comparative Review*. London: Sage, *187*

MILLETT, K. (1969) *Sexual Politics*. St Albans: Hart-Davis *22*

MILLWARD, N. (1968) 'Family Status and Behaviour at Work'. *Sociological Review*, 16(2), 149–66 *71, 73*

Minimum Wages for Women (1980) London: Low Pay Unit

MOLYNEUX, M. (1979) 'Beyond the Domestic Labour Debate'. *New Left Review*, 116, 3–27 *21*

MONCK, E., and LOMAS, G. B. (1975) *The Employment and Socio-Economic Conditions of the Coloured Population*. London: Centre for Environmental Studies *166, 168*

Monthly Digest of Statistics. CSO. London: HMSO

Morbidity Statistics from General Practice 1971–72 (1979). Second Study, Royal College of General Practitioners, OPCS and DHSS. Studies on Medical and Population Subjects No. 36. London: HMSO *3.4*

MORGAN, J. P. (1975) *The House of Lords and the Labour Government 1964–70*. Oxford: Clarendon Press *184*

MORRIS, A. (1981) *Women and Crime*. Cropwood Conference Series, No. 18. Cambridge: Institute of Criminology *261, 262, 266*

MORRIS, J. N. (1975) *The Uses of Epidemiology*. 3rd edn. London: Livingstone *57*

Mortality Statistics 1979 (1981) OPCS, Series DH2, No. 6. London: HMSO *44, 50; 3.12*

NACRO (1977) *Children and Young Persons in Custody: Report of a Working Party*. Chichester : Barry Rose *213*

NACRO (1980) *Women in the Penal System*. London: NACRO *222, 223, 227*

NAGEL, I. (1981) 'Sex Differences in the Processing of Criminal Defendants'. In Morris (1981) *221*

NATIONAL BOARD FOR PRICES AND INCOMES (1971) *General Problems of Low Pay*. London: HMSO *146*

NATIONAL COUNCIL FOR ONE-PARENT FAMILES (1980) *Annual Report and Accounts 1979–80*. London: National Council for One-Parent Families *79, 82*

NATIONAL LABOUR WOMEN'S ADVISORY COMMITTEE (1971) *Women Candidates in the Labour Party*. London: Labour Party *179, 193*

NATIONAL AND LOCAL GOVERNMENT OFFICERS' ASSOCIATION (1980) *NALGO Equal Rights Survey*. London: NALGO *155, 158, 161*

NATIONAL UNION OF TEACHERS (1980a) *Once Upon a Myth*. NUT Ad Hoc Committee on Equal Opportunities. London: NUT *161*

NATIONAL UNION OF TEACHERS (1980b) *Promotion and the Woman Teacher*. London: NUT *153, 161*

New Earnings Survey. DoE. London: HMSO *114, 132; 6.5, 6.7*

NEWSON, J., and NEWSON, E. (1976) *Seven Years Old in the Home Environment*. London: Allen & Unwin *219, 221*

NISSELL, M. (1980) 'Women in Government Statistics: Basic Concepts and Assumptions'. In EOC (1980b) *238, 239*

NORWOOD COMMITTEE (1941) *Curriculum and Examinations in Secondary Schools*. London: HMSO *103*

NOVITSKI, E. (1977) *Human Genetics*. London: Collier Macmillan *30*

OAKLEY, A. (1972) *Sex, Gender and Society*. London: Temple Smith *2, 13, 15*

OAKLEY, A. (1974a) *Housewife*. London and Harmondsworth: Allen Lane/ Pelican

OAKLEY, A. (1974b) *The Sociology of Housework*. Oxford: Martin Robertson *68, 72, 145*

OAKLEY, A. (1980) 'For Love or Money: The Unspoken Deal'. *New Society*, 18 December, iv–vi *144*

OAKLEY, A. (1981) *Subject Women*. Oxford: Martin Robertson *14, 133, 150, 172*

OAKLEY, A., and OAKLEY, R. (1979) 'Sexism in Official Statistics'. In Irvine, Miles and Evans (1979) *238*

Occupational Mortality (1978) The Registrar General's *Decennial Supplement* for England and Wales 1970–2, Series DS, No. 1. London: HMSO *5.3; 3.2*

OFFICE OF MANPOWER ECONOMICS (1972) *Report on the Equal Pay Act*. London: HMSO *170*

Official Journal of the EEC (1979) EEC Council Directive of 19 December 1978, 79/7. Luxemburg: EEC *60*

OPCS Monitor, PP1 78/2 (1978) London: HMSO *3.1*

OPCS Monitor, FM2 78/2 (1978) London: HMSO *56; 3.17*

ORMEROD, M. B. (1975) 'Subject Preference and Choice in Co-educational and Single Sex Secondary Schools'. *British Journal of Educational Psychology*, 45, 259–67 *100*

PAHL, J. (1980) 'Patterns of Money Management Within Marriage'. *Journal of Social Policy*, 9 (3), p. 313–37 *70, 74*

PARKIN, F. (1972) *Class Inequality and Political Order*. St Albans: Paladin *26*

The Part Time Trap (1978) London: Low Pay Unit *120, 158*

PENROSE, L. S. (1973) *Outline of Human Genetics*. 3rd edn. London: Heinemann *30*

People in Britain (1980) Census Research Unit, Department of Geography, University of Durham, OPCS and General Register Office (Scotland). London: HMSO *32*

PHILLIPS, M. (1980) *The Divided House: Women at Westminster*. London: Sidgwick & Jackson *176, 184, 242, 248*

PINCHBECK, I. (1930) *Women Workers and the Industrial Revolution 1750–1850*. London: Routledge *246*

PIPER, D. W. (1975) *Women in Higher Education*. London: University of London Teaching Methods Unit *255*

POLLAK, O. (1961) *The Criminality of Women*. New York: A. S. Barnes *204, 210, 214, 216, 217, 218*

POSTER, M. (1978) *Critical Theory of the Family*. New York: Continuum *22*

PREECE, M. (1979) 'Mathematics: The Unpredictability of Girls?'. *Mathematics Teaching*, 85, 27–9 *98*

PREST, A. R., and COPPOCK, D. T. (1980) *The UK Economy: A Manual of Applied Economics*. London: Weidenfeld & Nicolson *265*

PRICE, R. R. (1977) 'The Forgotten Female Offender'. *Crime and Delinquency*, 23, 101–8 *227*

Primary Education in England (1978) DES. London: HMSO *87, 88*

PULZER, P. G. J. (1967) *Political Representation and Elections in Britain*. London: Allen & Unwin *195*

PURCELL, K. (1979) 'Militancy and Acquiescence Amongst Women Workers'. In Burman (1979) *157, 159*

RAPOPORT, R. B. (1981) 'The Sex Gap in Political Persuading'. *American Journal of Political Science*, 25 (1), 32–48 *242*

RAPOPORT, R., and RAPOPORT, R. (1976) *Dual-Career Families Re-Examined*. London: Martin Robertson *145*

Recession 1974–75 and the Employment of Women (1976) Reprinted in Amsden (1980) *142*

Regional Trends. CSO. London: HMSO *144*

REID, I. (1978) *Sociological Perspectives on School and Education*. London: Open Books *247, 252*

REID, I. (1981) *Social Class Differences in Britain*, 2nd edn. London: Grant McIntyre *5, 29, 53, 239, 252*

REITER, R. R. (1975) *Towards an Anthropology of Women*. London: Monthly Review Press *2*

RENDEL, M. (1975) 'Men and Women in Higher Education'. *Educational Review*, 27 (3), 192–201

Report of the National Insurance Advisory Committee on a Question Relating to the Household Duties Test for NCIP for Married Women (1980) Cmnd 7955. London: HMSO   *62*

Report of the Work of the Prison Department (1979) Cmnd 7965. Home Office. London: HMSO   *223, 227, 228; 8.13, 8.15*

Report of the Work of the Prison Department: Statistical Tables (1979) Cmnd 7978. Home Office. London: HMSO   *225, 227; 8.16, 8.17*

Response of the Supplementary Benefits Commission (1978) 'Social Assistance: A Review of the Supplementary Benefits Scheme in GB'. SBA Paper, No. 9. London: HMSO   *206, 212, 220*

RICHARDSON, H. J. (1969) *Adolescent Girls in Approved Schools*. London: Routledge & Kegan Paul   *206, 212, 220*

ROBERTI, P. (1974) *The Distribution of Household Income in the UK 1957–72*. Cited p. 40, Royal Commission on the Distribution of Income and Wealth (1978a)   *150*

ROBERTS, H. (1981) *Women, Health and Reproduction*. London: Routledge & Kegan Paul   *243*

ROBINSON COMMITTEE (1977) *Committee of Inquiry into the System of Remuneration of Members of Local Authorities*. London: HMSO   *188, 190; 7.12*

ROGERS, C. S. (1980) 'The Development of Sex Differences in Evaluations of Others' Success and Failures'. *British Journal of Educational Psychology*, 50 (3), 243–52   *100*

Role of Immigrants in the Labour Market (1976) DoE. London: HMSO   *166*

ROSE, R. (1969) *Studies in British Politics*. 2nd edn. London: Macmillan   *195*

ROSE, R. (1974) *Electoral Behaviour: A Comparative Handbook*. New York: Free Press   *195; 7.15*

ROSENBLUM, K. (1975) 'Female Deviance and the Female Sex Role: A Preliminary Investigation'. *British Journal of Sociology*, 26 (2), 169–85   *205*

ROSS, J. F. S. (1955) *Elections and Electors*. London: Eyre & Spottiswoode   *179*

ROWBOTHAM, S. (1973) *Hidden from History*. London: Pluto Press   *13*

ROWBOTHAM, S. (1979) 'The Trouble with Patriarchy'. *New Statesman*, 28 December   *28*

ROWETH, B. (1981) 'Enigma APR = QLR × QPR'. *The Guardian*, 9 January   *86, 90*

ROYAL COMMISSION ON THE DISTRIBUTION OF INCOME AND WEALTH (1976) *Report No. 3: Higher Incomes from Employment*. London: HMSO   *126*

ROYAL COMMISSION ON THE DISTRIBUTION OF INCOME AND WEALTH (1978a) *Report No. 5: The Causes of Poverty*. London: HMSO   *79, 80, 81, 120, 126, 149, 150, 165; 4.2, 4.8, 4.9, 4.12*

ROYAL COMMISSION ON THE DISTRIBUTION OF INCOME AND WEALTH (1978b) *Report No. 6: Lower Incomes*. London: HMSO   *76, 126, 132; 6.23*

ROYAL COMMISSION ON THE DISTRIBUTION OF INCOME AND WEALTH (1980)

Report No. 8: Fifth Report on the Standing Reference. London: HMSO *138, 6.12*

RUSH, M. (1969) *The Selection of Parliamentary Candidates*. London: Nelson *179, 193*

SCASE, R., and GOFFEE, R. (1980) *The Real World of the Small Business Owner*. London: Croom Helm *147*

SCHUARD, H. (1981) 'Mathematics and the 10-Year-Old'. *The Times Educational Supplement*, 27 March *88*

SECOMBE, W. (1974) 'The Housewife and her Labour Under Capitalism'. *New Left Review*, 83, 3–24 *21*

SHACKLADY-SMITH, L. (1978) 'Sexist Assumptions and Female Delinquency'. In Smart and Smart (1978) *220*

SHARMA, S., and MEIGHAN, R. (1980) 'Schooling and Sex Roles: The Case of GCE "O" Level Mathematics'. *British Journal of Sociology of Education*, 1 (2), 193–205 *97, 99*

SHARPE, S. (1976) *Just Like a Girl: How Girls Learn to be Women*. Harmondsworth: Penguin *2, 13, 94, 95, 101, 103, 104*

SHIMMIN, S., McNALLY, J., and LIFF, S. (1981) 'Pressures on Women Engaged in Factory Work'. *Employment Gazette* (August), 344–9 *145, 148*

SHIPLEY, P. (1979) *Directory of Pressure Groups and Representative Associations*. Cambridge: Bowker *194*

SIEBERT, W. S., and SLOANE, P. J. (1981) 'The Measurement of Sex and Marital Status Discrimination at the Workplace'. *Economica*, 48 (190), 125–41 *165*

SILVERSTONE, R., and WARD, A. (1980) *Careers of Professional Women*. London: Croom Helm *259*

SIMON, R. (1975) *Women and Crime*. Lexington, Mass.: Lexington Books *206*

SLOANE, P. J. (1980) *Women and Low Pay*. London: Macmillan *257*

SLOANE, P. J. and SIEBERT, W. S. (1980) 'Low Pay Amongst Women'. In Sloane (1980) *130, 136, 269*

SMART, B., and SMART, C. (1978) *Women, Sexuality and Social Control*. London: Routledge & Kegan Paul *22, 269*

SMART, C. (1976) *Women, Crime and Criminology: A Feminist Critique*. London: Routledge & Kegan Paul *205, 206, 212, 216, 217, 220, 230; 8.8, 8.9, 8.10*

SMART, C. (1979) 'The New Female Criminal: Reality or Myth'. *British Journal of Criminology*, 19 (1), 50–9 *207; 8.1, 8.4*

SMELLIE, K. B. (1968) *A History of Local Government*. 4th edn. London: Unwin *188*

SMITH, D. J. (1974) *Racial Disadvantage in Employment*. London: PEP *166, 169*

SMITH, D. J. (1976) *The Facts of Racial Disadvantage: A National Survey*. London: PEP *167*

SMITH, D. J. (1981) *Unemployment and Racial Minorities*. London: Policy Studies Institute *149*

SMITH, S. (1980) 'Should They Be Kept Apart?'. *The Times Educational Supplement*, 18 July *100*

SNELL, M. (1979) 'The Equal Pay Act and Sex Discrimination Acts'. *Feminist Review*, 1   *14, 170*

Social Trends No. 5 (1974) CSO. London: HMSO   *146, 147; 6.10*

Social Trends No. 9 (1978) CSO. London: HMSO   *45, 53; 3.13*

Social Trends No. 10 (1979) CSO. London: HMSO   *34*

Social Trends No. 11 (1980) CSO. London: HMSO   *66, 89, 164; 4.5, 6.1, 6.2, 6.26*

SPARKS, R. F. (1971) *Local Prisons: The Crisis in the English Penal System*. London: Heinemann   *226*

SPARKS, R. F., GENN, H. G., and DODD, D. J. (1977) *Surveying Victims*. London: Wiley   *228; 8.19*

STACEY, M., and PRICE, M. (1981) *Women, Power and Politics*. London: Tavistock   *186*

STAGEMAN, J. (1980) *Women in Trade Unions*. Hull: University of Hull   *158*

STARK, T. (1972) *The Distribution of Personal Incomes in the UK 1949–63*. Cambridge: Cambridge University Press   *68*

START, K. B., and WELLS, B. K. (1972) *The Trend of Reading Standards*. Slough: NFER   *88*

Statistics of Education 1977 (1979–80) DES. London: HMSO   *93, 105, 109, 110; 5.4, 5.5, 5.7, 5.8, 5.9, 5.12*

Statistics of Education 1978 (1980–1) DES. London: HMSO   *85; 5.1, 5.2, 5.3, 5.10, 5.11*

STEED, M. (1975) 'Analysis of the Results'. In Butler and Kavanagh (1975)   *178*

STRADLING, R. (1978) *The Political Awareness of the School Leaver*. London: Hansard Society   *202; 7.21*

STRATTA, E. W. (1970) *The Education of Borstal Boys*. London: Routledge & Kegan Paul   *213, 252*

Strikes in Britain (1978) Manpower Paper No. 15. DoE. London: HMSO   *156, 158*

SULLEROT, E. (1977) 'The Changing Roles of Men and Women in Europe'. In *The Changing Roles of Men and Women in Modern Society: Functions, Rights and Responsibilities*, vol. 2. New York: United Nations   *188*

SUTHERLAND, M. B. (1981) *Sex Bias in Education*. Oxford: Blackwell   *97*

TAVRIS, C., and OFFIR, C. (1977) *The Longest War: Sex Differences in Perspective*. New York: Harcourt Brace   *235*

TAWNEY, R. H. (1931) *Equality*. London: Unwin   *251*

TEITELBAUM, M. S. (1972) 'Factors Associated with the Sex Ratio in Human Populations'. In Harrison and Boyce (1972)   *30*

TERRY, R. M. (1970) 'Discrimination in the Handling of Juvenile Offenders by Social Control Agencies'. In Garabedian and Gibbons (1970)   *212, 220*

THOMPSON, B., and FINDLAYSON, A. (1963) 'Married Women Who Work in Early Motherhood'. *British Journal of Sociology*, 14, 150–68   *145*

TODD, J. E., and JONES, L. N. (1972) *Matrimonial Property*. London: HMSO   *70; 4.4*

TODD, J. E., and WALKER, A. M. (1980) *Adult Dental Health*. Vol. 1: *England and Wales 1968–78*. Social Survey Division, OPCS. London: HMSO   *45*

TOWNSEND, P. (1963) *The Family Life of Old People*. Harmondsworth: Penguin *69, 72*

TRADES UNION CONGRESS (1978) *Homeworking*. London: TUC *136*

TRADES UNION CONGRESS (1980) *Women Workers 1980*. London: TUC *119*

TURNBULL, P., and WILLIAMS, G. (1974) 'Sex Differentials in Teachers' Pay'. *Journal of Royal Statistical Society*, 137 (2), 245–58 *147*

TURNER, H., CLACK, G., and ROBERTS, G. (1967) *Labour Relations in the Motor Industry*. London: Allen & Unwin *157*

VALLANCE, E. (1979) *Women in the House*. London: Athlone Press *183, 187, 193, 7.1*

VAN ARNHEM, C., and LEIJENAAR, M. (1981) *The Significance of Political Socialization for Dutch Political Practice*. European Consortium for Political Research Workshop. Lancaster: University of Lancaster *190*

VAZ, E. W. (1967) *Middle Class Juvenile Delinquency*. New York: Harper Adamson *272*

VERBA, S., NIE, N. H., and KIM, J. O. (1978) *Participation and Political Equality*. Cambridge: Cambridge University Press *203*

WAINWRIGHT, H. (1978) 'Women and the Division of Labour'. In Abrams (1978) *115*

WALKER, N. (1973) *Crime and Punishment in Britain*. Edinburgh: University of Edinburgh Press *206*

WALLER, I., and OKIHIRO, N. (1978) *Burglary: The Victim and the Crime*. Toronto: University of Toronto Press *231*

WARD, M. (1979) *Mathematics and the Ten Year Old*. Schools' Council Working Paper 61. London: Evans/Methuen *88*

WEST, D. J. (1980) *Sex Offenders in the Criminal Justice System*. Cambridge: Cambridge University Press *258*

WEST, J. (1978) 'Women, Sex and Class'. In Kuhn and Wolpe (1978) *17, 20*

WESTERGAARD, J., and RESLER, H. (1975) *Class in a Capitalist Society*. London: Heinemann *20*

WHITE, G. (1977) *Socialisation*. London: Longman *248*

WHITEHOUSE, M. (1967) *Cleaning-Up TV*. London: Blandford *194*

WICKHAM, M., and YOUNG, B. (1973) *Home Management and Family Living*. London: National Council of Women of Great Britain *144*

WIGRAM, M. (1980) *Survey of Female Manual Workers in Tower Hamlets*. London: Polytechnic of Central London

WILD, R., and HILL, A. (1970) *Women in the Factory*. London: Institute of Personnel Management *164*

WILES, P. (1970) 'Criminal Statistics and Sociological Explanations of Crime'. In Wiles and Carson (1970) *209*

WILES, P., and CARSON, W. (1970) *Crime and Delinquency in Britain*. London: Martin Robertson *272*

WILLIAMSON, P. (1981) 'Careers of Graduates'. *Employment Gazette* (May), 220–2 *137*

WILLIS, P. (1978) *Learning to Labour*. Farnborough: Saxon House *249*

WILSON, E. (1974) *Sexist Ideology in Casework*. Case Conference Womens' Issue *14*

WILSON, E. (1977) *Women and the Welfare State*. London: Tavistock *60*

WISE, N. B. (1967) 'Juvenile Delinquency among Middle-Class Girls'. In Vaz (1967)   *210, 212*

WITTIG, A. M., and PETERSEN, A. C. (1979) *Sex Related Differences in Cognitive Functioning*. London: Academic Press   *92*

WOLFGANG, M. E. (1958) *Patterns in Criminal Homicide*. Philadelphia, Pa: University of Pennsylvania Press   *217, 219*

WOLPE, A. (1977) *Some Processes in Sexist Education*. London: Women's Research and Resource Centre

Woman's Own (1975) 'How Inflation is Hitting our Homes'. October. London: IPC   *73*

Women and Employment: Policies for Equal Opportunities (1980) Paris: OECD

Women and Work: A Review (1975) Manpower Paper No. 11. DoE. London: HMSO   *6.13*

Women of Europe: Supplement 5 (1980) Brussels: Commission of the European Communities   *238*

WOMEN'S STUDY GROUP: CENTRE FOR CONTEMPORARY CULTURAL STUDIES (1978) *Women Take Issue*. London: Hutchinson   *262*

WOOD, R. (1978) 'Sex Differences in Answers to English Language Comprehension Items'. *Educational Studies*, 4, 157–65   *101*

WORMALD, E. (1981) 'Women, Socialisation and Political Reality'. *Proceedings of the American Political Science Association Annual Meeting*. New York: APSA   *203*

WORMALD, E. (1982) 'Apolitical Women: the Myth of Early Socialisation'. *International Journal of Political Education*, 5, 1   *242*

WRONG, D. (1961) 'The Over-Socialised Conception of Man in Modern Society'. *American Sociological Review*, 26, 184–93   *248*

YOUNG, M. (1952) 'Distribution of Income Within the Family'. *British Journal of Sociology*, 3, 305–21   *72*

YOUNG, M. (1974) *Poverty Report*. London: Temple Smith   *272*

YOUNG, M., and SYSON, L. (1974) 'Bethnal Green'. In Young (1974)   *73*

YOUNG, M., and WILLMOT, P. (1973) *The Symmetrical Family*. London: Routledge & Kegan Paul   *145*

YUDKIN, S., and HOLME, A. (1963) *Working Mothers and their Children*. London: Joseph   *18, 19*

ZARETSKY, E. (1976) *Capitalism, the Family and Personal Life*. London: Pluto   *22*

ZWEIG, F. (1961) *The Worker in an Affluent Society*. London: Heinemann   *68, 69, 70*

INDEX

The figures which follow a semi-colon refer to tables

273